The Old World and the New

EDITED BY WALTER E. RIEDEL

The Old World
and the New 🙟

Literary Perspectives
of German-speaking
Canadians 🙟🙟

UNIVERSITY OF TORONTO PRESS

Toronto Buffalo London

© University of Toronto Press 1984
Toronto Buffalo London
Printed in Canada

ISBN 0-8020-2516-1

Canadian Cataloguing in Publication Data

Main entry under title:
The Old World and the New: literary perspectives of
German-speaking Canadians

Includes index.
ISBN 0-8020-2516-1

1. Canadian literature (German) – History and
criticism – Addresses, essays, lectures.* I. Riedel,
Walter, 1936–

PS8075.G4043 1984   c830   c84-098665-3
PR3917.C3043 1984

This book has been published with the help of a grant from
the Canadian Federation for the Humanities, using funds
provided by the Social Sciences and Humanities Research
Council of Canada, and with further financial assistance
from Multiculturalism Canada.

Hermann Böschenstein

IN MEMORIAM

North my love north
we came from all directions
to be free
from poverty and persecution
from all the evitable
burdens of being human –
and found them
waiting for us in ambush.

Henry Beissel, *Cantos North*

You have to go home again,
in some way or other.

Margaret Laurence, *The Diviners*

It is meaningless to call anyone a foreigner in
this country. We are all foreigners here.

John Marlyn, *Under the Ribs of Death*

Contents

The Old World and the New

Canada's Cultural Mosaic and the Literature of the German-speaking Canadians

WALTER E. RIEDEL

The search for identity has become a characteristically Canadian pre-occupation. Although Canada's existence as an independent nation dates back to just over a century, its historical development encompasses a far greater span. Its history comprises the original inhabitants of a vast continent, the exploration and the settlement emanating primarily from Europe and resulting in a colonial allegiance – first to France, then to Britain – and the colonies' resistance to the varied and powerful influences coming from their southern neighbour, the United States. In his study *The Canadian Imagination*, David Staines aptly describes Canada's history as 'a series of attempts to unify a land so vast as to defy unity.'[1] The vastness of the country and the diversity of its people explain why Canada's road to nationhood has been so long. It is therefore not surprising that the combination of bilingualism and multiculturalism – a compromise solution – has become the basis for Canada's cultural policy. The concept of Canada as a cultural mosaic recognizes the existence of various regional and ethnic groups, and, in the spirit of 'unity in continuing diversity,' encourages each to maintain and to cultivate its different heritage with a view to enriching the Canadian community with its specific contribution to the development of a Canadian identity. The multicultural concept reflects a democratic spirit; it is based on mutual acceptance, respect, tolerance, and cooperation. Evidently, if the experiment called Canada is to continue, each group's willingness to regard

Canada as something more than the sum of its various parts – be they regional, ethnic, or other – is imperative.

The multicultural concept obliges us to ask the question who we are as a Canadian community. The Canadian historian J.M.S. Careless reminds us that within this multicultural context nothing less than the ancient maxim 'Know Thyself' ought to be applied: 'we need to know who we are as a Canadian community ... how we got that way and where we stand now, at home and in the world at large.'[2] The German-Canadian contribution to the multicultural mosaic of Canada forms a part of such an endeavour.

The two dominant ethnic groups of Canada – the British and the French – have done a great deal to examine their contributions to Canada. Spurred on by Canada's centenary, historians, politicians, economists, linguists, literary historians, and others have debated few questions more avidly than that of Canadian identity. Undoubtedly this has contributed to a greater Canadian consciousness of self. The preoccupation with questions pertaining to Canadian identity has produced a movement in literary criticism, led by Northrop Frye, in which the attempt to define the Canadian experience in terms of specifically Canadian myths is central. Proceeding from the physical reality of Canada – the 'huge, unthinking, menacing and formidable physical setting' – from its geography and its history, the vastness of the country, its colonial origins and its nearness to the United States, Frye postulated a concept of a specifically Canadian 'garrison mentality.'[3] Following in his wake, Margaret Atwood in her thematic study of (selected) Canadian literature written in English, French, and to a small extent German, claimed that 'Survival' was the collective Canadian experience and elevated it to a central symbol of typically Canadian literature.[4] Atwood regarded the characteristically Canadian protagonist as a victim, a view that led to both an intensifying search for myths in Canadian literary criticism and to the inevitable reactions to this approach. The need to interpret the Canadian experience as reflected in Canada's literature in terms of central poetic symbols has been noted;[5] it is evident even in titles, such as Ronald Sutherland's 'Twin Solitudes' (an adaptation of the title of Hugh MacLennan's novel *Two Solitudes*),[6] in D.G. Jones's *Butterfly on Rock*,[7] Warren Tallman's 'Wolf in the Snow,'[8] and others. Occasionally this preoccupation has produced humorous and satiric commentaries, such as Philip Stratford's reference to the 'great Canadian ice-cube tray with its many ethnic minorities zealously nursing European memories and traditions, remaining happily frozen in their own separate identities.'[9] Reacting against the overemphasis and the restrictedness of myth-orientation in Canadian literary criticism, Eli Mandel and others called for new approaches to the study of Canadian literature which would do greater justice to the Canadian reality, to both the real world and the literary imagination. In his Introduction to *Contexts of Canadian Criticism*, Mandel calls for a widening of the context to include sociological and historical criticism, structural and interpretative criticism, and the study of the literary tradition of Canada's literature. [10]

One of the most interesting discoveries of Canadian literary criticism was the problematic nature of the question 'What is Canadian?' Myth-oriented critics tended to exclude all literature not specifically relevant to the Canadian experience. At the same time it was problematic to include in Canadian literature works written by recent immigrants or by visitors to Canada, even though – as for example in the case of Louis Hémon, a visitor from France and the author of *Maria Chapdelaine* – they dealt with aspects of the so-called Canadian experience. Questions whether and where such authors as Malcolm Lowry, Brian Moore, and Arthur Hailey, who deal with typically Canadian themes in at least some of their books, can be considered as belonging to Canadian literature are not easily answered, especially in view of the fact that these authors chose to leave Canada after brief stays.

Only a century ago the most important English literary critic of his time, Matthew Arnold, in his essay 'Civilization in the United States,' maintained that the United States in literature had 'as yet produced little that is important'[11] – despite the work of Henry David Thoreau, R.W. Emerson, Edgar Allan Poe, Herman Melville, Walt Whitman and others. It is hardly two decades since the first courses in Canadian literature were introduced at Canadian universities – and that despite a considerable Canadian literary tradition. It could be argued that now is the opportune time for Germanic Studies in Canada to begin to focus on what is closest: the literary contributions of German-Canadians to the Canadian mosaic.

The German-Canadians have made a rather late but nevertheless noteworthy beginning. With the publication of the *German-Canadian Yearbook* (now in its seventh volume), and with a series of monographs, Hartmut Fröschle of the University of Toronto was the first to establish an important forum for the study of questions concerning the German-Canadians.[12] In addition, three colloquia organized by Karin Gürttler of the Université de Montréal have yielded three volumes of published proceedings, further important milestones in matters of 'Canadiana

Germanica.'[13] The purpose of this collection of essays is to deal with the main figures of what is loosely referred to as German-Canadian literature within the larger spectrum of Canadian literature, a spectrum that George Woodcock has characterized most fittingly with the term 'variegation.'[14] By focusing on the specific literary perspectives which these representative German-Canadian authors have brought to Canada's literature, the essays attempt to assess the contributions of German-Canadians to Canadian literature in relation to the traditions of their cultural origins. The 'then and now,' the 'Old World and the New,' or a variation of this contrast is essential to the experience of these 'new' Canadians. For some the experience was that of the immigrant, for others it was that of exile; still others draw consciously and intensely from two homes, Canada and Europe.

If within the context of Canadian literature the term 'Canadian' is problematic, the term 'German-Canadian' is beset with even more problems. An acceptable definition of 'German-Canadian' should comprise linguistic and national characteristics. However, if national origin and knowledge of German are used as criteria, our definition would not embrace all those who are generally included in Canada's third-largest ethnic group. German is also spoken by the Austrians and the Swiss, who are, obviously, more appropriately referred to as Austrian- and Swiss-Canadians. German is also the language of the Mennonites who came to Canada from Russia and who adhered more tenaciously to their language than did any other German-speaking group. Language alone cannot reasonably serve as our only criterion; in an ethnic context, a German-Canadian will remain the same hyphenated Canadian for many years, even though, owing to the forces of assimilation or acculturation, he might have long ago begun to speak English or French. Therefore, rather than using the term 'German-Canadian' with an all-inclusive connotation to refer to those ethnic groups whose language was German when they came to Canada (Germans, Austrians, Swiss, and Mennonites), we shall use the term 'German-speaking Canadians'; this change of emphasis makes allowance for the fact that the literature of the so-called German-Canadians may have been written in their native German, or later, after the effects of assimilation and acculturation, also in English or French.

It is hardly surprising that the immigrant experience forms the essence of the writings of German-speaking Canadians. The immigrant experience is also highly relevant to Canadians in general. J.M.S. Careless reminds us that 'a great series of migrations formed and built our present Canadian society' and that 'we are all immigrants from one time or another, even the native peoples who first arrived from Asia before recorded history.'[15] Significantly the immigrant experience includes both the new beginning in a new country whose culture and language are foreign to the newcomers and the time and place left behind. Thus behind the often glossy legends and success stories about the immigrants there is a reality made up of the experience of the New World *and* the Old, or the then *and* now. The New World is experienced by the immigrant in terms of his cultural origins, and the writings of the newcomers reflect this perspective in the form of unique structural elements. I do not intend to propose another Canadian or a German-Canadian myth; the term 'Canadian experience' is used in this context not with a myth-oriented connotation, but with a literal one. Robin Mathews, in defining Canada's literature – the literature of a community which talks 'about its own experience' – describes *experience* simply as 'being born, loving, suffering, seeking a home, desiring community, finding value, naming a god, dying,' and stresses that these experiences are 'universal' though they happen 'uniquely in different societies.'[16] Naming the nameless or giving voice to the voiceless is, after all, central to all literature, that of the German-speaking Canadians included.

Because of the nature of the hitherto not clearly defined and perhaps not clearly definable area under investigation, the most appropriate method seemed to be a combination of predominantly biographical, historical, thematic, and comparative approaches; the literary perspective of German-speaking Canadians on both the Old World and the New, of necessity, brings about an emphasis on biographical and historical aspects. Since some of the writers are less widely known than others, bibliographies will be included in the few cases where these have hitherto not been readily accessible.

A typically Canadian theme, the pioneer experience, forms the subject of the first essay, Rodney Symington's study of Else Seel's immigrant experience. With a three-pronged emphasis on survival, assimilation, and alienation, Symington deals with the life and *oeuvre* of Else Seel, who exchanged the big city (Berlin) for a quiet life in a log cabin in the remoteness of the Ootsa Lake area in British Columbia. He shows how, in her diary, her poems, and her short stories, Else Seel transformed human experiences of twenty years of pioneer life in the backwoods of British Columbia – birth, death, joy, suffering, toil, celebration – into aesthetic form characterized by simplicity of expression and sincerity of feeling. Her literary achievement, according to Symington, was to have captured pioneer life and to have 'distilled out of it its universal significance.' Comparing her life and literary achievement to that of typically Canadian women writers who dealt with pioneer life in Canada, Symington interprets Else Seel's *oeuvre* as a German-Canadian version of the survival theme and places it in the tradition of imaginative Canadian pioneer literature. Else Seel's is a late pioneer experience; her literary achievement is an echo of that of Catharine Parr Traill and Susanna Moodie except in the modern ending of environmental destruction.

Ever since Douglas Spettigue's astonishing literary detective work[17] established that the Canadian writer Frederick Philip Grove and the German novelist, poet, and translator Felix Paul Greve were one and the same, Grove's *oeuvre*, which had been regarded as a realistic portrayal of the Canadian experience, has been seen in a new perspective. Both personal experience and his affinity with the literary tradition of Germany, with Naturalism and neo-Romanticism in particular, play a much greater role in Grove's writing than has hitherto been realized. In his essay, 'The Case of Greve/Grove: The European Roots of a Canadian Writer,' Anthony Riley explores this dimension of Grove, who in the novels he wrote in Canada remained faithful to 'his European heritage.'

Günter Hess's study of Walter Bauer focuses on the immigrant writer's experience of Canada in terms of what Bauer himself called the burden of his European 'luggage.' That burden, made up of 'the events of the past' – memories and experiences connected with two world wars, which left him with personal feelings of shame and guilt – stayed with him during his Canadian 'journey.' A tension between the then and now, between the Old World and the New, is central to Bauer's perception of Canada. Sometimes even the beauty and grandeur of the Canadian landscape are subjectively idealized when seen against a background of his European experiences. Walter Bauer is at his best in his portrayal of the immigrant experience in terms of man's search for meaning, of humanity's existential situation. Bauer's *oeuvre*, of which to date only a small part is accessible in English translation, provides a unique glimpse of Canada.

In the next essay Harry Loewen examines the development of the literature of the Mennonites against a background of the fate that brought them from Russia to Canada. Loewen interprets the growth of the Mennonites' creative literature as an expression of their sense of loss and considers the 'longing for a lost homeland' central to their literature. He points out that during the time the Mennonites lived securely in Prussia and later in Russia, they wrote religious and didactic, but little creative, literature. The events connected with World War I, the Communist Revolution, and civil war brought chaos and finally the end to their world. Their first significant creative literature dates back to these chaotic times and is essentially an expression of their losses: their home, their identity, their values. They retained German as their language for decades in Russia as well as in Canada, where they added English. Their latest and perhaps most significant literary contributions are now beginning to be made in English rather than in German.

For some writers, internment and exile constituted the beginning of their Canadian experience. Hitler's Germany and the *Anschluss* of Austria sealed the fate of Jewish writers. The fortunate among them left their homelands and sought asylum in any country that would accept them. Those who continued to write in exile experienced the harsh reality of having lost their natural audience and of having to write in a country whose language and culture were foreign to them. Consequently their writings frequently reflect that experience of exile. In German literature the term 'Exilliteratur' has come to denote specifically the literature written in exile between 1933 and 1945. To writers such as Thomas and Heinrich Mann, Bertolt Brecht, Leon Feuchtwanger, Alfred Döblin, Carl Zuckmayer, and numerous others, the United States served as country of exile. Because of a restrictive immigration policy, Canada admitted fewer people who sought asylum during World War II.[18] In fact, Canada became a country of exile only in 1940, when Britain, seized by wartime panic, resorted to the measure of interning as 'enemy aliens' some thirty thousand German, Austrian, and Italian citizens (among them a great many Jewish refugees) and then requested that Canada accommodate as many as possible in special camps.[19]

Three writers who came to this country by way of internment in Britain, then in Canada, are Henry Kreisel, Carl Weiselberger, and Charles Wassermann. Karin Gürttler's essay, 'Henry Kreisel: A Canadian Exile Writer?,' deals with the theme of exile in this writer's novels, which, though written after the actual period, reflect his exile experience. Clearly discernible exile structures permit us to regard Henry Kreisel as a special kind of exile writer. The essay on Carl Weiselberger focuses on that writer's Canadian experience in terms of his Jewish-Austrian origins. His perception of Canada is a reflection of the different stages of his sojourn: exile and internment, freedom and the new beginning in a foreign country. His creative literature, written in German and in English, his art and music criticism, and his reports on Canada for the Old World are a remarkable testimony to a writer who, in a short time, successfully mastered the English language as a medium of expression and became a significant cultural intermediary, and who responded with gratitude and enthusiasm to his new homeland. Helfried Seliger's essay on Charles Wassermann deals with another important cultural intermediary between the Old and the New Worlds. As author of more than ten books (in German) and over two hundred radio and television plays (in English), as professional radio and television correspondent for the CBC and European networks, Wassermann brought Canada closer to his German-speaking audience in Europe, and Europe closer to his audience in Canada. With his TV programmes on Canada he also contributed to the mutual understanding between Canada's 'two solitudes.' Able to speak German, English, and French and to use various media, he reached a wide audience. Seliger aptly observed that Wassermann's narrative and dramatic talent and his contribution as an important cultural ambassador for Canada deserve far greater recognition in this country than has hitherto been the case.

Peter Liddell's essay is a first assessment of the young writer Ulrich Schaffer, who draws intensely from his two homes, Canada and Germany. Schaffer's work transcends the immigrant experience. His books, from the first experiments with the newer poetic forms to his 'meditations,' followed by meditations accompanying his own photographs, down to his most recent prose parables, reflect a clear sense of the writer's spirit concerned with the search for meaning in today's world. Schaffer has said that he derives peace from his North American homeland, but his audience from Germany and other parts of Europe. He tends to write first in German and then rewrite the version for his English-speaking audience. His books – twelve titles to date in over four hundred thousand copies[20] – have also appeared in French, Dutch, Spanish, and Japanese translation. With his genuine concern for finding meaning he has been able to reach a loyal international readership.

The late Hermann Böschenstein, Swiss by origin and Canadian by choice, was first and foremost internationally renowned as a very distinguished professor of German. In this volume Armin Arnold examines a hitherto less known side of the scholar: his remarkable creative literary achievement. Focusing on an autobiographical novel written in the heyday of Expressionism, Arnold proves that Böschenstein wrote one of the earliest and most interesting parodies of Expressionist prose.

Böschenstein's response to Canadian literature took the form of the first and so far the only anthology of Canadian poetry in German translation; his response to Canada was a collection of short stories entitled *Unter Schweizern in Kanada*. Böschenstein was fascinated by the immigrant experience both from the point of view of leaving one's native country and from that of returning to it. A returning emigrant is the central character in a recently published novel; his counterpart, the person leaving, is the central character of an unfinished novel that occupied him during the last years before his death.[21] Arnold also gives us glimpses of three didactic comedies due to be published shortly.

This collection of essays on the literature of the German-speaking Canadians not only gives an impression of the literary voice of Canada's third-largest ethnic group, but also reflects the variety of Canada's literary culture. The literary voice contains a remarkable thematic unity that relates to Canadian literature in general. It is a unity based in some writers on their immigrant experience, in others on their exile experience in the sense of the German term 'Exilliteratur,' and in still others on that of exile in a general, unlimited sense, as in the literature of the Mennonites, which is interpreted here as a reflection of their longing for a 'lost homeland.' The literary perspective incorporating both the Old and the New World can be considered as a variation of what Friedrich Schiller termed the elegiac mode, the contrast between then and now, or there and here.[22] This theme of the Old World and the New also comprises the search for identity, which, although perceived by many as characteristically Canadian, also relates, with its posing of existential questions, to the main literary currents of modern Europe.

NOTES

1 David Staines, Introduction to *The Canadian Imagination: Dimensions of a Literary Culture*, ed. David Staines (Cambridge, Mass.: Harvard University Press, 1977), p. 2.
2 J.M.S. Careless, 'The Concept of Canadian Studies and the Task of the Multicultural History Society of Ontario,' *Deutschkanadisches Jahrbuch. German-Canadian Yearbook*, 5, ed. Hartmut Fröschle (Toronto: Historical Society of Mecklenburg Upper Canada, 1979), 1.
3 Northrop Frye, Conclusion to *Literary History of Canada*, ed. Carl F. Klinck (Toronto: University of Toronto Press, 1976) II, 342.

4 Margaret Atwood, *Survival: A Thematic Guide to Canadian Literature* (Toronto: Anansi, 1972).

5 See Walter Pache, *Einführung in die Kanadistik* (Darmstadt: Wissenschaftliche Buchgesellschaft, 1981), esp. pp. 82–8, for a succinct discussion of myth criticism.

6 Ronald Sutherland, 'Twin Solitudes,' *Canadian Literature*, 31 (Winter 1967), 5ff.

7 D.G. Jones, *Butterfly on Rock: A Study of Themes and Images in Canadian Literature* (Toronto: University of Toronto Press, 1970).

8 Warren Tallman, 'Wolf in the Snow,' *Contexts of Canadian Criticism*, ed. Eli Mandel (Chicago: University of Chicago Press, 1971), p. 232ff.

9 Philip Stratford, 'Is There a Distinctive Canadian Prose?' Paper given at the Symposium on Canada held in Washington, DC, 1977.

10 Eli Mandel, Introduction to *Contexts of Canadian Criticism*, p. 4.

11 Matthew Arnold, *Civilization in the United States* (1888; repr. Freeport, NY: Books for Libraries Press, 1972), p. 183.

12 *Deutschkanadisches Jahrbuch. German-Canadian Yearbook*, ed. Hartmut Fröschle (Toronto: Historical Society of Mecklenburg Upper Canada); *Deutschkanadische Schriften. Serie: Bellestristik*, ed. Hartmut Fröschle and Hermann Böschenstein (Toronto: German-Canadian Historical Association), *Deutschkanadische Schriften. Serie: Sachbücher*, ed. Hartmut Fröschle and Victor Peters (Toronto: German-Canadian Historical Association).

13 *Annalen. Symposium 1; Annalen 2* ('Tradition, Interpretation, Rezeption'); *Annalen 3* ('Kontakte, Konflikte, Konzepte'), ed. Karin Gürttler (Montréal: Université de Montréal, 1976, 1978, 1980).

14 George Woodcock, 'Canadian Literature – How a Fragile Flower Grew to Bloom,' reprinted in part in *Sunday Star* (24 May 1981) from *Books in Canada*, 10 (May 1981), 6–9.

15 Careless, p. 2.

16 Robin Mathews, *Canadian Literature: Surrender or Revolution* (Toronto: Steel Rail Educational Publishing, 1978), p. 9.

17 Douglas O. Spettigue, *FPG: The European Years* (Ottawa: Oberon Press, 1973).

18 Cf. Irving Abella and Harold Troper, *None Is Too Many: Canada and the Jews of Europe, 1933–1948* (Toronto: Lester and Orpen Dennys, 1982).

19 Cf. Eric Koch, *Deemed Suspect: A Wartime Blunder* (Toronto, New York, London, Sydney: Methuen, 1980).

20 This figure is based on Peter Liddell's recorded interview with Ulrich Schaffer, made in July 1981 in preparation for his study of Schaffer's writing.

21 Cf. letter from H. Böschenstein to A. Arnold (Jan. 1982) in *Seminar*, 19 (1983), 1–5.

22 Cf. Friedrich Schiller's essay 'Über naive und sentimentalische Dichtung,' especially the part entitled 'Elegische Dichtung.' Also Theodore Ziolkowski, *The Classical German Elegy: 1795–1950* (Princeton: Princeton University Press, 1980), esp. pp. 55–88.

Else Seel ◦—◦ Survival, Assimilation, and Alienation

RODNEY SYMINGTON

I

> Among the many books that have been written for the instruction of the
> Canadian emigrant [sic], there are none exclusively devoted for the use of
> the wives and daughters of the future settler, who for the most part, possess
> but a very vague idea of the particular duties which they are destined to
> undertake, and are often totally unprepared to meet the emergencies of their
> new mode of life.
>
> Catharine Parr Traill[1]

Thus wrote Catharine Parr Traill in the opening sentence of the Preface to
her 'Manual of Canadian Housewifery,' *The Canadian Settler's Guide*
(1855). This eminently practical book – with hints on everything from
curing the ague to making soap – would have been of considerable help to
Else Lübcke, if she had known of it, on her arrival in Canada seventy-two
years later, in August 1927, on the *Empress of Australia*. The CPR brought
her safely from Montreal to Vancouver, where she was met by George
Seel, a forty-year old expatriate Bavarian, who earned his living as a
prospector and trapper in the area to the south and west of Burns Lake,
BC.

They had never met before, only corresponded briefly; but they were
married the next day, 6 September 1927. Immediately they travelled by
steamer up the coast to Prince Rupert, by rail to Burns Lake, and then a

hundred miles by truck and boat to George Seel's isolated (and unfinished) two-room log cabin on the shores of Ootsa Lake. The nearest neighbours were several miles away.

Within a week George Seel made ready to go on a prospecting and trapping trip in the mountains – reminding us somewhat of the man whom Frederick Philip Grove saw ploughing his field scarcely more than an hour after his arrival on his homestead. '"You aren't losing much time about it," I said. "Nothing else to do." he replied.'[2]

George Seel certainly did not lack for things to do when he left his wife of one week in mid-September. When would he be back? 'Before Christmas.' In less than a month Else Lübcke-Seel had come from overcrowded, dynamic, bustling Berlin to total isolation in the backwoods of BC: the shock on her twentieth-century sensibilities must have been comparable to that experienced by those European emigrants who had arrived in similarly sparsely settled Eastern Canada a hundred years earlier. Susanna Moodie, for example, landing in Canada in 1832, was guided to what she thought was going to be her 'new abode,' but she could hardly believe her eyes at what she beheld.

> I gazed upon the place in perfect dismay, for I had never seen such a shed called house before. 'You must be mistaken; that is not a house, but a cattle-shed, or pig-sty.'
>
> The man turned his knowing, keen eye upon me, and smiled, half-humorously, half maliciously, as he said: 'You were raised in the old country, I guess; you have much to learn, and more, perhaps, than you'll like to know, before the winter is over.'[3]

Like Susanna Moodie almost a century earlier in Eastern Canada, Else Seel had to face her first winter as a settler's wife in Western Canada in total ignorance of pioneer life. She, too, was told: 'Forget what you have learned; conditions are vastly different here.' But the contrast between Mrs Moodie and Mrs Seel could not, in at least one respect, be greater. Whereas the former remained hyper-critical, aloof, and snobbish ('a one-woman garrison,' as Northrop Frye remarked),[4] Else Seel demonstrated from the start an unremitting humility and curiosity towards the new land, its people and customs.

But in most other respects there is a remarkable congruence between the experiences of the two women who, after all, came to Canada a century apart. In fact, Else Seel's *Canadian Diary* (1964) is in many ways the mid-twentieth-century counterpart to Susanna Moodie's *Roughing It in the Bush* (1852). Robin Mathews wrote of the latter work that it 'deals with ecstatic religious experience, attempted suicide and suicide, murder, madness, rejection, personal cruelty, and physical struggle to survive the extremes of frost and fire.' And of the author herself, he said: 'As a character typical of Canadian immigrants, in her mixture of ingenuousness and sophistication, she can involve the reader in her own character and in its growth and transformation.'[5] To the letter those comments could be applied to Else Seel's *Canadian Diary*.

A comparison of the two works reveals remarkable parallels: the unity of pioneer experience demonstrated by these two books which were written a century apart is testimony not only to the relatively unchanging sameness of a Canadian settler's existence, but also to the common denominator of *human* experience in the Canadian environment. If Susanna Moodie and her sister, Catharine Parr Traill, stand at the beginning of the imaginative autobiographical tradition of pioneer writing, then Else Seel represents the continuation of it in the second half of the twentieth century. The editor of the US edition of *Roughing It in the Bush* in 1852 called Mrs Moodie 'a true heroine, and her simple narrative is a genuine romance, which has all the interest of an imaginative creation.'[6] Else Seel's odyssey is likewise heroic in its own way, and her autobiographical 'novel'[7] stands four-square in the tradition of imaginative Canadian pioneer literature beginning with Susanna Moodie and continuing via Frederick Philip Grove and beyond. In an author's note to the fourth edition of *A Search for America* Frederick Philip Grove wrote: 'Every work of so-called imaginative literature, good or bad, is necessarily at once both fact and fiction; and not only in the sense that fiction is mingled with fact. In every single part fact and fiction are inextricably interwoven.'[8] We now know that there is a certain irony in Grove's words, but they are also literally true for the works of Else Seel.

But who was Else Lübcke-Seel, where had she come from, and was she in any way prepared 'to meet the emergencies of [her] new mode of life,' when on 18 August 1927 she set sail from Hamburg en route to Canada?

II

> The female of the middling or better class, in her turn, pines for the society of the circle of friends she has quitted, probably for ever. She sighs for those little domestic comforts, that display of the refinements and elegan-

cies of life, that she had been accustomed to see around her. She has little time now for those pursuits that were even her business as well as amusement.

Catharine Parr Traill[9]

What 'refinements and elegancies of life' had Else Lübcke given up in order to emigrate to Canada and marry George Seel? On the surface her sacrifice would appear to have been extraordinary, for she had exchanged a life of growing literary fame in the dynamic cultural metropolis of Berlin for the hard and often lonely life of a settler's wife deep in the Canadian bush. If we look deeper, however, we shall find that her decision to give up the seeming advantages of civilization was based on a phenomenon common to many emigrants from the Old World: she was what the Germans call 'Europamüde': tired of Europe.

Scepticism about the value of European civilization as compared with the comparative 'purity' of North America has a long history that goes back to Rousseau and Chateaubriand, and even an eighteenth-century German visitor to North America had been 'enlightened' on this score. Johann Gottfried Seume (1763–1810) had been shanghaied into the Hessian army in 1780 and sent to North America. He served here for three years, in which he gathered the impressions and opinions which we find expressed in his poem 'The Huron':

> A Canadian who had not yet encountered
> Europe's artificial sham politeness
> And who had a heart – still free from culture
> As God gave it to him – in his bosom,
> Came to sell what he had shot and captured,
> While in Quebec's ice-covered forests
> He had been hunting with his bow and arrow.
> After having – without sly orations –
> Parted with the birds from rocks and mountains
> For as little as he then was offered,
> Quickly he returned with little profit
> Home to his far-distant living tribesmen,
> To his tawny wife and her embraces.[10]

The 'Canadian' is, of course, the Huron, and the poem is sheer Rousseauism, but it contains precisely the elements of purity, self-sufficiency, honesty, freedom, contentment, and loyalty that so many emigrants from Europe throughout the nineteenth and twentieth centuries came searching for in the virgin forests of Canada. 'There is something in the nature of man which has kept him seeking in this country the new Eden.'[11]

Emilie Luise Emma Else Lübcke was born in Schivelbein, Pomerania, which is now called Swidwin and belongs to Poland. Both her birth and baptismal certificates give her date of birth as 9 November 1894, although later she herself always claimed her date of birth was 1898 and spoke of having been born 'at the turn of the century.' The discrepancy might appear irrelevant, but her age was very probably a significant factor in her decision (in 1927 at the presumed age of almost thirty-three) to accept the offer of marriage from a man she had never met.

Else's father managed a country estate for an absentee owner, and they lived in a large house. Her first memory, she wrote, was of being 'in the arms of a nurse, reaching through – the open window for grapes.'[12] When she was seven years old her father died, the family had to move and took up residence with various relatives. In her teens she received a classical education at the Girl's High School (Lyceum) in Kolberg, but both her education and her life were disrupted by the outbreak of the First World War.

After the war Else Lübcke moved with her mother and her aunt to Berlin. Their small inheritance had been swallowed up by inflation and it seems to have been Else's decision to move to Berlin in the hope of finding a job to support her two aging relatives. She took a position in the German Annuity Bank, where her function was to scour various foreign-language newspapers for information which would help in compiling a daily economic report for the bank's directors. It was by no means an ideal life. 'I live with the two old women and cannot make up my mind to get married.'[13]

The stifling narrowness of this existence is portrayed in an unpublished autobiographical story: 'She lived with two old aunts, whom she supported by means of her work ... He heard how she sought to grasp in her own way a little piece of life. She ran away from the two old women and let herself be driven by the current which washed her up in different places – in a lecture hall, in a theatre, an amusement park or a meeting.'[14] In the same story she even writes of having slept in the same room as her two relatives.

The Berlin of the Weimar Republic was enjoying a cultural renaissance.

The collapse of the Second Reich, the revolutionary aftermath of war, and the continuing social and political unrest contributed to a cultural effervescence in which movements, tendencies, and individuals alike were able to flourish in an atmosphere of freedom that bordered on licence.

These years in Berlin were seminal and crucial for Else Seel. In the evenings, apart from the activities described above, she also took university courses and began writing seriously. In 1921 a short story by her appeared in *Die Welt am Montag*, the first of many such publications in various newspapers and periodicals over the next several years. 'As I travel to work, people are reading the products of my intellect.'[15]

One of the most enlightening literary products of these early years in Berlin is a series of what she called 'transfer-pictures' ('Abziehbilder'). Written in 1921, these are six somewhat caustic portraits in words of people she knew. The following is her description of herself: 'My father was a farmer and drank schnaps and read travel books in order to endure life. My mother was his best servant and under him she lost the pride and the abilities of an old family. I don't drink schnaps and I describe my own travels, but pride and ability are like young dogs within me and can endure any life.'[16] One must remember that she was seven years old when her father died; perhaps her memory of him was coloured not only by her own imagination but also by the reminiscences of her mother and her aunt. In any event, the importance of the above portrait lies rather in what it demonstrates about her own character: independence, tenacity, and courage. There is, of course, an unwitting irony in the last four words, in view of her future destiny.

Her independence of spirit is also revealed very clearly in the first of these pictures, which concerned the famous German dramatist Gerhart Hauptmann – portrayed following a public reading. The portrait is headed 'A Name – Fame!' ('Ein Name – Reklame!') and begins: 'An old gentleman, all dressed up like a Christmas-tree reads first bombastic, then majestic phrases by another old gentleman – namely God. ...' And a definite anti-bourgeois bias can be seen in her conclusion: 'Everyone is disappointed, but no-one shows it. After all, they possess jewels, good boots and a good upbringing ...'[17] She seems to have associated in these years with a number of artists and writers who shared a radical, anti-bourgeois bias.

Another of her portraits depicted the Expressionist writer Walter Hasenclever (1890–1940), who, by her own account, fell in love with her and paid homage to her in both word and deed. In 1913 he had written a revolutionary play, *The Son* (produced in 1916), in which a tyrannical father locks his rebellious son in a cage and threatens to whip him. At the end of the play the son aims a pistol at his father, who thereupon dies of a stroke! It is by no means too far-fetched to extend the imagery to Else Lübcke's position: 'caged' up with her mother and her aunt and feeling 'whipped' by them into working at a job she does not particularly like in order to support them. It is understandable that she and Hasenclever would have had much in common, including pacifistic, pan-European tendencies which were the inevitable legacy of the First World War among the younger generation.

In an obvious reference to his notorious play, she described him in her 'transfer-picture' thus:

> Mr. Walter Hasenclever has, according to his own 'decision,' left the political arena. He has done the right thing. Writers who can so stupidly make fun of a revolution – no matter of what kind – don't need to be shot in their plays, for they have been shot already ... Every person who comes from a bourgeois milieu is subjected to inhibitions and constantly has to fight with his milieu and himself; if he does not or cannot do that any more then he withdraws gradually back into that bourgeois milieu that he so youthfully despised. The yearning was honest, but the fulfilment philistine.[18]

In the long run Walter Hasenclever's 'fulfilment' was compellingly honest: in 1940, as the German army approached, he committed suicide in an internment camp at Milles, France.

But Else Lübcke's most significant and fateful meeting of these years was with the Danish writer Martin Anderson-Nexö, whose fame at that time in Europe was at its zenith. 'Jupiter comes from the North, Thor with thunder and lightening and leads me up to the stars. Europe lies at his feet, and he lies at my feet.'[19] Anderson-Nexö was twice her age and married into the bargain. It made no difference to her: she fell in love with him. In the course of their affair, he seems to have treated her somewhat callously.[20]

The unhappy outcome of this relationship, growing disenchantment with life in Europe, the narrow confines of her domestic and professional situation, her advancing years (in 1927 she was thirty-two and still unmarried!), and not the least her independence of spirit – all these culminated in a decision to emigrate to Canada in order to marry George

Seel, to whose advertisement in a Berlin newspaper she had recently responded. It was, no doubt, a decision made out of disillusionment and depression, as well as out of desire for change and adventure. But once she had made her decision, she quickly cut both her ties and, symbolically, her hair. 'One day I had my long hair cut off and laid it on the table in tissue paper, next to a ticket to Canada. Mother, no lamenting; help me pack quickly, for in a week I must travel from Hamburg to Quebec on the "Empress of Australia."'[21] She left behind the rich cultural tradition of a European metropolis, gave up all the modern 'refinements and elegancies of life,' and embarked on her new existence with the total commitment of both mind and body. Although later she inevitably made comparisons between her new life and the one she had left behind, she never regretted her decision. Despite all the hardships and miseries which were unavoidably part of the settler's lot, Else Seel did consider her new life for the most part more Elysian than Stygian.

III

> 'What are the necessary qualifications of a settler's wife; and the usual occupations of the female part of a settler's family?' are your next questions.
>
> To the first clause I reply, a settler's wife should be active, industrious, ingenious, cheerful, not above putting her hand to whatever is necessary to be done in her household, nor too proud to profit by the advice and experience of older portions of the community, from whom she may learn many excellent lessons of practical wisdom.
>
> Catharine Parr Traill[22]

For almost twenty-five years Else Seel lived the life of a pioneer. Her initial experiences reveal her naïveté and helplessness. For example, the day after her husband, George, had left on his trip she found that she couldn't even light a fire. Never having heard of kindling, and never having watched her new husband closely, she attempted to light damp logs with newspaper. She was forced to sit freezing in her overcoat until a passing neighbour noticed the absence of smoke from the chimney – in the backwoods always a sign that something is wrong.[23]

On another occasion she had her first experience with native people:

> One evening Indians landed in their canoes on the shore and built a great camp fire. Quickly I extinguished the kerosene lantern. Axes split up trees and logs, children and dogs howled, strange sounds shrilled across

to me. Then I ran in the dark to Old King's place. There they all laughed resoundingly, when they heard why I had run away. The Indians were going hunting in the mountains and were completely harmless. Unfortunately I had read in the old country too many tales of the terrible deeds of the Indians. Only a Finn showed understanding when he learned that I had been in Canada only two weeks.[24]

These early prejudices quickly dissolve and Else Seel not only befriends many Indians, but learns about their culture and eventually translates their songs and legends into German.[25]

The significance of these and many other episodes related in her *Canadian Diary* lies in the utter open-mindedness and willingness to learn everything anew. She does not relinquish her own culture, but she is ready to absorb into her being her new environment and its customs. Inappropriate material things – such as silver cutlery and damask tablecloths which she had brought with her from Europe – are put aside, but traditional customs, such as the important religious celebrations of the Advent season and Christmas, are retained as part of a cultural and personal heritage that should not be lost.

The absorption of the new environment occurs through a variety of means: work, observation, reading, and listening all contributed to her adaptation to the unfamiliar surroundings.

Work played the most significant role in the life of any pioneer. While the Seels were not completely typical settlers – George Seel earned (or rather tried to earn) his living by trapping and prospecting rather than by farming – there was still an immense amount of work to be done, as there is on any homestead. Land was cleared for crops to fill their family needs, a beaver farm was started, and eventually two children had to be cared for and brought up.

The record of pioneer life is circumscribed by the three events: birth, marriage, death. In between occur the myriad episodes that not only give their hues to this particular form of existence but also imbue it with a significance beyond the practical and everyday. The planting of seeds (which also becomes a symbolical act), the nurturing of plants, animals, and children alike, the battle against the elemental forces of nature and the equally destructive forces of distant economic events (against which they are totally impotent), and the necessary acceptance of every day's mixture of misfortune and joy: all this is woven into the tapestry of a life that most would consider narrow and insignificant, but which is here revealed to have a fulfilling richness.

This life, in that particular form and in that particular place, was brought to an abrupt end by the building of the Nechako Dam and the consequent flooding of the areas behind it, including Ootsa Lake and the settlement of Wistaria. Else Seel's quest for a new life had brought her to Canada: the products of a quarter-century of toil were now to be inundated. It would all be a memory.

Nor was this the only blow: George Seel, working as a guide in the mountains for the engineering survey connected with the Dam, returned from an arduous trip and died on 1 April 1950. Else Seel had to bury him, negotiate compensation for her land, and take her family elsewhere. The Ootsa Lake period of her life was over:

> Flooded is everything. Water covers
> the loghouse on the shores of Ootsa,
> water covers the acres of fertile soil,
> the planted shrubs and the pines,
> water covers the little schoolhouse
> and the neighbours' dwelling-places.
> Water stopped only before the church
> and the grave of the last pioneer.[26]

The above lines from her poem 'Last Pioneer,' written in English and commemorating the life of her husband, exemplify the transition from autobiography to art. From the first lines of the poem: 'George was forty years when he went to Vancouver to get his bride, a young girl from Berlin ...' (the young girl was thirty-two) there is a manipulation of autobiographical fact aimed at producing something of more than individual and more than transitory value. We must now turn to the question: What did Else Seel, the writer, make of her twenty-five years of pioneer life?

IV

[*Roughing It in the Bush*] in spite of its non-fictional subject matter ... bears all the formal characteristics of a work of the imagination.

John Moss[27]

The literary, in Canada, is often only an incidental quality of writings which, like those of many of the early explorers, are as innocent of literary intention as a mating loon.

Northrop Frye[28]

How does Else Seel's *Canadian Diary* relate to the two quotations above? In the first place, the title of her book is misleading: it was the preference of her German publisher, who believed that the word 'Canadian' in the title would make the book more attractive to potential purchasers.

It is true that Else Seel kept at all times a fairly voluminous diary. But what appeared in book form was quite different from the original. The published version of her *Canadian Diary* is the result of selecting, reworking, reordering, and shaping her original diary entries: in brief, it is a conscious work of art, with a definite form and infused with a consistent vision. It is, moreover, the tale of only a segment of her life, and that segment constitutes, in fact, almost exactly half her life in Canada.

Thus the *Canadian Diary* attempts to present us with a picture of the nearly twenty-five years that Else Seel spent on the shores of Ootsa Lake. It is a portrait not only of her own life, but also of the geographical and human environment in which she lived. It offers us a picture of pioneer life filtered through the eyes of an artist who was at the same time both participant and observer. The immediacy of the original diary entries is, so to speak, 'recollected in tranquillity.'

Thus, as in the works of Frederick Philip Grove, there is a certain manipulation of autobiographical detail, but by no means to the extent to which Grove is now known to have done it. However much Else Seel might have insisted on calling her book the 'novel of my life,' it was not what in any age would normally be called a novel. If it does contain a mixture of 'poetry and truth,' then it must be said that the truth is the preponderant element: the 'poetry' largely consists in the creative elaboration of the events and episodes.

All autobiographies contain varying degrees of 'poetry and truth.' What makes one, as literature, more valuable than another depends on the more or less successful combination of three elements: form, language, and vision.

The last element, vision, is initially the most important. Without a consistent vision or perspective there can be no work of art. Of Else Seel's vision we can say that it demonstrates an attempt to penetrate to the human and universal significance of seemingly 'unimportant' lives. To her, every life had some significance and every person she met was of interest. In essence, all lives are potentially of equal importance, and in the backwoods of Canada, stripped of sophistication and superficiality, life is more real, more immediate, more sharply defined.

A host of small episodes in the *Canadian Diary* underscore this point.

For example, she receives a book from Germany entitled 'I have lived falsely' (*Ich habe falsch gelebt* by J.M. Frank). 'I couldn't make the people here understand the title; they simply didn't comprehend that one could live "falsely." And a Frenchman asked: "*Loved* falsely?" – I, too, do not believe that one can live falsely.'[29] The structure of this paragraph hints at the possibility that this was another lesson that Else Seel had learned from the settlers. But here again we have evidence of the dichotomy between Old World and New: the terrible suspicion of a misdirected life occurs to the 'civilized' European, but is incomprehensible to the settlers of the woods.

We should also not forget that her 'diary' was published in the 1960s in West Germany: the contrast between the society which it describes and the society in which it appeared is both striking and significant. For many Europeans the word 'Canada' still evokes the strong polarity between an old, overcrowded, polluted, dying continent and a land of pioneers enjoying wide open spaces, unlimited opportunity, clean air and water, and cheerfully overcoming all adversity. In sum, their vision is half-Rousseau, half-Crusoe.[30]

But they would not find that vision realized in Else Seel. Her works are far removed from the proselytizing rural idyll, typified by many French-Canadian works of the late nineteenth and early twentieth centuries.[31] There is nothing idyllic about an existence where in winter the temperature is forty to sixty degrees below zero, where in one year the family's total income is $69.50, or where, while walking through the forest during wartime, mother and daughter are shot at by hateful but cowardly neighbours. Above all, the destruction of a life's work by the so-called march of progress, by that very 'civilization' that she thought she had left behind in Europe, is a minor tragedy.

> After all the difficult years life seemed to be getting easier. Suddenly the terrible news spread that Ootsa Lake was to be included in a great power dam project and that its banks would be flooded. We could hardly believe it. … Our hearts stood still. All at once everything seemed to have been in vain. Everything that in more than 25 years we had cleared, planted, built and fenced was now to be placed under water. … The water would flood everything, and nothing would remain of all our work and worry – nothing.[32]

At the end of her autobiographical account Susanna Moodie is thoroughly disillusioned with pioneer life – at least for the well-born:

To the poor, industrious working-man it presents many advantages; to the poor gentleman, *none!* ... If these sketches should prove the means of deterring one family from sinking their property, and shipwrecking all their hopes, by going to reside in the backwoods of Canada, I shall consider myself amply repaid for revealing the secrets of the prison-house, and feel that I have not toiled and suffered in the wilderness in vain.[33]

In other words: 'let my life be a lesson to you! Don't follow in my footsteps!' How different are Else Seel's conclusions: her bitterness is not at all with pioneer life itself, but with those forces that have destroyed the life's work not only of her own family, but of all the families around Ootsa Lakes in Canada and elsewhere.

Yet even when to this catastrophe is added the loss of her husband, her vision remains positive and optimistic. On the one hand, all the experiences, good and bad, of the past quarter-century were valuable and necessary, because 'they belonged to a life of fulfilment.'[34] And on the other hand, life continues, and a new life, with new experiences, awaits.

The *Canadian Diary* begins with Else Seel's arrival in Canada to embark on a new life, and it ends with her departure from Wistaria – likewise to commence a new life. In between there has been marriage, birth, death, joy and suffering, toil and relaxation, mourning and celebration: twenty-five years of human experience the locale of which may have been flooded, but the years themselves are not forgotten.

What is so pleasing about her *Canadian Diary* is its rightness of tone. The language is deceptively simple and laconic, but people and events are rendered accurately by a few understated strokes of the pen. When she meets two German women, for example, the one loud and domineering, and the other meek and mild, she says of the latter: 'one only learned anything about her from the other woman, for example: that she had seven children.'[35] Whether writing of the great solitude, the awesomeness of nature, or the most elemental experiences such as birth and death her sureness of tone never falters.

If we agree with Northrop Frye that 'literature ... is conscious mythology: it creates an autonomous world that gives us an imaginative perspective on the actual one,'[36] then Else Seel's *Canadian Diary* is far more than a mere social document; it offers us an 'imaginative perspective' on pioneer life that renders its significance universal. It likewise represents a step forward from the straightforward recounting of events to be found in *Roughing It in the Bush*, or in *The Backwoods of Canada*; yet it refrains from going all the way into fiction, as, for example, does the work of Frederick

Philip Grove. The *Canadian Diary* thus occupies a middle ground between autobiography and fiction: it is none the less a work of considerable imagination and it exemplifies the truth of the statement that 'the Canadian writer has been one of the fighters for humanization of Canadian life, for life lived with nature and not over it.'[37]

V

> Even when it is literature in its orthodox genres of poetry and fiction, it is
> more significantly studied as a part of Canadian life than as part of an
> autonomous world of literature.
>
> Northrop Frye[38]

Both the poetry and the short stories of Else Seel are far more than a mere record of personal concerns or a simple reflection of pioneer life. It is true that if one reads her poems that have as their themes various aspects of pioneer life, one could conjure up a mosaic of that existence: poems about the land and the animals and humans that inhabit it. On a modest level Else Seel's poems about Ootsa Lake and Wistaria might be compared to Dylan Thomas's *Under Milk Wood* or Edgar Lee Masters's *Spoon River Anthology*. For in each poem one finds a small but priceless gem of human significance. Thus 'Beatrice' commemorates the first woman to welcome her when she first arrives in Ootsa Lake. They live as neighbours for twenty-five years, sharing joy and pain; then the end comes and they have to leave:

> And for the last time
> we stood opposite each other,
> as at the beginning we
> shook hands, smiling.

> Ootsa Lake flooded everything
> that once we'd loved.
> Under water lay our houses,
> under water lay our seasons,
> lay our hearts, too,
> lay our love and understanding;
> yet the waves still whispered:
> Beatrice, Beatrice,
> goodness lasts for ever.[39]

Clearly, Else Seel's poems concern her own experiences as a settler's wife, but her most striking achievement as a pioneer poet is the way in which she captures the nature and suffering of *other* people. Perhaps her most successful and poignant poem concerns a neighbour whose life was so hard and unremittingly humdrum, whose poverty was so unrelieved, and whose family grew so quickly, that one night, in total despair, she walked into the lake to drown herself. (The same neighbour is portrayed in the short story 'A Small Silver Cloud ...').[40] This is one of the finest and most moving poems ever written about pioneer life and it deserves to be quoted in full (albeit in translation):

The Neighbour

Saw you coming o'er the rise
saw your fluttering dress,
Ootsa blew into your eyes,
drove you to excess.

Oh, your hands they were so fine
and so thin your face and hair,
you came from London's poorest quarter
and life was hard to bear.

Oh, too long the winter was
and he whitened all your face,
and he whitened all your hair,
but of strength gave not a trace.

Idle fell your hands beside you,
idle fell your house and garden,
a hundred times I saw you waving
and saw your features harden.

I wanted then to give you courage
wanted, too, to do the best,
yet with all life's blows behind you
all you wanted was to rest, to rest.

And in a Summer's night

you walked silently into the lake;
your children sleeping tight,
no-one woke for your own sake.[41]

Such poems are no mere social documents, they are testimonies to human concerns. As William Henry Drummond captured the life of the 'habitant' in his 'Habitant Poems,'[42] so Else Seel has provided the same service for the settlers of the backwoods of British Columbia, although significantly with scarcely a trace of humour.

In like manner Else Seel also captures the essence of the people of the BC Interior in her short stories. Here again we witness repeatedly the loneliness and the frustrating and often futile attempts to forge human contacts. The fragility of such bridges is demonstrated by the story 'Sled Dogs,' in which an old settler from Scandinavia, Anders (in German: other, different), lives on the opposite side of the lake and crosses it in summer by boat (two hours hard rowing) and in winter by dog-sled, in order to visit Mrs West (that is, Else Seel) and her children. When the lake begins to freeze the boat can't get through and the ice is not yet safe enough for the sled. Such conditions can last for weeks. The yearning for human contact is too great: he hears Mrs West calling him and he can wait no longer; he sets out. 'Twice the ice broke open in narrow clefts, but twice the sled sprang over them ... fog and light snowflakes swirled around like a wet blanket and covered everything up ... Anders must have reached the middle of the lake. Then a wide crack appeared in the ice ... The dogs reared up and refused to cross the dangerous place. But the whip cracked and the last "ho-ho" cleaved the early morning, and Anders plunged into the open ice.'[43] The brittle bridge of ice stands as a natural symbol for the fragility of human relationships and, indeed, of life in general.

In another masterful story, 'Hephata: Faith, Hope, and Charity,'[44] a strange, deaf man arrives one day at the door of the log-house and introduces himself to the wife (Mrs Wertin). He can only communicate by writing on a pad, seems awkward, even helpless. He lives in a tiny cabin and barely ekes out a living. But in a time of crisis he appears as if summoned by telepathy and saves the wife from death. He not only saves life, he fosters it: he plants seeds in the earth and when they grow, they form the shape of a heart, an anchor, and a cross: faith, hope, and charity. When he finally leaves the area, his flower-pattern remains as a visible and articulate symbol of a lesson that he, the deaf man who had trouble communicating, was able to transmit in a natural, lasting manner. His 'inner' ear had a message for those who were apparently not as handicapped as he was.

Else Seel had no need to fabricate either stories or images: the episodes that filled her life were material enough, and nature itself provided the most fitting images and symbols. All that was left for the artist to do was to mould events and images into a suitable form. Thus her stories and poems have no need of artificial stimulants to make them interesting; the material is of inherent interest because it springs from genuine human sources. This is not to belittle her achievement: the transformation of raw experience into aesthetic form still requires artistry of a high order, and this she indubitably possessed.

If she was able so successfully to capture in diary, in poems, and in short stories the nature of pioneer life, and also to distil out of it its universal significance, what effect did that ability have on her own life? Was she able to come to terms with the inevitable problems every immigrant settler has to face: survival, assimilation, alienation?

VI

> These new aliens faced an unintelligible language, strange customs and stranger laws; an apparent cultural vacuum. ... There was no impetus for the non-English-speaking immigrant to participate in a common dream and, in many cases, he was actively committed to oppose assimilation of any sort. He learned the language and the laws of his new place – not in order to adopt them but to adapt to them where necessary to protect his alien status.
>
> John Moss[45]

Except for the fact that the language, customs, and laws were indeed strange to her, none of the above is true of Else Seel (or indeed of many German-Canadian writers). Just the very opposite: her whole striving was to learn, to understand, to absorb, to assimilate as much of Canadian culture – history, geography, literature, and so on – as was humanly possible. While it is true that there have been, and presumably always will be, immigrants who react in the way described above by John Moss, it is also true to say that there is a significant body of immigrant writing that takes the opposite view: namely, that assimilation is desired by every fibre of mind and body, but that a perfect and harmonious blend of two different cultures from two different continents is simply not possible. The result is indeed a perpetual feeling of alienation, but one tinged with sadness rather than arrogance or antipathy.

German-Canadian literature manifests this dichotomy of the immigrant experience time and time again. The poems of Walter Bauer, for example, contain repeated statements like the following: 'An old emigrant says: Once I lived there, now I live here, in between lies the sea – but only the sea? Now I live in another land, once I lived over there; when one leaves, does one only change one's house and town?'[46] A collection of his short stories is significantly entitled 'Alien in Toronto,' and the everlasting schism of the immigrant soul is revealed in observations such as this: 'The oppressive consciousness of not having been born here, of being an alien, is suddenly set aflame by an inkling of endless freedom ...'[47]

Another example of this alienated mentality is a poem by Harry Loewen, 'Travelling': 'I am a wanderer on many paths ... much I have seen and much I've learned, the towns and countries are all known to me, but after so many years nowhere did I find a beloved home, a native homeland.'[48] Many more such examples could be cited to demonstrate the essential disharmony of the immigrant's attempt at cultural assimilation. In the Canadian immigrant's experience, there are more than just *two* solitudes.

But there is yet another dimension to this dilemma. The lack of roots – or perhaps better: the putting forth of roots that don't quite go deep enough in the foreign soil – leads to a metaphysical malaise, in which the immigrant's cultural rootlessness stands as a symbol for, and also thereby reinforces, the existential alienation caused by the loss of identity and, ultimately, the transience of life. 'Rootlessness' in this framework takes on its deeper significance. Walter Bauer's poem, 'The Great Inn' ('Das grosse Gasthaus'), for example, portrays the writer as being a guest not just in Canada, but on earth: 'I wasn't in a paradise, I was in an inn or shelter, which was simply called: "on earth."'[49]

The surmounting or suppression of this feeling is for many immigrants – both as individuals and as groups – a major aim, be it conscious or not. Whether a group be a communistic-religious body, such as a Hutterite or Mennonite settlement, or just the development of an 'immigrant neigh-bourhood' as is found in many cities and towns, its desire is the same: to preserve the old and the known and only slowly to absorb the new and the unknown. This is what John Moss had in mind, no doubt, when writing the passage at the head of this section, or when he wrote, somewhat hyperbolically, of 'the violent, often explosive collision of different, incompatible worlds.'[50] There are also immigrant writers who exemplify that attitude, such as Peter Klassen (1889–1953), who in a poem entitled 'My Confession' could write on the one hand: 'O Canada, my homeland ... I will be a true citizen in word and deed and life! What's mine is yours, what's yours is mine! And my whole striving belongs to you!' But at the end of the same poem he expressed a significant reservation: 'Yet if I am to be of use to you, I must not lose my self. There is "something" that is mine! I can feel it in my heart. This "something" is my German blood, the spirit of German ancestors ... The German language, German loyalty, and the belief of my fathers – I shall hold onto them wherever I be, no-one shall steal them from me!'[51] Such sentiments reveal more a 'garrison mentality' than a true desire for assimilation, although the preservation of 'self' is often both natural and involuntary. It is striking, however, how often one reads, particularly in German-Canadian poetry, not only of the desire to retain the mother tongue, but also of its unparalleled glories. In this respect Else Seel is no exception, though less intrusively insistent. Language is, after all, one of the primary roots of being: the cutting off of the native tongue and the inadequate growth of the second language's roots leave the immigrant clinging to a rather thin topsoil. Else Seel often quoted Santayana's well-known phrase: 'The roots of the English language do not quite reach my centre.' That quotation can stand for the experience of the vast majority of non-anglophone Canadian immigrants.

Is there then no middle ground between the cultural schizophrenia of the immigrant garrison and the involuntary alienation of the rootless wanderer or the unwilling exile?

As indicated at the beginning of this section, Else Seel undertook with heart, mind, and body to become a Canadian. Her trunk was full of her cultural heritage – from her Pomeranian feather-bed to the works of Goethe and Schopenhauer – but she brought these things, both material and spiritual, *to* Canada and attempted to plant them in her own piece of the new soil. 'To conquer a piece of the continent, to put one's imprint on virgin land, to say "there I am, for that I came," is as much a way of defining oneself, of proving one's existence, as is Descartes' *Cogito, ergo sum.*'[52] In this statement Henry Kreisel, himself an immigrant, was referring to the conquest of the land, but what he says is equally true of any activity undertaken by the immigrant in his new 'land of opportunity.' The establishment of a newly defined identity is the alpha and omega of the immigrant's exertions.

In Else Seel's case we can adapt Descartes's phrase into: 'Scribo, ergo sum.' Once her work was done, her work began. Alone for weeks and months at a time, her solace was twofold: firstly, the human contacts she made with other settlers, and secondly, the forming of these experiences into art. It has already been pointed out how Else Seel transmitted raw material of her experiences into aesthetic form. This activity of writing was a natural endowment, but it could not, of itself, overcome the cultural dichotomy that is the immigrant's lot.

Thus Else Seel's work is a laudable example of countless battles won, but in a war that never ends. She survived, only to be displaced; she assimilated a great deal, but a measure of alienation was always present. Her works, however, testify only to achievement, not to failure.

VII

> Whoever searches for a Canadian identity cannot avoid an encounter with a multitude of duplicities and contradictions. Does Canada actually have an identity of its own or does it mirror some foreign identity – or is Canada still in the process of personality development? Is literature dealing with the Canadian identity optimistic or pessimistic? Is identity rooted in the past or in the future, in the mental or in the physical landscape?
>
> James Foley[53]

The great themes of Canadian literature: the search for identity, the problem of isolation, the great adversary Nature, survival, conquering the continent, the problem of being alien, and so on – all these themes can be traced in both major and minor writers, in English-Canadian, French-Canadian, and also in German-Canadian literature.

The very last words of Northrop Frye's Conclusion to the *Literary History of Canada* praise the writers who 'have also left an imaginative legacy of dignity and of high courage.'[54] Although little known and scantily published, German-Canadian writers – and in particular Else Seel – are a part of that legacy. In setting out on a quest for a new life, for love, happiness, and fulfilment, she relinquished a rich cultural environment and with steadfast determination chose the 'small world.' But to this 'small world' she brought some unique values: the courage and strength to take on and survive the arduous existence of a settler, and the rare ability to record it as part of her poetic vision. She lived and wrote in isolation: she did not seek fame, nor was it thrust upon her. When we look now at what she left behind, it is perhaps a modest achievement, but it encompasses two qualities that are rarely found in modern literature: a combination of profound experience and utter sincerity of expression.

Inevitably, 'pioneer literature' is considered to be at the best 'regional' literature, and at the worst it is valued as no more than a document of social history. But it is not the locality that makes literature profound, or even meaningful; it is rather the ability of the artist to depict the breadth and depth of significant human experience. The people in Else Seel's works live on the edge of nature, face to face with the stark reality of existence. Simple lives are captured in simple language; there is nothing artificial or manufactured. When the 'urbane' and 'sophisticated' accoutrements of modern life are flung aside, we are all left with the same fundamental needs, desires, and emotions as her pioneers. Her works thus testify not just to the nature of pioneer life, but to the nature of life itself.

For the immigrant-settler the first challenge is that of survival: and it is an endless, ongoing challenge. Not only natural and elemental forces have been opposed and conquered, but also unnatural and invisible ones: world-wide economic developments and the so-called march of progress.

But survival is only a first step (albeit one that has to be taken each day anew). Thereafter the immigrant faces the problems of alienation and assimilation. These, too, are part of the unceasing challenge of life. However much the immigrant accepts his new life and attempts to assimilate it, there will always be a degree of failure and hence a crisis of identity.

NOTES

1 Catharine Parr Traill, *The Canadian Settler's Guide* (Toronto: McClelland and Stewart, 1969), p. xvii. Note Mrs Traill's use of the word 'emigrant' where we would normally expect to read 'immigrant.' Her choice of the former word reveals her biased perspective.
2 Frederick Philip Grove, *In Search of Myself* (Toronto: Macmillan, 1946), p. 259.
3 Susanna Moodie, *Roughing It in the Bush* (Toronto: McClelland and Stewart, 1962), pp. 68–9.
4 Northrop Frye, Conclusion to *Literary History of Canada*, ed. Carl F. Klinck (Toronto: University of Toronto Press, 1965–76), p. 351.

5 Robin Mathews, *Canadian Literature: Surrender or Revolution* (Toronto: Steel Rail Educational Publishing, 1978), pp. 41–2.
6 Moodie, p. xiii.
7 This is how she often referred to her work. See also Preface to Else Seel, *Kanadisches Tagebuch* (Tübingen: Erdmann, 1964), p. 5.
8 Frederick Philip Grove, *A Search for America* (Toronto: McClelland and Stewart, 1971), p. xvii.
9 Traill, *The Backwoods of Canada* (Toronto: McClelland and Stewart, 1929), pp. 190–1.
10 Translation by Walter Roome.
11 John Moss, *Patterns of Isolation in Canadian Literature* (Toronto: McClelland and Stewart, 1974), p. 3.
12 Else-Seel-Archive, unpublished poem: 'Letzte Pionierin.' All translations from the German are by me, unless otherwise noted.
13 Else-Seel-Archive, unpublished poem: 'Elses Gesang.'
14 Else-Seel-Archive, 'Der alte Löwe,' unpublished.
15 Seel, 'Letzte Pionierin.'
16 Else-Seel-Archive, 'Abziehbilder,' unpublished.
17 Ibid.
18 Ibid.
19 Seel, 'Elses Gesang.'
20 The long autobiographical story 'The Old Lion' in the Else-Seel-Archive presumably recounts this episode.
21 Seel, 'Letzte Pionierin.'
22 Traill, *Backwoods*, pp. 188–9.
23 Seel, *Kanadisches Tagebuch*, pp. 13–14.
24 Ibid., p. 15.
25 'Lieder der Haida' in Else Seel, *Ausgewählte Werke: Lyrik und Prosa* (Toronto: German-Canadian Historical Association, 1979), pp. 203–4.
26 'Last Pioneer,' Else-Seel-Archive, unpublished.
27 Moss, p. 84.
28 Frye, p. 334.
29 Seel, *Kanadisches Tagebuch*, p. 171.
30 The phrase is attributed by Northrop Frye (*Literary History*, p. 353) to Professor Alec Lucas. For German perspectives on Canada, see Walter E. Riedel, *Das literarische Kanadabild* (Bonn: Bouvier, 1980).
31 See Albert le Grand, Introduction to Ringuet, *Thirty Acres* (Toronto: McClelland and Stewart, 1960), p. xi.
32 Seel, *Kanadisches Tagebuch*, pp. 239–40.
33 Moodie, pp. 236–7.
34 Seel, *Kanadisches Tagebuch*, p. 245.
35 Ibid., p. 51.

36 Frye, p. 349.
37 Mathews, p. 129.
38 Frye, p. 334.
39 Seel, *Ausgewählte Werke*, p. 29. On the literary quality of Else Seel's work, see H. Böschenstein, 'Else Seel: Eine deutsch-kanadische Dichterin,' *German-Canadian Review*, 10:1 (Spring 1957).
40 Ibid., pp. 66–77.
41 Ibid., p. 28.
42 William Henry Drummond, *Habitant Poems* (Toronto: McClelland and Stewart, 1970).
43 Seel, *Ausgewählte Werke*, p. 65.
44 Ibid., pp. 78–93.
45 Moss, pp. 91–2.
46 *Nachrichten aus Ontario*, ed. Hartmut Fröschle (Hildesheim and New York: Olms Presse, 1981), p. 19.
47 Ibid., p. 145.
48 *Unter dem Nordlicht*, ed. George K. Epp (Winnipeg: Mennonite German Society of Canada, 1977), p. 84.
49 Fröschle, p. 21.
50 Moss, p. 91.
51 Epp, pp. 26–7.
52 Henry Kreisel, 'The Prairie: A State of Mind,' *Canadian Anthology*, ed. Carl Klinck and Reginald Watters (Toronto: Gage Educational Publishing, 1974), p. 623.
53 *The Search for Identity*, ed. James Foley (Toronto: Macmillan, 1976), p. 1.
54 Frye, p. 361.

The Case of Greve/Grove ʡ
The European Roots of
a Canadian Writer ʡ ʡ ʡ

ANTHONY W. RILEY

The case of Felix Paul Greve or Frederick Philip Grove, as he later chose to call himself, is an extraordinary and indeed probably unique one, not only in the literary history of Canada, but in world literature. There is, of course, a small but well-known group of creative writers who at some period in their lives deliberately changed their medium of literary expression from their mother-tongue to a totally different language; one thinks of Joseph Conrad, Vladimir Nabokov, or Samuel Beckett in this context. There are some others, but except for Grove (and possibly B. Traven, the still mysterious pseudonymous author of *The Treasure of the Sierra Madre* and *The Death Ship*, whose real identity will probably never be revealed)[1] none of these writers kept his linguistic heritage secret or contrived in the most elaborate fashion, as Grove did very successfully, to dupe the world into believing that the intricate web of fiction which he had spun around his own backround and autobiography was true.

Over a decade has now passed since Douglas O. Spettigue, as the result of brilliant literary detective work, was able to report in 1972 that the Grove enigma had been resolved and that the eminent Canadian novelist and author of some of the most important works of Canadian Realism, Fellow of the Royal Society of Canada, recipient of the Governor General's Award for Non-Fiction (awarded with supreme irony for *In Search of Myself*, an autobiography in which fiction outweighs fact by some large factor) was in fact of German origin and indeed had been a writer and translator of some repute in Germany before settling in Canada at the end of 1912.[2] With the publication of Spettigue's full-length study *FPG: The European Years* in 1973,[3] the same year that the first public discussion of his findings at the Grove Symposium at the University of Ottawa took place on 5–6 May, any lingering doubts in the minds of the vast majority of Canadian scholars about Grove's origins were put to rest.[4] Nobody who took part, as I did, in the Grove Symposium will forget the crackling tension in the lecture theatre where Spettigue's conclusions were subjected to quite intense scrutiny; the late Desmond Pacey, for example, still seemed sceptical at that time. By June 1974, when Pacey was preparing his edition of the letters of Frederick Philip Grove, he still did not appear to be completely willing to concede to Spettigue; while he writes in his preface that Spettigue's 'assiduous research' has established 'beyond reasonable doubt' that Grove was Greve,[5] Pacey maintains in his introduction to Appendix A of his edition, containing a group of Greve letters written in German, that the case 'is still not conclusively proven,' admitting at the same time that 'the circumstantial evidence for their identity' is very strong.[6] Unfortunately, Pacey died in 1975 while his book was still in production, so we will never know whether he would have finally accepted Spettigue's findings; nevertheless, by publishing the early German letters, even if they are printed in an appendix and not in the main body of the volume, Pacey performed a very valuable service to Grove scholarship, and at the same time, at least by implication, recognized that the Canadian Grove was in fact the German Greve. (In future, to avoid having to switch between Greve and Grove, I shall abbreviate the writer's name as FPG.) Since the mid-1970s critical interest on both sides of the Atlantic in FPG's early years in Germany and in their implications for his Canadian *oeuvre* has increased; the latest edition of one of the standard biographical reference works in Germany has, as it were, put its official stamp of approval on Spettigue's discovery;[7] Walter Pache (University of Cologne) and others have published stimulating articles dealing with FPG's European literary heritage;[8] excerpts from a number of previously published essays (1926–76) on FPG, including ones on his German period, have been reprinted in an American collection of twentieth-century literary criticism;[9] and in a new book, Edward D. Blodgett devotes a long essay to a detailed discussion of FPG's German novels and their relationship to European literature of the day, a point to which I shall return later.[10] In addition, the first English translation of FPG's *Maurermeister Ihles Haus* (1906) was published in 1976, and Douglas Spettigue and I are presently in process of editing an English translation of his other German novel, *Fanny Essler* (1905).[11]

'Three decades after Grove's death, ' Walter Pache rightly points out, 'his life and personal history have been thoroughly explored. The same cannot be said of his works and literary background, although both have moved once more into the centre of critical interest.'[12] It is important to note that FPG carefully concealed his *literary* as well as his personal ancestry, Pache continues, stressing above all the influence of *décadence*, of the *fin de siècle*, especially Oscar Wilde, on FPG's art. Similarly, though in far more detail, E.D. Blodgett carefully examines FPG's intimate knowledge of the German literary movement of *Neuromanik* (or Symbolism or neo-Classicism, as it is sometimes called) and in particular its relevance for his novel *Fanny Essler*, in which neo-Romantic ideology is not only 'treated with continuous satire but also ... is the fundamental explanation of Fanny's pathetic failure to endure.'[13] Blodgett's well-reasoned discussion of FPG's often merciless satire of some of the more pretentious aspects of German neo-Romantic literature and its practitioners has important implications for a proper understanding of FPG's later, Canadian novels in particular as well as for his narrative art and *Weltanschauung* in general. These aspects cannot concern us at present, though I shall touch upon a further dimension of FPG's satirical intent later on: *Fanny Essler* as a *roman à clef*. First, however, I wish to trace FPG's early career as a novelist, poet, and translator by comparing it with that of another German author on which my own research has been largely concentrated in recent years: Alfred Döblin. At first glance, this may appear to be a strange thing to do, for it would be hard to imagine two more dissimilar writers; yet they do have things in common which may serve to highlight some facets of their beginnings as creative writers in the turbulent society of Wilhelminian Germany in the last few years of the nineteenth and the first decade of the twentieth centuries. It was a period of incredible political, social, scientific, economic, literary and artistic ferment throughout Europe; and nowhere, one might add, was the intellectual yeast which caused this ferment more potent, or of more far-reaching consequences for the life of our century, than in Germany between the 1870s and 1914.

Alfred Döblin and FPG were born not only within a year of each other (1878 and 1879),[14] but also in the same general area of north-eastern Germany (all of which is now part of Poland), Döblin in Stettin (Szczecin), a port on the Baltic Sea in Pomerania, FPG in Radomno near Deutsch-Eylau (Ilawa), a railway junction in the then province of West Prussia, some three hundred and fifty kilometres to the east of Stettin. The family backgrounds and circumstances were different: FPG was the son of a fairly well-to-do estate steward or manager, but by no means a property owner or member of the landed gentry as FPG was later to imply, Döblin the son of a ne'er-do-well Jewish tailor, whose spendthrift ways left his family in dire poverty, forcing the mother to become the breadwinner when Döblin *père* ran away to America with one of his young seamstresses in 1888. But the coincidences are odd: the Greve family, slowly but surely descending on the social scale, had moved to Hamburg in 1881, where Greve *père* was employed as a tram conductor and ticket collector. For a brief period in 1890, the Döblin family lived in Hamburg, too, so in theory the paths of the two schoolboys and budding authors may have crossed. In both cases, however, it is the father who is the cause of the break-up of the family, a break-up ending in separation and divorce (the Greves were separated in 1892, the Döblins in 1890). Both mothers were abandoned and left to their own devices; Mrs Greve set up a boarding house with the help of a well-to-do relative, possibly her brother or brother-in-law, and her death in 1900 was brought about at least in part by her ruining her health to support her family. In Döblin's case it was also an uncle's financial help which enabled his mother to eke out a living in Berlin for herself and her five children. Alfred attended *Gymnasium* (or high school) in Berlin, Felix a similar institution in Hamburg. Both received their *Abitur*, the certificate required for university entrance, both began their studies, FPG in the Faculty of Arts at Bonn University, Döblin in the Faculty of Medicine at Berlin, in 1898 and 1900 respectively. Here perhaps the similarities between the two so dissimilar writers end; for Döblin not only became a successful physician and psychiatrist, but also in the fifty years of his literary career (he died in 1957) one of the most significant creative writers of this century, a major innovator in the avant-garde movement of Expressionism, and a world-famous figure in 1929 with the publication of his novel *Berlin Alexanderplatz*. One may say that Döblin occupies roughly the same position in German literature as James Joyce and John Dos Passos do in the English-speaking world. Both Döblin and FPG went to North America, but under very different circumstances. Döblin, a socialist and Jew, had to flee from Germany in 1933 and spend long years of enforced exile in Switzerland, France, and Hollywood until 1945, when he returned to his native Germany, a French citizen and convert to Christianity. He died, neglected by the literary world and in impoverished circumstances, in Emmendingen near Freiburg in 1957. It is only in the past ten years or so that the importance of his vast *oeuvre* is becoming recognized; Günter Grass has called him his teacher,[15] and Döblin's influence on twentieth-century German literature was truly seminal.

FPG's departure for North America in about 1909 was for very different reasons. In 1900 he withdrew from university, travelled extensively throughout Europe by dint of borrowing large sums of money from a fellow student, and on 29 May 1903 was sentenced to a year's imprisonment in Bonn for fraud. The news hit the press, and I like to think, though I have no proof at all for my supposition, that Thomas Mann chose the first name of his fictional confidence-man, artist, and jailbird, Felix Krull (the titular hero of an unfinished novel which Mann began as early as 1906) after reading an account of FPG's trial in a newspaper.[16] Whether this is true or not, FPG's double life, his suave appearance, smooth talk, and criminal activities make him the confidence-man *par excellence*. I am certain that Thomas Mann, had he known the facts, would in any case have enjoyed the humorous side of the following situation, alluded to by Spettigue in a newspaper article but not in his book.[17] In a letter dated 5 June 1939, when Thomas Mann was living in Princeton, he thanked FPG rather fulsomely for sending him what must have been the author's limited edition of *Two Generations*, which had just been published in Toronto.[18] (*Two Generations* is a novel set in Simcoe County where FPG was living at that time; father-son, husband-wife, parents-children conflicts dominate the novel just as they had in *Our Daily Bread*.) The unconscious irony of Mann's words, written in German (here in my translation) is delicious: 'the synthesis of tellurian and intellectual forces, for which I strive, is in your case a very charming, subdued, genuinely Anglo-Saxon humour, which does not die in the search to comprehend.'[19] If only Thomas Mann had known that his correspondent was a fellow German, whose sense of humour was anything but genuinely Anglo-Saxon! And FPG must have derived quiet amusement and satisfaction from the great ironist's letter.

Desperately trying to pay off his huge debts with his writing and especially translating – his productivity in this area was truly prodigious – between 1904 and 1909, FPG managed to cram in other activities as well; in 1902 he eloped with a friend's wife and married her (he probably divorced her in 1909); just after his release from prison in June 1904, as André Gide's diaries make abundantly clear, FPG even pretended to be a homosexual when visiting the French writer, whose proclivities in this direction were well known, in order to curry favour with him. Gide was not impressed, despite FPG's immaculate appearance: 'FPG was impeccably dressed, looking more English than German,' Gide notes, admiring the 'most elegant' silver cigarette case he had ever seen (with a matching silver match box), all of which were, of course, paid for with borrowed money.[20] FPG's final coup came some five years later: in order to escape his creditors and perhaps his wife, FPG faked suicide and disappeared from Germany, leaving a 'widow,' huge debts, and a death notice in the standard German necrological lexicon of the day. Where he lived between his disappearance in 1909 and his documented arrival in Winnipeg in December 1912 we shall probably never know. Perhaps FPG will have the last laugh after all.

But let us return to our comparison of FPG and Döblin. Despite all the many differences of character, of perceived artistic merit, of *Weltanschauung*, of their development as writers, Döblin and FPG do have some things in common; Nietzsche influenced them in their formative years, as he did the vast majority of writers of their generation, though Döblin, unlike most contemporary German *literati*, soon became an extraordinarily critical reader of Nietzsche's philosophy, as evidenced by his two essays of 1902–3.[21] FPG, on the other hand, continued to adhere to some of Nietzsche's vitalistic doctrines, even in Canada – a topic well worth further investigation. FPG and Döblin also both shared the same basic literary heritage of Naturalism, a point to which I shall return. Above all, as I have already mentioned, they both had unsuccessful, weak, and rather caddish fathers who left their wives and children in more or less desperate straits, and, balancing this, both had mothers whose self-sacrificing love managed to ensure that their sons received an education despite poverty. Were I a professing Freudian, which I am not, I could enjoy a critical banquet of Father Figures, feast on Oedipus complexes, and relish ids to my heart's content in the case of both FPG and Döblin. Some scholars, at least in Döblin's case, have done precisely this and their books sometimes suffer from severe post-prandial spasms of psycho-critical indigestion. Nevertheless, it is noteworthy that in the novels of both men, the relationships of fathers and mothers, of sons and daughters to their parents, and of marriage and sexual relations in general play an important role, a role which, particularly in the case of FPG, is almost invariably coupled with money, or rather the lack of it.

It is perhaps difficult for us to realize in these affluent days of medicare, social insurance, entrenched human rights, and minimum wages how extraordinarily repressive society in Wilhelminian Germany at the turn of the century was. Capitalism appeared to reign supreme, especially during the last decades in the nineteenth century: Germany advanced from a mainly agricultural economy to a highly industrialized juggernaut, advancing at breakneck speed towards the terrible clash in 1914–18 with the Western powers of France and England whose industrial might had been waning in proportion to the rapid advances of German science, technology, and industrial productivity. When FPG and Döblin went to school, German universities were at their zenith: scholarly research in all fields was booming, and German arts and letters enjoyed a similar prestige. And yet, in the midst of all this wealth and progress, there was crying poverty and misery for the masses of poor farmers and factory workers. Material progress had undoubtedly been made, but at a terrible price; it was the sort of progress scorned for vastly different reasons both by Nietzsche and by Karl Marx.

Women, in many ways, bore the brunt of the social and economic repression caused by unbridled capitalism; and women are the topic of both Döblin's first fragmentary narrative work, entitled 'Modern,' written in 1896 but unpublished until 1981,[22] and of FPG's first two novels, *Fanny Essler* and *The Master Mason's House*. The latter is readily available to Canadian readers, and since I have summarized the plots of both novels elsewhere,[23] I will not go into them in any detail here. However, it is worth pointing out that Susie, the main character of the novel, is a teenage girl whose development to womanhood and whose relationship with her ill-educated and tyrannical father are problematic and whose mother is driven insane by the strained marital relationship. The end of the novel is interesting – Susie's father marries again, and Susie's relationship with him and his wife is so bad that the master mason almost strangles Susie; but by this violent act Susie is at last 'free,' that is she can escape the stifling atmosphere of her parental home; and although the novel ends on an optimistic note – Susie is clearly going to marry Consul Blume, her admirer – we must note that marriage was the *only* 'escape' possible for a girl in Susie's circumstances.

Fanny Essler,[24] though published before the other novel, is in a sense a continuation of *The Master Mason's House*. While the latter is set in Pomerania in a little provincial town, the former's *mise-en-scène* is mainly Berlin and to a lesser extent other European cities. Berlin, of course, was the thriving, vibrant centre of Bismarck's reunified Germany; it is to Berlin that Fanny, the novel's heroine, escapes – once again from the repressive atmosphere of a lower-middle-class home in the province near Stettin (Döblin's birthplace, too, we recall). Typical of the age, Fanny has lost her virginity (she is nineteen when the novel opens and the year is pinpointed by FPG exactly: 1892) to a local member of the minor nobility.

But marriage is out of the question, since neither of the two fathers will agree to the union for reasons of social class and status. It cannot be overemphasized how accurate FPG's portrayals of the society of his day are; the physical appearance of people, the rooms they live in, the clothes they wear, their gestures, and above all their various levels of language (ranging from High German to the coarsest of dialects, of which there is an abundance in *Fanny Essler*) – all are 'photographed' or 'recorded' with loving care and attention to detail in the true Naturalist tradition. This type of naturalistic description is probably the novel's greatest weakness, since even minor characters who appear only once in a short scene are given the same 'close-up' treatment; the result is an inordinate proportion of descriptive *longueurs*, and in my view *Fanny Essler* could have been advantageously cut to about two-thirds of its present length. FPG, it may be added, does not avoid the crudities of gutter language in his attempt to reproduce the living language of the day. One of the characters in the novel is described as walking like a 'gev...... Henne' (p. 145); the prim but letter-numerically accurate ellipsis is FPG's, but not one of his readers could have failed to fill in the blanks with the German equivalent of the past participle of the English four-letter word for fornication. Or to take another example, tipsy students in the Berlin Café Monopol sing a ditty, in the presence of Fanny and her friend Bertha, the humour of which depends on a scatological pun of almost untranslatable vulgarity: 'Selbst der Eskimo – Wird seines Lebens froh – Nimmt sich eine Eskimöse ... (p. 117). There are other similar instances which need not concern us here, but FPG's words on the very first page of *A Search for America* (1927) take on a new significance if viewed from the standpoint of *Fanny Essler*, written some twenty years earlier; in his German novel, as we have seen, he was by no means above using the occasional vulgarity, but in his adopted language he simply did not have the linguistic facility to reproduce street language of this kind: 'I had acquired,' FPG writes, '– by dint of much study of English literature – a rather extensive reading and arguing vocabulary which however showed – and, by the way, to this day shows – its parentage by a peculiar stiff-necked lack of condescension to English slang.'[25] Slang aside, FPG's German linguistic 'parentage' frequently shows in most of his English writing – a topic well worth further research.

Döblin's ear for Berlin dialect, especially that of the lower classes, is evident in his first attempt at narrative prose, 'Modern: A Picture of Present-Day Life,' to which I have already alluded. Written while he was still a high school student in 1896, 'Modern,' short and fragmentary as it is, is in a sense the forerunner of Döblin's other Berlin novels, *Wadzeks Kampf mit der Dampfturbine* (1918) and above all *Berlin Alexanderplatz* (1929), in which his extraordinary artistic ability to reproduce lifelike everyday speech patterns comes to full flower. As has been recently established, 'Modern' – its genre is hybrid, consisting of a short story about a fallen working-class woman embedded in a kind of political-social tract on the emancipation of women – draws heavily on one of the most popular and influential studies on the role of women in society published in Germany in the late nineteenth century: August Bebel's *Die Frau und der Sozialismus*, the first edition of which appeared in 1883, reaching its fiftieth edition by 1910.[26] Bebel (1840–1913) was a Marxian socialist, and the main theme of his book, sometimes forbidden by the authorities and circulated clandestinely, is the exploitation of women in the capitalist society of his day. Although I have no proof (as I have in Döblin's case) that FPG actually read Bebel, my hunch is that he did; Bebel's book was after all part and parcel of the intellectual atmosphere of FPG's youth, especially from 1903 onwards when he had passed through his Oscar Wildean 'aesthetic' period (that is the period of close contact in person and by letter with members or would-be adherents of the *George-Kreis*) and when he was beginning to write his neo-Naturalist novels *The Master Mason's House* and *Fanny Essler*. Be that as it may, many critics have noted a passage in FPG's fictionalized autobiography, *In Search of Myself* (1946), which refers specifically to the role of women in his Canadian prairie novels. In 'pioneer countries' like America, FPG writes,

> woman is the slave; just as she is the slave in the uncivilized steppes of Siberia. A pioneering world, like the nomadic world of the steppes, is a man's world. Man stands at the centre of things; man bears the brunt of the battle; woman is relegated to the tasks of a helper. It is an unfortunate arrangement of nature that the burden of slavery, for such it is in all but name, should be biologically aggravated. As it is, it cannot be helped; and any artistic presentation has to take it into account. But it is not to be imagined that my sympathies were with the men. Quite the contrary. My sympathies were always with the women.[27]

Perhaps FPG may have been thinking, when he used the word 'always,' of his two German novels as well. For here, women are not only the heroines, around whom the whole of the plot revolves, but also the characters with whom FPG's sympathy undeniably lies. Many of the male characters in his German novels are portrayed negatively, or even ridiculed; the reader is compelled to empathize with Fanny and Susie, both young women in a man's world. August Bebel begins his famous treatise on women with a remarkably similar clarion call:

> Woman and the workingman have, since old, had this in common – *oppression*. ... However much in common woman may be shown to have with the workingman, she leads him in one thing: – *Woman was the first human being to come into bondage; she was a slave before the male slave existed.* All social dependence and oppression has its roots in the *economic dependence* of the oppressed upon the oppressor. In this condition woman finds herself, from an early day down to our own.[28]

It is an intriguing question why FPG as a Canadian writer chose to stress the repression of women as something peculiar to such 'pioneer' societies as Canada was at the turn of the century, for if anything the repression of women in the highly industrialized Germany at that same period was just as bad, perhaps even worse in some ways. Again and again, both Bebel in his treatise, Döblin in 'Modern,' and FPG in *Fanny Essler* explore the root causes of the oppression of women. The economic basis of prostitution, for example, is examined by all three writers in their different ways, but all come to similar conclusions. Young girls from the working classes or even the petite bourgeoisie, unable to make a decent living wage, are forced to resort to prostitution to make enough money to buy essential food and clothes. (This is precisely what Fanny does.) Lack of educational opportunities for women further exacerbates the problem, and it is worth noting that FPG's Fanny, though she did receive a sort of education at a ladies' 'Academy,' is in no way prepared for any sort of career suited to her intelligence. For Fanny is bright, intellectually curious, and reads a lot – a sort of haphazard self-educational process. The relationship between education and independence of women is, as Lorraine McMullen points out in her perceptive essay 'Women in Grove's Novels,'[29] particularly crucial in FPG's second published English-language novel, *Our Daily Bread* (1928); it is just as crucial in his German novels, and also in Bebel, who devotes a lot of attention to this same interrelationship.

Throughout *Fanny Essler*, we learn of Fanny's reading matter: Goethe, Schiller, Ibsen, Hauptmann, and Richard Voss (1851–1918), for example, a now forgotten writer belonging to the circle around the brothers Julius and Heinrich Hart. When Fanny becomes an actress she visits public libraries and reads 'quite indiscriminately: if a title took her fancy in the catalogue, she would take the book out; of all the authors she read only the names of Tolstoy, Dostoevski and Goncourt remained fixed in her memory' (pp. 278–9). On one occasion Fanny even forgets to go to the dress rehearsal of a play because she is so fascinated by Dostoevski's *Idiot*; arriving an hour and a half too late, she is promptly fired. Throughout the novel there are constant references to Goethe, and Fanny's distaste for his works is reflected in many conversations she has with her various well-educated lovers. FPG himself, as many of his letters reveal, was an admirer of Goethe;[30] here, FPG seems to be using Fanny's disdain for, and incomprehension of, the greatest German poet to highlight her lack of education; later in the novel when she has married Eduard Barrel, a member of a circle of neo-Romantic poets and writers, there is some indication that Fanny's *Bildung* is approaching the point when she can appreciate some aspects of Goethe, but in general she remains unrepentant in her dislike of his works. In this connection, Blodgett argues very cogently that although Fanny is the 'commanding figure' in the novel, her function in it 'would not be fully clear if it were not perceived that she stands in opposition to the values of the male world of her time.'[31] And this male world, Blodgett continues, is represented by neo-Romanticism and its ideologies, which are satirically and bitterly examined and found to be thoroughly wanting. 'Fanny's virtue, then, whether she is emancipated or not, is her refusal to be stereotyped,' Blodgett points out, 'to be as men want her to be, and to be as men are in the novel.'[32] Nevertheless, I think that FPG's merciless satire of German *Neuromantik* can also be explained at least in part by his own personal *engagement* with the ideologies of the movement before *Fanny Essler* was published. I am thinking here not only of his essays on Wilde,[33] but also of twenty-three of his own neo-Romantic poems, published privately and luxuriously under the title *Wanderungen* in 1902.[34] These poems, so obviously modelled on Stefan George's 'cycles' of poems that they read like parodies (rather bad ones in fact), received scant praise from the critics and were cruelly reviewed by Otto Julius Bierbaum;[35] a few years later, after his two novels had been published, FPG distanced himself from his own neo-Romantic lyrics by writing (in a *curriculum vitae*) that *Wanderungen* are 'bad if one fails to take their parodistic intent into account.'[36] This, I fear, is casuistry, for FPG's poems were almost certainly not conceived as parodies, but rather as a homage to the Master, Stefan George, with whom he visited and exchanged letters in 1902; clearly, by 1907 FPG deliberately emphasized his 'parodistic intent' in his *c.v.* because the poems had been so devastatingly reviewed. *Fanny Essler*, with its equally devastating satire of neo-Romantic aesthetes and their pretensions, is another matter altogether. For here the satire is intentional and deliberate: it is as if FPG were taking revenge on adherents of the very literary movement with which he had tried, in vain, to associate himself more intimately. Thus, FPG *combines* his portrayal of Fanny Essler's fate as a woman in a man's world with his own personal vendetta against the literary school which had to all intents and purposes rejected him. There is more than a little of FPG in his character Fanny; the novel kills, one might say, two birds with one stone.

Recent evidence, which I believe has not been noticed in print in Canada hitherto, tends to back up my thesis about FPG's taking revenge on the *Neuromantiker* in this novel. This evidence is contained in a letter to Ernst Hardt (1876–1947), a novelist, poet, and playwright with many contacts with the leading German literary figures at the turn of the century, from Marcus Behmer (1879–1958), a graphic artist and book designer of the *Art Nouveau* style; he definitely knew FPG, and designed the binding and drew other illustrations for FPG's multi-volume translation of Richard Burton's version of the *Arabian Nights*, which appeared in the prestigious Insel-Verlag in 1907–8. (FPG, it will be recalled, designed the dust-jacket of *Fanny Essler*, a fact which is recorded on its title-page; this was work FPG was to perform many years later in Canada for The Graphic Press.) On 19 February 1907 Behmer wrote to Hardt, gleefully referring to *Fanny Essler* and, not without *Schadenfreude*, making it quite obvious that he (and presumably others in the know) considered the novel to be a *roman à clef*:

> Fanny Essler is really marvellous: If Else Ti hasn't yet become a whore,
> despite her whore-like nature, well she has finally found her pimp, who is
> now prostituting her more than if he were to allow her to be mounted at 50
> pfennigs a trick. – The book is also excessively impudent regarding the
> other personalities depicted in it; and it hasn't had many readers? –
> Strange, in spite of its beastly vulgarity?! –[37]

This passage is interesting, since, as Pacey points out, FPG eloped with the wife of a friend in 1902, marrying her after her divorce and his release from prison in 1904, possibly in Switzerland.[38] This friend was the famous architect August Endell (1871–1925), who was in turn a friend of Hardt's and of Behmer's, and well known to many members of the George Circle in Munich (such as Karl Wolfkehl); Endell's wife was Else Hildegard, née Ploetz; an artist and the daughter of a master mason (!), she must have been a notorious *femme fatale* in her day. Thus, it becomes apparent from Behmer's letter (not known to Pacey or Spettigue when they published their books) that Fanny Essler is in fact a portrait of FPG's own wife Else – note also the similarity of 'Essler' and 'Else' – whom he probably divorced at the time of his 'disappearance' in 1909. But what about the mysterious name 'Ti' which Behmer uses? It is obviously not a surname, but a term of endearment or nickname. And it was precisily this intimate form of address, though Anglicized phonetically to 'Tee,' that FPG frequently used when writing to his second wife, Catherine, née Wiens, whom he married in 1914 in Manitoba. According to Pacey, Mrs Grove explained that her husband told her that 'Tee' meant 'mistress' in Chinese;[39] this is in fact true.[40] But really it is just another example of FPG's former habits catching up with him. One can only hope that Mrs Grove never knew that 'Tee' was the sobriquet which FPG applied to his first and notoriously immoral wife.

If one recalls the Canadian prairie novels of FPG, the role played in them by the *femme fatale* is certainly significant – one thinks of Clara Vogel in *Settlers of the Marsh* or Sybil Carter in *The Master of the Mill*. These and other women in FPG's Canadian novels seem to be an amalgamation of traits to be found in Fanny Essler: Fanny is a European prototype for many female characters in the later novels, for she combines innocence with lust, sturdy independence with dependence on her numerous lovers, love with hatred, cruelty with kindness, revulsion towards the sexual act with almost nymphomaniacal urges bordering on hysteria. Lorraine McMullen speaks of FPG 'moving in the direction of an androgynous society, in which roles are no longer sex-typed.'[41] It is, of course, for this type of society that Bebel was striving (though he does not call it 'androgynous' – a quaint word in this context since it really means hermaphrodite); Bebel, of course, felt that equality for women could be attained only through Marxian socialism – or as he puts it (how poignant and politically naïve his words seem today in light of recent events in Poland!):

> The complete emancipation of woman, and her equality with man is the
> final goal of our social development, whose realization no power on earth
> can prevent; – and this realization is possible only by a social change that

shall abolish the rule of man over man – hence also of capitalists over workingmen. ... The 'Golden Age' ... will have come at last. Class rule will have reached its end for all time, and, along with it, the rule of man over woman.[42]

Both Bebel and Döblin refer specifically to the plight of small-part actresses in Berlin; Döblin writes: 'There are said to be 20,000 prostitutes in Berlin alone, a figure which is almost certainly too conservative.' (Bebel puts the figure for 1890 much higher at not less than 50,000);[43] after demonstrating the economic causes of this sad statistic, Döblin continues: 'The chorus girls in the theatres are with rare exceptions almost all prostitutes. The more so if they are unfortunate enough to be beautiful. To earn enough to eat and to continue their education they have to work for miserable wages, and they themselves have to supply their own, extremely expensive costumes into the bargain.'[44] Bebel says almost the same and cites an actual example of an actress at a well-known Berlin theatre in 1891 engaged at a monthly salary of 100 marks, whose outlay for wardrobe alone ran up to 1000 marks a month; the deficit was covered by a 'friend.'[45] Precisely this happens to Fanny Essler. Soon after her arrival in Berlin, she is befriended by Bertha, the sort of young woman people referred to as a 'bourgeois girl with a house-key' (p. 106); that is she lived with her parents, but enjoyed night-life and luxuries by earning money from male admirers. FPG makes it clear that in Berlin 'Fanny learned that those distinguished, elegant ladies whom she had already seen on her walks late in the evening ... were in fact neither Countesses nor *grandes dames*. She discovered that their obvious luxury was earned in a manner which also lay within her grasp. There were gentlemen who loved this sort of lady, and love was the profession of these ladies' (p. 107). But Fanny is no slut, and one of the tragic elements of FPG's novel is that its heroine never does meet the fairy-tale prince for whom she yearns and wishes to love for love's sake. Nor does she (as FPG specifically says of her friend Bertha, p. 106) passionately devour the novels of Paul de Kock (1794–1871), a now-forgotten French writer of the nineteenth century, whose salacious, or at any rate rather risqué, tales delighted generations of readers – including, we may add, Dostoevski's Stepan Trofimovitch in *The Possessed*, who takes 'De Tocqueville with him into the garden while he had a Paul de Kock in his pocket.'[46]

Later, after Fanny has had an unsuccessful career as an actress at the Berlin Korso Theatre, she moves to the Provinces, to Kottbus, a small

garrison town, but with an ambitious theatre director, who has Ibsen's
Pillars of Society, Schiller's *Don Carlos*, and even Shakespeare's *Romeo and
Juliet* in his repertoire. But Fanny has no wardrobe and little money. In
FPG's novels we always find detailed facts and figures about money,
coupled with equally detailed descriptions of even the most minor
characters. Here is a typical example:

> Only one thing depressed her: *Don Carlos* was soon to be rehearsed and
> Mr. Timm [the theatre manager] told her that she would be given the part of
> Mondecar: she had neither wig nor even a trace of a wardrobe! Finally, she
> spoke to Mr. Timm about it. Mr. Timm was a small, thin man with a tiny
> head, dark-blond hair, a pleasant, clean-shaven face, and the gestures of a
> Berlin sales clerk. When he was standing behind a table and spoke with
> somebody he automatically bent forward, supporting himself with his
> knuckles pressed upon the table. 'Well, there's no way out,' he said to
> Fanny, 'you must have a wardrobe.' – 'But I don't *have* a costume,' Fanny
> said, 'and in any case, I can't afford to buy one on my 70 Mark salary.'
> (p. 245)

(Notice that Fanny's pay is even less than that of Bebel's actress.) For the
time being she is allowed to play modern roles, using her own clothes; but
when she wants to play Juliet, the advice given her by the theatre director
is brutally to the point: 'Get a rich admirer!' (p. 247). Unfortunately for
Fanny, the lover she does finally find is a debt-ridden army officer, who
cannot afford to pay for her wardrobe. And in the end, she is made to
leave town by the local police, after she has been denounced as an
immoral woman by local do-gooders. Yet, strangely, we do not feel that
Fanny is immoral: she is a victim of circumstances, of the society in which
she lives, of her own good nature, for she is unwilling to 'love' a rich man
for money alone. As I have previously pointed out, money with FPG is
always the key to happiness; but it is a key which talent, vitality,
intelligence, and even love alone cannot provide.

Northrop Frye once said that FPG was 'a pathological liar';[47] on the
surface, this seems to be true, as Spettigue has shown by his excerpts from
Gide's diaries, where FPG in June 1904 is reported to have said: '"I must
warn you, Monsieur Gide, that I am constantly telling lies." "[Your
friend] had warned me of that, too," [Gide replied]. "Yes, but he never
understood the point of my lies. ... it isn't what you think. ... I experience
the same need to lie, and the same satisfaction from lying, as another
person would in telling the truth ..."'[48]

And yet in a sense, FPG's need to lie is perhaps the secret of his artistry; fiction and fact are woven together to produce a many-coloured fabric of 'lies' in which poetic 'truth' shines through. And it is this kind of truth which matters to FPG. In this respect, he is backward- rather than forward-looking; and it is in this respect that he parts company with *avant-garde* writers like Döblin, who shared a common heritage of Naturalism and even art nouveau with FPG, but who, in the very years that FPG was publishing his two novels, were already beginning to produce works signalling the tumultuous advent of Expressionism, the dominant movement in German letters from about 1910 to 1925. FPG's abrupt departure from Europe meant that he had unwittingly cut himself off from exciting new developments on the German literary scene, which left works like *Fanny Essler* or *The Master Mason's House* far behind them. FPG missed the boat, as it were, by catching one.

Very early in his career Thomas Mann noted the proximity of the criminal and the artistic mind. In *Tonio Kröger*, published in 1903, he writes: 'One might be rash enough to conclude that a man has to be in some kind of jail in order to become a poet. But can you escape the suspicion that the source and essence of his being an artist had less to do with his life in prison than they had with the reasons that *brought him there*?'[49] I like to think that in this regard FPG was the archetypical Mannian artist and writer of the turn of the century, and that, as his moving, well-wrought Canadian prairie novels prove, artistic integrity and morality far outweigh their author's personal mendacity. In *Fanny Essler*, which appeared only two years after *Tonio Kröger*, there is a clear echo of Mann's novella: Tonio speaks of the 'benevolent pity' he feels when he is surprised to learn that an officer, a lieutenant and 'man of the world,' has written a sentimental poem – 'something about love and music, as deeply felt as it is inept.'[50] Fanny's lover in Kottbus, also a lieutenant, does precisely this: he shows Fanny one of the terribly amateurish poems he has secretly written. 'Fanny was dumbfounded,' FPG writes, 'A lieutenant does things like this!' (p. 253). FPG knew, as Mann did, that the dilettante approach to art was doomed to failure; as he wrote in a letter to Willard Holliday on 11 December 1940 (by that date FPG was a reasonably well-established author in his adopted country, with nine published books to his credit): 'You see, to me publication means nothing. What matters is solely that the work be done, the book be written, the beauty created.'[51] In the same letter he speaks of unpublished novels which he doesn't dare to publish, for 'the people of Canada would have *me* stoned or call *them* pornography.' Despite the fact that books of his were barred from libraries during his life, FPG remained true to his own strict brand of artistic integrity and morality; it is the morality he had succinctly expressed, many years before, in the epigraph to *Fanny Essler*: 'All true art is, in the strictest sense of the word, moral.'[52] Despite his pillorying of neo-Romanticism in his first novel, FPG always remained faithful to his European heritage of the first decade of our century.

NOTES

The present article is a revised version of a lecture given by me as a Lansdowne Visitor at the University of Victoria, British Columbia, on 10 February 1981; I have attempted, whenever possible, to retain the oral flavour of the original.

1 The case of B. Traven is far more complex and enigmatic than that of Grove; it seems possible that his early novels may have been the result of a strange kind of 'collaboration' between the mysterious German-speaking revolutionary Ret Marut and an American 'Erlebnisträger'; but as M.L. Baumann concludes: 'Almost 30 years of journalistic detective work has ended in failure, and the texts have yielded all the biographical clues that they are ever likely to yield' (Michael L. Baumann, 'Who Was B. Traven?' *Pennsylvania Gazette*, April 1976, pp. 15–42, here p. 42); for a more detailed study see the same author's *B. Traven: An Introduction* (Albuquerque: University of New Mexico Press, 1976). In any case, Traven, unlike Greve/ Grove, never assumed a new public persona, nor did he openly write and achieve nation-wide recognition under the guise of this new identity; Traven became internationally famous despite (or because of) the fact that both the reading public and literary scholars were aware that 'B. Traven' was in fact the pseudonym of a writer who deliberately went to extraordinary lengths to conceal his identity from them.

2 See D.O. Spettigue, 'The Grove Enigma Resolved,' *Queen's Quarterly*, 79 (Spring 1972), 1–2.

3 Spettigue, *FPG: The European Years* (Ottawa: Oberon Press, 1973); see also Spettigue (with A.W. Riley), 'Felix Paul Greve *redivivus*: Zum früheren Leben des kanadischen Schriftstellers Frederick Philip Grove,' *Seminar*, 9 (1973), 148–55. I gratefully acknowledge my debt to Douglas Spettigue for much of the information I have used in this article.

4 Eight of the papers delivered at the Grove Symposium were published in a special issue, edited by John Nause, of *Inscape* (11:1, Spring 1974), 1–110.

5 See *The Letters of Frederick Philip Grove*, ed. Desmond Pacey (Toronto and

Buffalo: University of Toronto Press, 1976), p. ix (Pacey's Preface is dated 10 June 1974).

6 Ibid., p. 515 (Pacey's Introduction to the German letters is undated).

7 See Wilhelm Kosch, *Deutsches Literatur-Lexikon*, 3rd completely reworked edition (Bern and München: Francke Verlag, 1978), vi, col. 778–9. Although Kosch lists a large number of FPG's publications, including his many translations, they are not complete; D.O. Spettigue and Paul Hjartarson are presently compiling an exhaustive FPG bibliography (primary and secondary) to be published in the series 'Bibliographies of Major Canadian Writers' by ECW Press, Downsview, in 1984.

8 See Walter Pache, 'Der Fall Grove – Vorleben und Nachleben des Schriftstellers Felix Paul Greve,' *Deutschkanadisches Jahrbuch*, 5 (Toronto, 1979), 121–36, and also his 'The Dilettante in Exile: Grove at the Centenary of His Birth,' *Canadian Literature*, no. 90 (Autumn 1981), 187–91; K.P. Stich's article, 'Grove's New World Bluff,' in the same issue of *Canadian Literature* (pp. 111–23), is a Jungian interpretation of *Settlers of the Marsh* with some discussion of *Fanny Essler*. The 'cornerstone' of Stich's unusual interpretation is the 'ambiguity' of FPG's phrases 'the big bluff' (referring to a clump of trees) and the 'Big Marsh,' which in FPG's bilingual world have, according to Stich, 'covert significance' (p. 113) of a symbolical and psychological nature: they allude to the only German meaning of the loanword *Bluff* (= a 'lie' or 'false front') and *der* and *die Marsch* (= 'march' and 'marsh,' respectively). Unfortunately, one may add, there are dozens of linguistic *faux amis* of this kind in German and English, and it would not be hard to project 'covert meanings' into the text of all of FPG's novels on this rather shaky basis. For example, if FPG talks about having a 'lump in his throat' (as he does in *A Search for America*) is he really also alluding to *der Lump* (= scoundrel)? Would the English word 'shield' conjure up *das Schild* (= a label or signboard) as well as *der Schild* (= a shield or buckler)? And when FPG refers to 'fall' (autumn or any other English meaning of the word) could he not also be cryptically alluding to *der Fall* (a grammatical of legal case) as well as to *das Fall* (a halyard)? To base interpretations of literary texts on 'punning' words which are phonetically or morphologically similar in two different languages is a dangerous game, even if the odd bilingual *double entendre* may be potentially amusing.

9 'Frederick Philip Grove,' in *Twentieth-Century Literary Criticism*, ed. Sharon K. Hall, vol. iv (Detroit: Gale Research Company, 1981), pp. 132–45 (contains excerpts from essays by A.L. Phelps, I. Skelton, B.K. Sandwell, N. Frye, L. Pierce, T. Sanders, D.O. Spettigue, R. Sutherland, D. Pacey, and A.W. Riley).

10 I am grateful to Professor Blodgett for having kindly allowed me to read a draft typescript of his essay, '*Alias* Grove: Variations in Disguise,' which

has since been published in his book *Configuration: Essays in the Canadian Literatures* (Downsview: ECW Press, 1982), pp. 112–53; future page references will be to this volume.

11 Frederick Philip Grove, *The Master Mason's House*, ed. A.W.Riley and D.O. Spettigue, trans. Paul P. Gubbins (Ottawa: Oberon Press, 1976); an English version of *Fanny Essler* (trans. Christine Helmer, A.W. Riley, and D.O. Spettigue) is scheduled for publication in 1984.

12 Pache, 'The Dilettante in Exile,' p. 188.

13 Blodgett, p. 128.

14 Biographical data used in the present essay have been taken from two major sources: D.O. Spettigue's *FPG: The European Years* and Jochen Meyer's 'Döblin-Chronik,' *Zu Alfred Döblin*, ed. Ingrid Schuster, LGW-Interpretationen 48 (Stuttgart: Ernst Klett, 1980), pp. 7–40. For a general introduction to Döblin's life and works in English, see Wolfgang Kort, *Alfred Döblin*, TWAS 290 (New York: Twayne, 1974).

15 Günter Grass, 'Über meinen Lehrer Döblin,' *Akzente*, 14 (1967), 290–309 (and frequently reprinted); very recently, Grass established a substantial Alfred Döblin Prize for Literature, devoting the royalties from his novel *Der Butt* (1977) to this end.

16 Thomas Mann, *Bekenntnisse des Hochstaplers Felix Krull: Der Memoiren erster Teil* (Frankfurt a.M., 1954); fragments of *Krull* were published as early as 1911 and 1922. Independently of me, K.P. Stich, in 'Grove's New World Bluff,' p. 111, also draws attention to similarities between Krull and FPG.

17 Spettigue, 'A Monument to Pacey and to This Elegant Dilettante and Suffering Hero Called Grove,' *Globe and Mail* (3 Jan. 1976), p. 30.

18 FPG, *Two Generations* (author's limited edition; Toronto: Ryerson Press, 1939).

19 There are two letters from Mann to FPG extant, both typed in German, and dated Princeton, 19 April 1939 and 5 June 1939. The originals are in the possession of Mr Leonard Grove (Toronto), and I am most grateful to him for sending me (at the request of D.O. Spettigue) photocopies of both in January 1971, at which time I sent further copies of the letters to the Thomas Mann Archives at Zürich; since then part of the text of the letter of 5 June 1939 has been published, including the sentence which I have paraphrased in English in the present article (see *Die Briefe Thomas Manns: Regesten und Register* ed. Hans Bürgin and Hans-Otto Mayer [Frankfurt a.M.: S. Fischer, 1980], II, 319). In the letter of 19 April 1939, Mann thanks FPG for his letter of 10 February 1939 and writes that he is looking forward to the 'luxury edition' of the novel (i.e. *Two Generations*) that FPG proposes to send him; in the longer letter of 5 June 1939 Mann also mentions that he is looking forward to reading FPG's *A Search for America* on his return from a summer trip to Europe (this took place from mid-June to mid-September

1939). It is not known whether Mann ever read FPG's 'Odyssey of an Immigrant' (*A Search for America* was reissued by Ryerson in 1939); it is however, worth noting that Mann's praise of FPG's 'Anglo-Saxon humour' is characteristic of Mann's view of the literature of the English-speaking world in general: the quality he admired most was its 'robust humour' (cf. my 'Notes on Thomas Mann and English and American Literature,' *Comparative Literature*, 17 [1965], 57–72).

20 The Gide quotations are from Spettigue's English translation in his *FPG: The European Years*, pp. 120 and 123.

21 'Der Wille zur Macht als Erkenntnis bei Friedrich Nietzsche' and 'Zu Nietzsches Morallehre[n].' The essays remained unpublished until 1978, when Bruno Hillebrand edited them in his two-volume *Nietzsche und die deutsche Literatur* (München: dtv; Tübingen: Niemeyer, 1978), I, 315–58; Hillebrand's volumes and his introduction to them are by far the best available scholarly documentation of the reception of Nietzsche by German writers from 1873 to 1963, and of the research literature on the topic.

22 Alfred Döblin, 'Modern. Ein Bild aus der Gegenwart,' *Jagende Rosse/Der schwarze Vorhang und andere frühe Erzählwerke* ed. A.W. Riley (Olten and Freiburg i.Br.: Walter-Verlag, 1981), pp. 7–25.

23 See my article 'The German Novels of FPG,' *Inscape*, 11:1, pp. 55–66.

24 Felix P.[aul] Greve, *Fanny Essler: Ein Roman*, 1st edition (Stuttgart: Axel Juncker Verlag, [1905]); a '2. Aufl.' (2nd edition) appeared the same year. It is noteworthy that FPG changed the dedication of his novel between editions: the first is dedicated to 'meinen Eltern' ('my parents'), the second to 'Ernst Engel,' the famous German statistician (1821–96), who was mainly interested in the sociology of the masses. What caused FPG to make this change is unknown, but one may assume that it was (a) because he felt some of the novel's characters were a little too close to home for comfort (see my remarks later in the present essay on *Fanny Essler* as a *roman à clef*) and (b) because the dedication to Engel made the novel appear closer in intent to 'scientific Naturalism.' Future page references in the text of this article to *Fanny Essler* will be to the German first edition, but the English versions are taken from the uncorrected draft translation mentioned in n.11, above.

25 FPG, *A Search for America: The Odyssey of an Immigrant*, New Canadian Library 76 (Toronto: McClelland and Stewart, 1971), p. 3.

26 See my editorial notes and afterword to 'Modern' (n.22, above), pp. 223–7 and 288–92. Two separate English translations of Bebel's *Die Frau und der Sozialismus* (1883) soon appeared (by H.B. Adams Walter, under the title *Woman in the Past, Present, and Future* [London: Modern Press, 1885], and by Daniel de Leon, entitled *Woman under Socialism* [New York: Labor News Co., 1904]); both translations have been recently reissued (by AMS Press,

New York, 1976, and Source Book Press, New York, 1970, respectively). Future references in my essay will be to the de Leon translation in the 1970 edition.

27 FPG, *In Search of Myself*, New Canadian Library 94 (Toronto: McClelland and Stewart, 1974), pp. 223–4.

28 Bebel, p. 9 (Bebel's italics).

29 Lorraine McMullen, 'Women in Grove's Novels,' *Inscape*, 11:1, pp. 67–76.

30 See for example *Letters*, ed. Pacey, pp. 6 and 308.

31 Blodgett, p. 126.

32 Ibid., p. 133.

33 FPG, *Randarabesken zu Oscar Wilde* (Minden: Bruns, [1903]), 50 pp.; *Oscar Wilde. Moderne Essays*, Nr. 29 (Berlin: Gose und Tetzlaff, 1903), 46 pp.

34 FPG, *Wanderungen* (München: I. Littauer, 1902); in all, 120 copies were privately printed on hand-made paper – another nod in the direction of the aesthetic exclusiveness of the George Circle, members of which always paid extraordinary attention to the quality of the paper and design of the books they published. See also Peter A. Stenberg, 'Translating the Translatable: A Note on a Practical Problem with F.P. Greve's *Wanderungen*,' *Candian Review of Comparative Literature*, 7: 2 (Spring 1980), 206–12; Stenberg prints several stanzas of the poems in the original German with some examples of his own verse translations into English. Since the poems read like bad parodies of George, the translator's task is extremely difficult, if not impossible.

35 Part of Bierbaum's review is reproduced (in English translation) by Spettigue, *FPG: The European Years*, pp. 71–2; Spettigue also gives his own free translation of one complete poem, two stanzas of which Bierbaum had quoted in his review to show how poor the verse was (ibid., pp. 66–7).

36 FPG, 'Biographical Notes' attached to letter to Franz Brümmer, dated Berlin, 6 March 1907, in *Letters*, ed. Pacey, p. 541.

37 *Briefe an Ernst Hardt: Eine Auswahl aus den Jahren 1898–1947*, ed. Jochen Meyer, Marbacher Schriften 10 (Marbach, 1975), p. 53 (my translation). It remains to be seen whether further study of the unpublished papers and letters of Hardt and Behmer (or indeed those of many of their other correspondents) will reveal further traces of FPG.

38 See *Letters*, ed. Pacey, p. 552.

39 Ibid., p. 83 (many of the letters FPG wrote to his wife begin with 'My dear Tee').

40 I am grateful for this information to Professor Jan Walls, University of Victoria, who is presently with the Canadian Embassy in Peking; in the transliteration of the day, 'Ti' was the standard German spelling of the Chinese word; its meaning is 'concubine' or 'mistress,' and FPG may well have come across it in one of the many translations of Chinese poems,

dramas, and stories which enjoyed a tremendous vogue in Germany from the 1890s onwards. Otto Julius Bierbaum (who reviewed FPG's *Wanderungen*) was one of the first translators of the period to introduce Chinese lyrical poetry to German readers (see Ingrid Schuster, *China und Japan in der deutschen Literatur 1890–1925* [Bern and München: Francke, 1977], p. 91 et passim).

41 McMullen, p. 75.
42 Bebel, p. 349.
43 Ibid., p. 159, and Döblin, 'Modern,' p. 18.
44 Döblin, pp. 18–19.
45 Cf. Bebel, p. 161.
46 Fyodor Dostoyevsky, *The Possessed*, trans. Constance Garnett (New York: Modern Library, 1963), p. 16.
47 Quoted by Spettigue, *FPG: The European Years*, p. 125.
48 Ibid., pp. 122–3.
49 Mann, 'Tonio Kröger,' in *Death in Venice*, trans. H.T. Lowe-Porter (Harmondsworth: Penguin Books, 1957), p. 153.
50 Ibid., p. 160.
51 FPG, *Letters*, ed. Pacey, p. 396.
52 Title-page (unnumbered) of *Fanny Essler*.

The German Immigrant Writer Walter Bauer ᅟ The Burden of His European 'Luggage' ᅟᅟ

GÜNTER HESS

In a letter to the Canadian poet John Robert Colombo the seventy-year-old Walter Bauer remarked that he had come to this country as 'a German who had been mortally wounded and crippled by events of the past.'[1] The 'events of the past' remained his burdensome 'luggage' throughout the twenty-five years of his Canadian journey. It contained the memories of two world wars and the holocaust, as well as his personal feeling of shame and guilt. It was mainly through this 'luggage' that Bauer experienced Canada. He was fully aware of this. He even hoped that 'it may be exactly that kind of past combined with the present of my life which may prove to be a unique foundation for the work I shall do or at least try to do.'[2] This explains why much of his Canadian writing is dominated by the tension between the present and the past, the 'here' and 'there,' the New World and the Old. In order to illustrate this double perspective and to assess to what extent the work of the German immigrant writer Walter Bauer contributed to Canadian literature, we must first recapture, although only briefly, his personal and creative life prior to his arrival in Canada in 1952.

He was born in the Saxon town of Merseburg in 1904. As the fifth child of a working-class family he soon learned that there was literally no room for him at the kitchen table, so he sat beneath it. From there he viewed the world around him; there he began to read and to write. After his graduation from teachers' college in 1925, Bauer taught in schools usually in areas of heavy industry. The pale and hungry students reminded him of the difficult years of his own childhood. They strengthened his commitment to speak out against social injustice. With the publication of his first book of poetry in 1929, *Kameraden, zu euch spreche ich* ('Comrades, I speak to you'), he joined the ranks of writers who deplored the exploitation of the proletariat. During the next two years two more books appeared: the volume of poetry, *Stimme aus dem Leunawerk* ('A voice from the Leuna Factory'), and the novel, *Ein Mann zog in die Stadt* ('A man moved to the city').[3] Both of these works firmly established his reputation as a young writer. Influential critics of the day praised his ability to depict with deep compassion the plight of the working class and the inhuman conditions of their proletarian milieu.

By the time Hitler came to power in 1933, Bauer had added one more novel to his list of publications. All of them were immediately banned. The Third Reich showed little sympathy for a pacifist who advocated a free, egalitarian Europe and international brotherhood. Many of Bauer's socialist and Jewish friends were imprisoned or had to go abroad. His own fate became at times rather precarious. He was fortunate, for instance, that the authorities did not intercept a letter he had sent to his Jewish publisher Max Tau. 'We,' he wrote on 31 March 1933, 'for whom the fatherland was only a stage on the great road to mankind ... have to bear witness to something that is more important than this throw-back to barbarity, to the fact, namely, that there is good in man and that our faith in this world is worthier than this frenzy of "race" instincts ... Only Germans could stage such anti-Semitic witch-hunts; by comparison the ghetto of the Middle Ages was human. It is our task to stand together more closely and to bear witness that the madness of mass instincts is the product of the intoxication with nationalism; let us be fellow humans. ...'[4] Such condemnation of fascism could, of course, never be voiced in public. Even the suspicion of tacit solidarity with people opposed to the regime jeopardized one's freedom. Bauer himself came close to being arrested for his secret meeting with Stefan Zweig in Zürich in 1935. He was demoted instead; as the friend of a Jewish writer he was declared unfit to teach certain subjects to the children of the Third Reich. Attempts to leave Germany with his wife – they had married in 1930 – were at times seriously considered, but never carried out. And so Bauer stayed and continued to write. In spite of the many difficulties he encountered – his manuscripts, for example, were usually scrutinized by the authorities – the record of his literary output was quite impressive.[5] It included volumes of poetry and short stories, novels, biographies, books for children, reviews, and numerous essays. With all of his writings, Bauer 'attempted to keep burning a tiny flame of the human spirit throughout those dark and terrible years.'[6] In his essays on Georg Forster, Livingstone, Nansen, Pestalozzi, Michelangelo, Flaubert, Goethe, to mention only a few, he wanted to bear witness to the forces of humanity and the indomitable spirit of the past which recognize no national boundaries and outlive any dictatorship. Much of his work was easily accessible since it was published in newspapers and journals. Particularly popular was his book *Tagebuchblätter aus Frankreich* ('A diary from France'),[7] which appeared in 1941, one year after Bauer had been drafted. By the end of the war, he had become an officer in the army fighting for a cause he bitterly hated. This complicity was to haunt him for the rest of his life.

When Hitler's tyranny had finally collapsed, Bauer was among those who hoped that a new Germany and a better Europe would emerge. He believed that after years of barbaric madness the writer's task was to aid in the recovery of the respect for human values. In a spirit of regeneration he wrote copiously. Within only six years he published some twenty books as well as numerous radio plays. The characters we meet in his post-war writings are still the simple people, but they have very little in common with the exploited proletariat of his earlier work. They are mostly German soldiers returning home after World War II and trying to find new roots in their desolated country. Some of them are shocked and deeply humiliated when they learn of Nazi atrocities. Often they share the author's own feeling of shame and guilt. The hero Wellner, in the prose work *Das Lied der Freiheit* ('The song of freedom'), speaks for Bauer too when he admits: 'And then I thought I was a coward. Yes, that's what I am. When there was still time to act, I did nothing.'[8] Distrustful of all political slogans and ideologies, Wellner gives his life a new turn by working for the welfare of war orphans, following closely in the footsteps of the Swiss pedagogue and humanist Pestalozzi. Other characters in Bauer's work represent Germans of the post-war period who simply swept the past under the carpet, unwilling to acknowledge and to accept responsibility for the crimes committed in the Third Reich. It was precisely this prevailing attitude, as Bauer repeatedly tells us, which eventually shattered his optimism. 'The dawn we hoped for did not come. Restoration and reaction are taking its place ... and the sight of a large part of Germans incapable of learning from the past fell like iron across my hands,'[9] he wrote in a farewell letter to his publisher. His disillusionment was intensified by Germany's so-called economic miracle and by the spreading commercialism in the book market. In spite of his own remarkable success as a freelance writer, he felt the new developments in Germany to be increasingly intolerable. Determined 'not to suffocate from shame, revulsion, anger and resignation.'[10] he assures us, he reached his decision to go to Canada.

Bauer's correspondence and diaries seem to suggest, however, that the events leading to his emigration were far more complex, at times more confusing, than he himself perhaps realized or was willing to disclose. Writing to Hermann Hesse in 1954, he draws attention to the fact that a recent book of his referred only to the political aspects of his decision to leave Germany. It did not mention, he points out, the deeper reasons closely linked with the very essence of his personal and creative life which he found virtually impossible to define clearly.[11] There is now enough evidence to believe that at least one of the 'deeper reasons' for his emigration was his marital problems. Actually it was his second wife, Jutta, who had initially suggested emigration to Canada.[12] When Bauer finally made up his own mind, his decision rested, to some extent, on the illusion that a fresh start in a new country could possibly save his broken marriage. Even after their four-year-old marriage had been officially dissolved a few days prior to their departure from Genoa, Bauer kept hoping their journey together would be the beginning of a better relationship. As it turned out, the first few months in Toronto put an end to that illusion. It is probably against this background that the following diary entry should be read:'24 years ago the "Argentina" approached the coasts of Newfoundland and Nova Scotia. Tomorrow I shall go on land. Everything was impenetrable, confused, painful.'[13]

Fortunately, Bauer had no illusion about the difficulties awaiting him as an immigrant. He had been sufficiently warned that he must expect to work extremely hard and, of course, under much less favourable conditions than in Europe. He was not afraid of this challenge. For some time he worked as a packer, dishwasher, factory worker; then, as a mature man of fifty, he began to study at the University of Toronto where eventually he became associate professor in the Department of German. During his early hardships as a manual labourer, he rediscovered, so he tells us, a few simple truths, like that of 'the air tasting, when you step outside after ten hours' work, like fresh water, and the truth about the safeness and warmth of being part of a team, the wisdom of the seventh day as a day of rest.'[14]

Earning his living through manual labour, Bauer regained confidence not only as a man but also as a writer. Unskilled labour had recharged, as it were, his creative energies. During his first four years in Canada, he published two volumes of poetry, one of short stories, and one children's book, as well as biographies of two explorers, Sieur de la Salle (*Folge dem Pfeil*, 'Follow the arrow') and Fridtjof Nansen (*Die langen Reisen*, 'The long journeys').[15] The Nansen book received the first International Albert Schweitzer Prize for Literature in 1956. The next twenty years of Bauer's Canadian sojourn were no less productive. He wrote about one book a year. Many of his works are specifically Canadian in content, including *Ein Jahr: Tagebuchblätter aus Kanada* ('One year: a Canadian diary'), the biography of Grey Owl, *Der weisse Indianer* ('The white Indian'), and a volume of short stories with the appropriate title *Fremd in Toronto* ('Stranger in Toronto').[16] That Bauer, the author, did not long remain a stranger in this country must be credited to the excellent translations of his poetry by his long-time colleague at the University of Toronto, Humphrey Milnes, and his younger poet-friend, Henry Beissel. Milnes's *A Slight Trace of Ash* and Beissel's *A Different Sun*[17] were both published shortly before Bauer's death in 1976. Beissel's first major translation of Bauer's poetry, *The Price of Morning*,[18] had already appeared in 1968.

In one of his poems, Bauer says that his immigrant 'luggage' contains far more than what the Canadian custom officers could possibly have noticed: his 'desperate love for Europe' (*Sun*, p. 15). Why the poet calls his love for Europe 'desperate' is not explained in this particular poem, but it becomes clearly evident even on a cursory reading of his Canadian writings, for Bauer returns time and again to the subject of his European past and the dark history of his own people. To be sure, his work of the immediate post-war period also concerns itself, as we have already pointed out, with this problem, but hardly ever with the painful intensity and almost terrifying obsessiveness of his Canadian *oeuvre*. Even fourteen years after his arrival in his adopted homeland, Bauer would admit to his publisher: 'It is only now that the full significance of my leaving Germany is being revealed. Everything before was just a prelude.'[19] Living under 'the cold refugee sky here' (*Sun*, p. 28) made him more aware that he was 'a German of his time' (*Sun*, p. 43) and that he had to come to terms with his identity more completely than ever before. 'Here,' he tells us in his poem 'Toronto Means Meeting-place,' 'Here I encountered myself / and had long conversations with myself' (Sun, p. 27). It was in Canada that the German immigrant writer rigorously and incessantly questioned his own past. He was convinced that his silent opposition to the Nazi regime was not enough to vindicate him. And the fact that he had served in Hitler's army, although reluctantly, increased the torment of his guilt-ridden conscience. The speaker's confession in the 'Interview with an Older Man' is Bauer's own confession:

> 'To have been cowardly
> When I should've been courageous.'
>
> 'To have survived
> When so many died and so many better ones.'
>
> 'To have trembled with fear
> When I should've been fearless.'
>
> 'To have crawled
> When I should've walked upright.'

(Sun, p. 43)

Bauer carried with him not only the burden of his personal guilt feelings but also what he called 'this horrible piece of rock of the German Sisyphus,'[20] the memories of hideous crimes committed during Hitler's dictatorship. They remained part of his immigrant's luggage throughout his Canadian journey.

> ...
> Tomorrow I shall travel west across the North American continent:
> Will the smoke follow me?
> I shall see the vast plains and the mountains' silver flames:
> Will the smoke melt away there and vanish?
> And when I dive with a shout of joy into the Pacific ocean
> Will my eyes still be tearing?
> Yes, it's the kind of smoke that will follow me everywhere.
> It'll always be burning in my eyes.

(Sun, p. 13)

The kind of smoke that never ceased to burn his eyes does not come from 'the autumn campfire' around which he gathered in his childhood years; it comes from 'the cities that fell to ruins in a hail of bombs' and 'those ovens heated with flesh!' (Sun, p. 12f.). 'For people my age' (Sun, p. 13), Bauer points out, the memory of the past will never fade away; 'knowledge /

Excludes forgetting' (*Sun*, p. 62). Moreover, he believed that 'the future poets – and this is not only the problem of German poets – are going to be those who will not forget Auschwitz and Belsen, and who accept the burden of history' (*Jahr*, p. 72), a burden which Bauer's Canadian work does not neglect. Whether the horrors of the past would have echoed as strongly in his work if he had never left Germany remains a matter of speculation. What we do know, however, is that his preoccupation with the tragic events of Germany's history was definitely intensified by his Canadian experiences, especially by his many encounters with European refugees who had personally suffered under the Nazi regime. His Jewish landlady, his Dutch watchmaker, his Ukrainian shoemaker, not to mention the hundreds of Jewish students in his classes at University College in Toronto, were all constant reminders to him of the unredeemed past. 'Sometimes I have the idea of writing a short story or a novel about a young German coming to Canada because he wants to live in the present and yet ends up finding the past,'[21] Bauer informed a friend. Although this particular plan was never carried out, we can easily perceive that such a project would have been dominated by the same tension we find so often in his Canadian work, the tension between the present and the past. The astute observations that F.W. Watt makes with regard to Bauer's poetry apply equally to most of his other Canadian writings: 'The perspective in many of his poems is irreducibly double: he sees the immediate Canadian scene, the city, the country, the people who inhabit it, with fresh and searching eyes, but always behind are the spectres of other cities, other landscapes, other human beings which are engraved upon his imagination with the intensity of an apocalyptic vision.'[22] His poem 'The Sun Here' clearly exemplifies this double perspective.

> The sun here must be a different sun
> From the one under which I could live no longer.
> The sun here has heard the cry of eagles
> And the patient whispering of ice ages,
> The sound of axes, the triumphant whistle of trains –
> Not the thunder of Last Judgments returning night after night
> Not the moaning of nations forced to their knees,
> Not the sounds of shots, or of sighs,
> Not the cry for freedom,
> The sun here has heard nothing, nothing at all.
> The sun here never turned black, never went into hiding, never knew
> shame.   (*Sun*, p. 10)

It is not lack of knowledge about Canada's history that leads Bauer to claim that the sun here 'never knew shame.' He knows otherwise. Yet, measured against the atrocities of war that had plagued Europe, Canada's history seemed to him to be unstained. 'Here I am,' he wrote in his diary, 'a man who was not born here, a European blackened and scarred by catastrophe, and up there is perfect emptiness, untouched by history' (*Jahr*, p. 18). By juxtaposing the peaceful and natural grandeur of the Canadian landscape with the horrors of warfare and persecutions, Bauer conjures up a Canada that assumes an almost idealized reality. Such a vision on his part is mainly determined by his need to create a positive counterpart to a war-stricken Europe and, more to the point, a Nazi Germany. Since the poet perceives his life 'here' with a consciousness which is simultaneously German and Canadian, he succeeds in blending the past and the present, Europe and Canada. The double perspective in his work contributes a more universal dimension to Canadian literature. The past Bauer evokes is also a warning to take nothing for granted, for recent history has shown how suddenly people and cities can perish:

> This city, like any other, will never know
> That I was here, that I am gone; it doesn't care.
> And yet I wish it luck and that its luck may last –
> I underline *last*, because the city's loud voice frightens me.
> Experience taught us all that cities too can die,
> Quickly, unexpectedly – or have we forgotten already?
>   It's but a few years ago.
> They die, and nothing is left of them but smoke to indicate
> That there, for God's sake, stood a big city;
> Now there is only the surging emptiness of light.
> That's why you have to wish this city luck, like a friend you found.
> I wish the city, that never knew me and yet was home to me, a long life.
>
> (*Sun*, p. 21)

It was in the city of Toronto, which he hardly ever left, that Bauer observed and encountered the many immigrants whose experiences are woven into the tapestry of his writings. Just as his working-class roots had once made him a spokesman for the proletariat, his sympathies as an immigrant turned naturally to the Canadian newcomers. In *Fremd in Toronto* ('Stranger in Toronto'), a volume consisting of thirty-six auto-biographical short stories or prose sketches, the author gives us a moving record of the many difficulties and hardships the immigrants face in establishing themselves in the new country. Their problems are usually very basic, finding a decent job, a place to live, a friend to talk to. In the story 'A Mozart Quartet,' Bauer skilfully introduces four players who share not only a profound love for music but also a sad awareness of their uprooted existence as European refugees: 'the gnawing loneliness in the unfamiliar vastness of a new land, ... the stammering in another language, and always the look back, a look of injured and betrayed love, of desperation, of anger and hatred at being shut out. ... The sensation of walking on land and yet of being without a land. The slow, painful growing into new relationships, into embraces and tenderness, whispered in a language that one did not speak, that consisted only of words that had not grown inside, of words that held no memories; the birth of a child that would never know of its father's flight. And then, years later, the startling realization that one could not go back again, never.'[23] Many of the other immigrants convey the same sense of loneliness and isolation, they are 'like a leaf torn from a tree.' Their simple lives, mostly spent in rooming-houses and humble jobs, oscillate between hope and despair, initial success and failure. Of the city itself we rarely get more than a few glimpses, as for example when the narrator in the short story 'The Breakfast' sits with an old Italian immigrant on a bench in Toronto's Queen's Park sharing with him some bread and cheese. If the author had merely changed the names of the streets, places, and buildings, Toronto could have easily been replaced by any other Canadian city. Interchangeable are also most of the characters, for their efforts to establish themselves in their adopted land and their reactions to their new environment are noticeably linked to Bauer's own experiences. Since the author tends to perceive the world lyrically, his characters are seldom depicted in real flesh and blood and their life stories remain fragments and impressions. This is true, of course, for much of Bauer's work. Time and again, he prefers the description of a fleeting moment to a detached and thorough analysis of the people around him. Yet it is in these brief encounters that he responds compassionately to his fellow men. 'Bauer's strength,' remarks Hermann Böschenstein, 'is in silencing the noise of everyday-life and then putting the stethoscope to his bodies; with the amplifying power of his own humanity he discovers an innate kindness in most of his acquaintances.'[24] His poem about the old Slavic woman on Toronto's streetcar shows the poet's ability to endow the people he meets with human dignity and to describe them to us with sympathy and tenderness:

...

Calmly she sat down, there was no embarrassment, no shame,
She sat down as if on the wicker chair by the stove after a long day's work,
And she looked out with tranquillity as if she were looking across fields.
Kerchief and pleated skirt. Her hands like brown, now crumbling earth in
    her wide lap,
And in her face the years of her village.
She carried everything with her: the summer wind, stillness,
The stillness of an unbroken world through which time flows as it should.
I saw her get up and then – she seemed to grow and look beyond us –
Out in the street she walked slowly as if she had plenty of time
And as if there were still the ploughed fields in the spring wind,
An old woman with the kerchief of Slavic peasants,
An old mother of the earth.

(Sun, p. 31)

For twenty-four years, Toronto remained the centre for all of Bauer's Canadian experiences. From this focal point he made his observations about the whole of Canada. Walking on Yonge Street he could hear the storms of the northern regions bringing, as he tells us, 'messages of gigantic arctic freedom, / Singing songs of inhuman solitude' (*Price*, p. 63). 'Here I am ... in an enormous city, while up there ice floes are colliding with northern lights flaring over them in mute play' (*Jahr*, p. 18). The Toronto sky seemed to him to be as lonely and empty as the sky that covered the rest of the country. Whether he sat at his desk in a rooming-house or in his apartment on top of a high-rise building, Bauer drew inspiration from the immense size of Canada and its stillness that came from endless space. In his poem entitled 'Canada' he says:

This earth does not bestow
The wisdom of Plato.
Aristotle did not live here.
Nor did Dante pass here through the inferno
In the fellowship of Virgil.
And Rembrandt? Not here the glamour of great lords
And then the drunken unknown king in exile.

Here you receive another kind of wisdom,
Bitter and icy and not to everybody's taste.

This earth says:
I was here long before you and the likes of you came;
Unmolested I conversed with wind and rivers,
Don't forget that, my friend. –
The wind blows cold from Labrador:
I have a message for you from the ice age,
But I shall not decode it for you. –
The forests of the north surge like waves:
We shall last longer than you. –
The Yukon and the Mackenzie flow with quiet patience:
Son, don't make things too hard for yourself;
Different times will come when you are gone, stranger. –
The arctic expresses the sum total of all wisdom:
Silence. Nothing but silence. The end of time.

(Price, p. 65)

In a noble and monumental, yet occasionally colloquial language Bauer is able to capture Canada's gigantic size, its eternal stillness, its lack of traditions, its indifference to man's struggle. 'Here is strong and vibrant poetry rooted in the Canadian landscape,'[25] says Fraser Sutherland in his comment on this poem. The silence of the arctic regions provides the poet with no answer as to the outcome of human aspirations, nor does it erase the memory of the cruel past. But his constant reckoning with the past is at least curbed, if only temporarily, in the face of the country's immeasurable stretches of time and space, the quiet and patient flow of its great rivers: 'Son, don't make things too hard for yourself.'

Bauer's preoccupation with the unredeemed past was linked to the fact that his whole existence was inseparable from his mother tongue. Throughout his Canadian period, he never stopped reproaching himself for having kept on writing in German. This might have been the only chance, he thought, to grow completely in the second language and to communicate directly with Canadian readers. But like so many other immigrant writers, he was unable to disassociate himself from 'the most basic feature' of his luggage – his native language.[26] He was fully aware of this dilemma. 'As soon as my hand touches a sheet of paper, I think in German,'[27] he informed his publisher. Thinking in German made it difficult for him to escape the associations dictated to him by the language itself, which in his case meant to return to the German past. 'Mother tongue,' he confessed near the end of his life, 'she carried me here for a long time – too long. And then she becomes your prison. To live on another continent without expressing the core of one's existence is absurd and results in a death sentence or, which is the same thing in the long run, in exile.'[28]

Bauer's voluntary exile was a double one: as a German author writing about experiences that were no longer German, he paid the price of having fewer and fewer readers in Germany, and as an immigrant writer publishing in a foreign language, he isolated himself from his potential Canadian public. The very feeling of being a stranger both 'here' and 'there' seemed almost to have crushed him at times. Yet he never had any regrets for having come to Canada. On the contrary, he conceived a passionate love for the country which had enabled him to write more than he would probably ever have written 'over there' (*Jahr*, p. 52), and with a freshness which is remarkable when compared with his pre-Canadian period. Our analysis of his Canadian work has shown that he writes intensely and compassionately about the immigrants' difficulties in living and striking roots in their adopted homeland. This important aspect of the Canadian mosaic plays a prominent role in his writing. We have also noticed that in his distinct ability to blend experiences of the present and the past, of the New World and the Old, he contributes a more universal dimension to Canadian literature. Furthermore, Bauer's own situation as a writer living in voluntary exile is exemplary of a phenomenon which extends far beyond our Canadian borders, namely of today's dislocation of refugees all over the world. His overall contribution to the Canadian literary scene seems to me convincingly summed up by F.W. Watt's statement that the 'Canadian readers are fortunate to be able to catch a glimpse of mankind, the world, and Canada through the eyes of Walter Bauer.'[29]

NOTES

1 Letter to J.R. Colombo, 30 Dec. 1974. A copy of the letter is among Bauer's posthumous papers which are housed in the Weldon Library (Special Collections) of the University of Western Ontario. The term 'luggage' used in the title and throughout this article is based on Bauer's poem 'My luggage,' from his collection *A Different Sun* (see note 17).
2 Letter to Colombo.
3 Bauer, *Kameraden, zu euch spreche ich* (Dresden: Kaden, 1929); *Stimme aus dem Leunawerk* (Berlin: Malik, 1930); *Ein Mann zog in die Stadt* (Berlin: Cassirer, 1931).

4 Quoted from Henry Beissel's pertinent and penetrating introduction to his translation of Bauer's poems, *The Price of Morning* (Vancouver: Prism International, 1968), p. 13. The original German letter was first published in Max Tau, *Das Land, das ich verlassen musste* (Hamburg: Hoffman u. Campe, 1961), p. 230.

5 Although Bauer's early books remained on the black list, the authorities found the work he had written since Hitler had come to power to be 'harmless' and too apolitical to warrant censorship. However, Bauer's secret meeting with Zweig in 1935 resulted in a temporary ban of his books written since 1933. This ban was revoked in March 1937.

6 Beissel's introduction to *The Price of Morning*, p. 13.

7 Bauer, *Tagebuchblätter aus Frankreich* (Dessau: Rauch, 1941).

8 Bauer, *Das Lied der Freiheit* (München: Desch, 1948), p. 60. All translations are mine unless otherwise indicated.

9 Letter to Ernst Tessloff, quoted from *The Price of Morning*, p. 15.

10 Ibid.

11 Letter to Hermann Hesse, 16 Aug. 1954.

12 Jutta was the stepdaughter of the successful German writer Ernst Wiechert. Bauer's friendship with him began in 1933 when Wiechert had written a favourable review of his novel *Das Herz der Erde* ('The heart of the earth'). During the following years both Bauer and his first wife Clärle were frequently guests at Wiechert's estate in Wolfratshausen. It was there that Bauer stayed for several months immediately after his release from prisoner-of-war camp. Living under the same roof, the two writers became increasingly critical of each other. Much of the growing tension between them resulted from the problems they both were encountering in their private lives. Bauer did not return to his wife in Halle; he was falling in love with his host's stepdaughter. Wiechert was experiencing difficulties with his own marriage.

13 Quoted from Henry Beissel, 'Walter Bauer: From the Last Year of His Diary,' *Tamarack Review*, no. 77/8 (Summer 1979), 54.

14 Letter to Ernst Tessloff, quoted from *The Price of Morning*, p. 15.

15 Bauer, *Folge dem Pfeil* (München: Desch, 1956); *Die langen Reisen* (München: Kindler, 1956).

16 Bauer, *Ein Jahr, Tagebuchblätter aus Kanada* (Hamburg: Merlin, 1967); *Der weisse Indianer* (Frankfurt: Ullstein, 1960); *Fremd in Toronto* (Hattingen: Hundt, 1963).

17 Bauer, *A Slight Trace of Ash*, trans. Humphrey Milnes. Block prints by Aba Bayefsky (Toronto: Roger Ascham Press, 1976); Bauer, *A Different Sun*, trans. Henry Beissel (Ottawa: Oberon Press, 1976). Further references to *A Different Sun* will be given in the text.

18 Further references to this work will be given in the text.

19 Letter to Andreas J. Meyer, 23 Jan. 1966.

20 Bauer, *Ein Jahr: Tagebuchblätter aus Kanada*, p. 150. Further references to this work will be given in the text.

21 Letter to G. Gaupp, 14 Jan. 1968.

22 F.W. Watt, 'A Different Son [sic]: Walter Bauer's Canadian Poetry,' *Canadian Forum*, 49:692 (1979), 24. See also Beissel's response to Watt's article in *Canadian Forum*, 49:694 (1979), 25.

23 Translated by Alexa Petrenko, *Tamarack Review*, no 77/8 (Summer 1979), 39. In *Fremd in Toronto* the title of the short story is 'Quartett der Fortgegangenen.'

24 Hermann Böschenstein, 'Is there a Canadian Image in German Literature?' *Seminar*, 3:1 (1967), 17.

25 Fraser Sutherland, review of *The Fixed Landscape* by Andy Wainwright, *Canadian Literature*, no. 44 (1970), 82.

26 Watt, p. 21.

27 Letter to Andreas J. Meyer, 14 Nov. 1966.

28 Quoted from Beissel, 'Walter Bauer,' p. 51. In the same issue, 77/8 of the *Tamarack Review*, Beissel has published some of the few poems Bauer wrote in English. It is noteworthy that with his retirement from university teaching in 1976 Bauer's ambition to write in English grew considerably. Poems, plays, and a novel were among the works that he planned to write in English.

29 Watt, p. 24.

Canadian-Mennonite Literature ᴈ Longing for a Lost Homeland ᴈᴈᴈ

HARRY LOEWEN

Much creative literature is an expression of a sense of loss – be it the proverbial loss of paradise or the loss of real or imagined values. Writers thus either recreate their lost world and values, or they portray a world which is devoid of stated or assumed values. As Friedrich Nietzsche observed, the heroes which an author creates are expressions of the author's longings and aspirations; if an author were like his heroes, he would never have created them.[1] This theory of the creative impulse also applies to so-called realistic works and novels of social criticism. In describing the deplorable social conditions, the authors of such works write against a background of ideals and values which have been lost or neglected.

This interpretation of literature holds especially true for the Russian-Mennonite fiction which forms the basis for Canadian-Mennonite literature. When the Mennonites lived securely in Prussia and Russia for almost three hundred years they wrote almost no creative works. They read such pietistic literature as Jung-Stilling's *Das Heimweh*[2] and in the nineteenth century began to write devotional poetry themselves. But such writers as Bernhard Harder (1832–84), outstanding teacher and minister in Russia, while laying a basis for later Russian-Mennonite fiction, cannot be considered original writers. Harder's poems and songs were written to edify and to promote the religious faith of his fellow Mennonites.[3] While some of Harder's poems had the making of folksongs, the Mennonite soil in nineteenth-century Russia was not ready to receive them as such.[4] Even the patriotic poems of Harder and Heinrich Heese (1787–1868) were of a religious nature and shamelessly didactic in content and purpose.[5]

Many reasons have been advanced for the lack of literature among the Mennonites,[6] but as far as the Russian Mennonites are concerned, they did not write much because they lived in what they perceived to be a whole and harmonious world which they had fashioned in their own image. The nineteenth-century Russian Mennonites were at peace with themselves and the world around them. Their tsar was, like God, their protector and benefactor. In keeping with the paradise image, the Mennonites had dominion not only over the vast expanses of the steppes which they had developed into prosperous colonies, but also over the non-Mennonite world within their reach. Since the Mennonites had all they needed and wanted and felt no loss of any kind, the creative impulses continued to slumber their *Dornröschenschlaf*.

The early Anabaptists who were severely persecuted had their martyrs' ballads and their Ausbund songs,[7] and the later Dutch Mennonites, when they sensed that they were losing or had lost their Anabaptist vision and ideals, wrote their *Wandelnde Seele* (1635) and *Martyrs Mirror* (1660), but the Russian Mennonites who had not experienced any such loss did not write. Not even the religious reform upheavals centring upon the formations of the Kleine Gemeinde (1814) and the Mennonite Brethren Church (1860) were of sufficient dynamic force to cause genuine and fervent religious fiction to emerge. Those who wrote did not write literature. The writings of Martin Klaasen and Claas Epp Jr towards the end of the nineteenth century, for example, dealt primarily with pietistic views of church history and prophecy. And even a voluminous historical work like Peter Martin Friesen's *The Mennonite Brotherhood in Russia* (1911) is a spiritual history of the Russian Mennonites. It is significant, it might be added, that this work, which includes sketches of Mennonite education and culture in Russia, does not mention a single work of fiction written by Mennonites.

There were, however, a few Mennonite writers who began writing poetry and prose prior to World War I: Peter B. Harder (1868–1923), son of Bernhard Harder, Jacob H. Janzen (1878–1950), Johannes Heinrich Janzen (1868–1917),[8] and Gerhard Loewen (1864–1946). These writers are in a way transitional figures between the whole and harmonious Mennonite world before 1917 and the literature which began to flower after the collapse of the Mennonite 'Commonwealth' in Russia. They are significant trailblazers on the Mennonite literary scene, but their poetry and prose still lack focus and originality, and are imitations of older, mostly German, literary forms.

In 1910 Jacob H. Janzen published his *Denn meine Augen haben Deinen Heiland gesehen*, a collection of twelve stories of a devotional and didactic nature. Arnold Dyck observes: '[Janzen's] tales are not just Christian stories in the usual sense of the word; they are also and always sermons designed to cause reflection and from reflection to occasion a "conversion" ... he is never far removed from sermonizing as he himself called his moralizing deviations from his main topic.'[9] Also Janzen's Low German one-act plays such as *De Bildung*, *De Enbildung*, *Daut Schultebott*, and *Utwaundre* were designed to teach and edify 'my people,' as Janzen called his Mennonite brotherhood.

Peter B. Harder published his novel *Schicksale: oder die lutherische Cousine* and his *Lose Blätter* just prior to World War I. As Al Reimer comments, *Schicksale* does not meet the test of universal appeal: 'It is a strange mixture of crude domestic melodrama and shrewdly observed, realistically rendered Mennonite life around the turn of the century.'[10] Moreover, since Harder did not sufficiently disguise his characters, he was severely criticized by his readers who felt themselves exposed by his work.[11]

One of the first poets in pre-World-War-I Russia was Gerhard Loewen.[12] Jacob H. Janzen writes of Loewen: 'Poems became music when he uttered them. His own poems all breathe a heartwarming joy that is closely allied to nature.'[13] Loewen characterized his poems as follows: 'Feldblümchen sinds; denn nicht in dumpfen Räumen, / Im engen Haus nicht sprossen sie empor: / Im freien Feld und unter Waldes Bäumen / Erblühte wonnig ihr bescheidner Chor.'[14] According to Arnold Dyck, Loewen's 'poems are flawless in form and diction. ... It may be, however, that the very stress on the outward form has hindered ... the easy flow of poetic thought and is the reason for the limitation in the power to interpret the original, deepfelt experience which gave the poem its birth.'[15]

By their own admission, these first poets and novelists were still very much under the influence of German nature poetry. In imitation of the *Hainbund* of the early German lyrical poets, Jacob H. Janzen, Gerhard Loewen, and others organized their own league of young poets; however, they could never clasp their hands 'by moonlight and dance around the oak tree,' as Janzen writes, 'for thousands of miles lay between the individual members of this league.'[16] This ironic comment no doubt indicates that these early Mennonite writers realized that genuine art cannot be an imitation of older forms but must spring from new experiences which give rise to new forms and content.

During World War I, the Communist Revolution, and the subsequent civil war in Russia, the Mennonites experienced a collapse of their world as never before in their four-hundred-year history. The Mennonites not only lost their land, homes, way of life, and many their lives in a most brutal way at the hands of bandits, but they were also threatened with the destruction of their religious faith and identity as a people. Their past vanished almost overnight, their present was bleak and dismal, and their future was unknown to them. Out of this chaotic and hopeless situation Mennonite literature was born. The Russian Mennonites experienced what Goethe's Torquato Tasso expressed in the depth of his anguish at the end of the drama:

> Nein, alles ist dahin! – Nur eines bleibt:
> Die Träne hat uns die Natur verliehen,
> Den Schrei des Schmerzens, wenn der Mann zuletzt
> Es nicht mehr trägt – Und mir noch über alles –
> Sie liess im Schmerz mir Melodie und Rede,
> Die tiefste Fülle meiner Not zu klagen:
> Und wenn der Mensch in seiner Qual verstummt,
> Gab mir ein Gott zu sagen, wie ich leide.

(v,5)

So strong was now the urge among Mennonites to express suffering and loss in words that go beyond simple prose that even a journal or diary came close to being poetic. Dietrich Neufeld (1886–1958), recording the chaotic events and anarchy during the years 1919 and 1920 (published in 1921 as *Ein Tagebuch aus dem Reiche des Totentanzes*), is not only concerned about facts, events, and historical accuracy, but also about the artistic quality of what he writes. In fact, like a true artist, he *must* write. 'I am writing in darkness ... I must use this time to pour out my feelings, even if I can't decipher it all later. Writing for me, is like conversing with a friend who hasn't been part of all this, whose mind and soul are free to relieve me of some of the heaviness ... I have to write myself free of this crushing burden.'[17]

Al Reimer, who has translated the journal and published it as *A Russian Dance of Death* (1977), says about Neufeld as a writer: '[Neufeld] felt his experiences deeply and had the artistic skill to record them without distortion in crisp, living language. With a sharp eye for detail, he also knew how to pick the significant out of the tangle of impressions. ... His strongest point as a writer was his ability to give his personal narrative universal significance. ...'[18]

Neufeld belonged to those Russian-Mennonite writers who began writing in Russia at the end of Mennonitism as it had been known in that country and then continued in North America. In their German and later English writings, be they prose or poetry, these writers develop themes which tell the story of their various losses: their world, land, and homes; their identity as a people in closed communities; and the values, beliefs, and practices that had characterized them for many generations. The older, German-speaking, Mennonite writers, who themselves had experienced the breakup of their world, deal primarily with the loss of the physical world. The younger generation of writers, most of them born in Canada, also 'remember' the external, physical world of their forebears, but their 'remembering' is more spiritual and existential. It is interesting to note that it is the young writers who, through the loss and uprootedness of their ancestors, 'remember' the spiritual home of the Anabaptists and Mennonites of the sixteenth century and deal with questions of identity and what it means to be Mennonite in today's society. Nevertheless, the land or home motif, whether understood in the physical-geographical-historical sense or in the spiritual-symbolic sense, runs like a red thread through most of Canadian-Mennonite prose and poetry.

The question of language has always been a problem among Mennonites. Some have pointed out that one reason for the lack of Mennonite literature is 'the fact that Mennonites have never been able to evolve a single linguistic fiction.'[19] There may be some truth to this. In church and in the schools Mennonites used High German, at home and on the street they spoke the Low German dialect inherited from West Prussia, and in their dealings with Russian officials they increasingly used Russian. When the Mennonites came to Canada towards the end of the nineteenth century and after the two world wars, they exchanged Russian for English, but retained, at least for several decades, the High and Low German languages. Thus some of the literature which began to emerge in the second decade of the twentieth century was written in High German and some in Low German. Canadian-Mennonite writers continued writing exclusively in the two German languages until the 1950s. Since Russian had never been close to the Mennonite soul, no Mennonite writer ever wrote in that language. In Canada, however, beginning with Rudy Wiebe in the 1960s, Mennonites have begun to make significant literary contributions in English.

Once the fountain of Mennonite literary art had found an outlet in the revolutionary upheavals in Russia, it began to flow in an ever widening and deepening stream. Among the better Mennonite writers who left Russia and came to Canada were Gerhard Toews (Georg De Brecht), Arnold Dyck, and Gerhard Friesen (Fritz Senn). Hans Harder, who immigrated to Germany after the Communist Revolution, should be mentioned here as well, since one of his early novels has been recently translated into English and published in Winnipeg, thus making Harder more accessible to Canadian readers than any other of the older Mennonite writers.

Hans Harder was one of the first Mennonite writers to give artistic shape to the tragic experiences of the Russian Mennonites. Almost thirty years before Alexander Solzhenitsyn wrote his significant *One Day in the Life of Ivan Denisovich* (1962), a novel about Russian prisoners in Stalin's camps, Harder published in Germany his first novel, *In Wologdas weissen Wäldern* (1934), also about the life, misery, and death of Mennonite and non-Mennonite exiles. The novel was 'freely translated from the German, edited, and expanded' by Al Reimer and appeared as *No Strangers in Exile* (1979).[20]

In *No Strangers in Exile* the Mennonite-German and Russian exiles ('they are called voluntary resettlers'!) have not only lost their homes, friends, and relatives, but have also become confused about the meaning of life and their worth as human individuals. Many of the exiles die miserable deaths in the northern taiga, but those few hardy souls who survive, including Alexander Harms, the narrator, survive because of their determination to live, their faith, and their acceptance of 'nothingness' as a pre-condition for living and spiritual liberty. As the characters conclude at the end of the novel: 'we have earned the right to bless and forgive not only those who put us here, but also those who do not even know of our existence. Through our suffering we have won the freedom to bless!'[21] In exile they have found their spiritual home.

In 1933 and 1936 there appeared two novels by Gerhard Toews (Georg De Brecht) written and published in Canada. Both *Die Heimat in Flammen* and its sequel *Die Heimat in Trümmern* deal with the civil war period in the Soviet Union, specifically with the atrocities committed by the anarchist Nestor Machno and his bandits. Toews 'is a novelist in the full sense of the word. He is a born story teller, a writer who revels in dramatic action and romantic adventure, the more violent the better,' as Reimer puts it. 'Among Mennonite novelists only Rudy Wiebe is his equal when it comes to the handling of fast-paced narrative action.'[22] Whether Toews describes an escape from the Reds or the Anarchists, a love affair, or the preparation of the German and Mennonite *Selbstschutz* (Self-Defence) units for action – there is always suspense, animated dialogue, drama, and fast action. Having experienced the anarchy in southern Russia, Toews is always frank in his opinion about the necessity of the existence of the controversial Self-Defence and realistic in portraying its often bloody activity. But in all this dramatic physical action, Toews also shows the sense of loss which the Mennonites experienced. Jacob H. Janzen writes: 'Toews sees not only the tumult of the physical struggle in the great slaughter of the Russian Revolution and civil war, but also the destruction of the human soul which trembled and often was shattered by the brutal attacks on the prevailing life of that day.'[23]

The following description of a mass funeral is characteristic of Toews's portrayal of contrasts and irony:

> Auf dem Friedhof zu Rotenfeld blühten die Blumen. Im grünen Versteck der hohen Bäume zwitscherten um ihre Nester die besorgten Vögel ... Die Natur stand im Zeichen des vollen Lebens. Inmitten dieses Lebens jedoch standen die Menschen um eine grosse Grube und nahmen Abschied von den drei Opfern falscher Freiheit und sangen ihnen ein trauriges Abschiedslied.[24]

One of the greatest of the Canadian-Mennonite writers is no doubt Arnold Dyck (1889–1970). He was born in Russia, studied art in Germany and Russia before World War I, and immigrated to Canada in the 1920s. There is no Mennonite author writing in German who has captured the Mennonite sense of being lost as well as Arnold Dyck. In his autobiographical novel *Verloren in der Steppe*, illustrated with sketches and published in Steinbach, Manitoba, in five separate volumes between 1944 and 1948, Dyck recreates the lost world of the Russian Mennonites in the form of a German *Bildungsroman*.[25] Hans Toews, the young hero of the novel, is in spite of his conservative background intelligent, striving, and artistically inclined. He feels hemmed in by his narrow, anti-intellectual environment, and yearns against almost overwhelming odds to break out and become free and cultured. Ironically, the vast expanse of the Russian steppe keeps the hero enslaved, with no place to go. The theme of loss takes on a new form in this novel: the Mennonite artist experiences a sense of loss in a world which for the majority of Mennonites was home and paradise. At the end of the novel, Hans, still 'lost in the steppe,' stands on the threshold of a new life and era as he considers his future in the New World.

While Dyck describes the oppressive Mennonite world in the novel, he nevertheless portrays his love for the Russian-Mennonite landscape, the Mennonite villages and institutions, and the Mennonite customs, traditions, and way of life – in a word, the world which no longer existed when he wrote about it. But there is more to the novel. The Russian steppe and the lost Mennonite world in the novel become by implication the Canadian prairie and Mennonite life in Canada. The narrow limits and conservative ways, Dyck seems to be saying, are still evident on Canadian soil, but in the hopes and aspirations of the young hero a new, brighter, and more cultured future is dawning.

Verloren in der Steppe is a mature work of art. For the first time in Mennonite literature there is a sense of freedom and ironic detachment in the author's handling of the material and characters. Reimer is correct when he observes that Dyck is the one author among the Russian-Mennonite writers 'who is always in perfect control of his tone, always safely above his material. He knows exactly how to set up a teasing, ironic interplay between subject ... and the narrator, the mature recording voice.'[26]

This freedom and irony find their most vivid expression in Arnold Dyck's most popular *Koop enn Bua* stories, written in Low German, the language in which Dyck found himself most at home. While *Lost in the Steppe* describes the Russian-Mennonite environment prior to its destruction, the *Koop enn Bua* stories, with their comic, earthy characters, portray a new-found Mennonite world in southern Manitoba. The comedy arises from the author's effective juxtaposing of the narrow world of the two bushfarmers and the larger society and world around them. Koop and Bua are always on the move – they travel to their brethren in the western provinces, to Toronto and other eastern centres, and even across the Atlantic to Germany. They are symbolic of the Canadian Mennonites seeking to establish contact with the larger world beyond them. In their communication with others, they excel when they can speak in their beloved Low German, but when it comes to speaking High German or English with those who do not understand the Low German, they are inept – and very funny! In laughing at and with Koop and Bua, the Mennonite reader actually laughs at himself, knowing that while there are still traits of these bushfarmers among present-day Mennonites, the majority of Canadian Mennonites are no longer like them.

Of the other short stories by Arnold Dyck *Twee Breew* (*Two Letters*) should be mentioned as a work which treats a serious theme – that of loss, separation, guilt, and death – in eloquent Low German. The author's device of alternating between hope and despair, love of life and miserable conditions, and between the past in which there was beauty and warmth and a present in which sadness and cold prevail, is not only most effective but also emotionally compelling. *Twee Breew*, translated into English by Elisabeth Peters,[27] is considered by some admirers of Dyck as his masterpiece.[28]

The best of the Mennonite-German poets is undoubtedly Gerhard Friesen (Fritz Senn), now living in Wilhelmshaven, West Germany. In the 1920s he came from Russia to Canada and prior to World War II he moved back to Germany. Recognizing Friesen's significance as a poet, Jacob H. Janzen wrote in the 1940s: 'it is not altogether impossible that he alone, of all of us, will be remembered by future generations.'[29] Elisabeth Peters, who has published a collection of Friesen's poetry,[30] observed correctly: 'Gerhard Friesen ... establishes the Mennonite identity in his verse which is often strangely haunting in its lyricism, and at times intensely dramatic as he depicts the Mennonite *Erlebnis* of the past.'[31] Moreover, Friesen's images and symbols move on many levels and express universally valid themes. The best of his poems are those which deal with the old Mennonite world in Russia, with land and farm life, and scenes of tranquillity and haunting music on the Russian steppes.

In the poem 'Hinterm Pflug I' the creation of mood and nostalgia for the past are most effective:

> Im Dämmern liegt das Herbstgelände
> Von Ruhesehnsucht überhaucht –
> Das Feuer ferner Stoppelbrände
> Versinkt, verhaucht.
> ...
> Wär' Friede zu erwandern auf der Welt,
> Hier fände ihn verborgen, wer ihn sucht
> Hier unter der Akazien grünem Zelt ...
> Doch wir sind in der Fremde, auf der Flucht.[32]

This sentiment is echoed in 'Fritz Senn Stimmungen' by Abram J. Friesen: 'Es weckt dein ernster Sang in meinem Herzen / Ein tiefes Sehnen mir. / Ich lausch ihm unter Lust und unter Schmerzen / Und möchte fort von hier.'[33]

The poet Gerhard Friesen lives in the past; his roots remained in Russia. Neither Canada nor Germany could provide him with the cultural soil needed for a successful transplantation. When he left Canada for Germany, he left a Mennonite cultural background which had also become to a certain extent rootless and even more narrow than the Mennonites had been in Russia. But in Germany, while cut off from the past, he could at least write in peace.[34]

While Gerhard Friesen is the best Mennonite poet writing in German, there are several other German-writing Canadian-Mennonite poets that deserve to be mentioned in this survey. Valentin Sawatzky, living and writing in Ontario, has published several small volumes of poetry dealing with many subjects in more or less conventional forms.[35] He makes a conscious effort to develop themes which express gratitude on the part of Mennonites for their new-found Canadian homeland. Poems such as 'Der alte Trapper,' 'Niagara,' 'Winter in Ontario,' 'Nordland-Frühling,' 'Dem Land des Ahorns' are among the best of these.

Nikolaus H. Unruh, another Canadian-Mennonite poet, reflects on the past Mennonite homeland and the changing seasons in such poems as 'Lied des Landmanns,' 'Mein Heimatdorf,' 'Sommernacht,' 'Herbststimmung,' and 'Verlassenes Farmhaus.'[36]

Abram J. Friesen, professor of German at the University of New Brunswick, is most probing in some of his lyrical-philosophical poems. In 'Heimweh' the author is reminded of his spiritual home: 'Eure alten frommen Lieder / Von dem Kreuz, vor das ihr tretet, / Von dem Gott zu dem ihr betet, / Heute hörte ich sie wieder.'[37] In 'Meditationen 1' the poet philosophizes: 'Es ist das Leben / Ein tiefer Schlaf, der uns umfangen hält. / Und uns umschweben / Im Traume Bilder einer schönern Welt. / Doch bald mit Beben / Seh'n wir, wie auch das schönste Traumgebild zerfällt.'[38] Friesen's lyrics are full of music, nostalgia, and symbolism. In 'Das Mädchen mit der Rose' the poet meets in the morning a young girl with a rose in her hair which at noonday is gone: 'Der klare Blick, das feine Lächeln – / 's war alles noch, wie es am Morgen war ... / Doch hatt' der Wind, liebkosend, ihm entblättert / Die Ros' in seinem Haar.'[39]

With the passing of Canadian-Mennonite writers who still wrote in the German language, some felt that an era in Mennonite writing in Canada had come to an end. Both Jacob H. Janzen and Arnold Dyck lamented this passing, but both also expressed the hope that Mennonite literature, which had barely begun, would not die when the writers of the old generation were gone. Janzen wrote in the 1940s: 'I feel as if I am writing epitaphs on tombstones. Would God that I could see a new generation of poets and artists arise among us. But even if I do not see my hopes realized in my lifetime, new poets will come.'[40]

New poets and novelists did come indeed – some even continuing to write in German[41] – but it was a generation of writers who were born and raised in Canada, who did not know the lost physical world in Russia, and who wrote mostly in English. The young writers, writing poems, novels, and short stories, include the novelist Rudy Wiebe and the published poets Clint Toews, Menno Wiebe, David Waltner-Toews, and Patrick Friesen. There are others, but in the rest of the article I wish to deal with these five. I shall begin with the most accomplished of them, Rudy Wiebe.

Rudy Wiebe has written several full-length novels and short stories,[42] including two novels which deal with Mennonites. *Peace Shall Destroy Many* (1962), which was originally written as an MA thesis in creative writing at the University of Alberta, exploded like a bombshell in the Canadian-Mennonite world. This novel portrayed an isolated Mennonite community in northern Saskatchewan so realistically and critically that many Mennonites felt themselves exposed and attacked by one of their own. Many were not so much concerned about what the novel said about the closed and narrow world of the Mennonites as about what other Canadians would think about the Mennonites as a group of people who tried to live by the principles of the gospels and their forefathers and yet in practice fell short of their professed ideals. There were cries of outrage against this talented young author, with some demanding that he be excommunicated from the church. As a result of the outcry, Wiebe lost his position as editor of the *Mennonite Brethren Herald* in Winnipeg. Wiebe found that a writer is often appreciated as long as he does not rock the ethnic boat. Wiebe had rocked the boat, had broken out from the fold as it were, and then went on to become an 'ethnic writer' who also had something to say to non-Mennonites.[43]

Set against the background of World War II, *Peace Shall Destroy Many* develops on several levels. It describes the conflict between the Mennonite belief in pacifism and the loyalty on the part of the young for their Canadian homeland; it registers the conflict between the traditional

Mennonite values brought to Canada in the 1920s by the Russian-Mennonite immigrants and the attempts on the part of the younger generation to come to terms with a set of new values and a new social-cultural environment. In all these conflicts the characters of the novel wrestle with the question of what it really means to be a Mennonite in today's society.

One motif which has not been analysed sufficiently in the literature surrounding the novel is that of land and the soil. Deacon Block, the most fully developed character in this novel, is very conscious of what the Mennonites lost in the Soviet Union – their homes, their land, and a way of life. In Canada Block seeks to establish and preserve for his son – and the young Mennonite generation – that which they lost in the Old Country. Thom, the hero of the novel, and his young friends, however, begin to realize that the Mennonites were not the first to come to the prairies but that others had been there long before them and that this places responsibilities and obligations upon them. This realization is effectively symbolized by the buffalo skull Thom finds in the field: 'Staring at the broken skull ... a vista opened for Thom. Why was Canada called a "young" country?'[44] And to his friend Peter, Thom says:

> 'the Indians – a people living in nearly half of the world – lived here for thousands of years, and we don't know a single thing that happened to them except some old legend muddled in the memory of an old crone. A whole world lost. Not one remembered word of how generations upon generations lived and died.'[45]

This is a most significant observation. Perhaps for the first time in their history Mennonites realize (at least some of their authors do) that the land which they have come to occupy belonged to others, to a native people which had called this land their own for many generations. Thus we have here in a sense a lost-found-and-lost-again situation; that is, the Mennonites who lost their homeland in Russia and found another in Canada realize that the land they acquired does not really belong to them. This idea is reinforced when at the end of the novel Deacon Block realizes that the Mennonite community which he tried to establish for his children is collapsing: 'The Deacon bowed his scarred grey head to his hands, and the men of Wapiti community, Métis and Mennonite, standing in an old barn, heard the sobs of a great strong man, suddenly bereft, and broken.'[46]

The land and homeland motifs are developed more fully in Wiebe's second Mennonite novel, *The Blue Mountains of China* (1970). The novel is a Mennonite epic, spanning four continents and interpreting four and a half centuries of Mennonite history and life. Wiebe's portrayal of the destruction of the Russian-Mennonite world in chapter 2, 'Sons and Heirs,' forms one of the most powerful sections of the novel. Young Jakob Friesen comes home from a Soviet prison ('Mutti, papa, I'm home! They let me out!'),[47] only to find that his 'house was a black hole,'[48] and that strangers, their former servants, have taken over their home. In this unexpected new situation Friesen's beliefs and ethics with regard to non-resistance and moral purity are severely tested. Friesen's subsequent failure and death symbolize the failure of the Russian Mennonites to come to terms with a changing society and a new historical period. The Mennonites, bereft of their homes and homeland, move in the direction of the 'blue mountains,' which symbolize their longing and ideals and their search for a new homeland in the distance. They find new land, freedom, and homes in North and South America, but in the end some of them realize that their home is nowhere on earth. They manage to establish their roots on foreign soil (Paraguay, Manitoba, Mexico, Alberta), but in doing so many lose their former vision of what it means to be Mennonite-Christian.[49] This loss is symbolized in the character of Willms who becomes prosperous in Canadian society, and then changes his name to Williams, while maintaining that 'Church and business don't mix,'[50] and in Elizabeth Driedger, who as Dr Cereno, a university professor, has moved far away from what Mennonites believed and practised.

Yet in this new homeland, Canada, there are Mennonites like Samuel U. Reimer and his brother John who not only remember their spiritual roots but also recognize their responsibility as Mennonite-Christians to the larger society beyond the Mennonite world. Ironically, however, Samuel, who hears the Vietnam call and recognizes the responsibility that goes with it, is not only misunderstood by his family and fellow Mennonites but also by his church and pastor. Similarly John has to drag a cross through Alberta in order to demonstrate repentance and what it means to be a Christian in today's society. For Samuel and John Reimer Canada may have become a physical home; spiritually, however, they are part of a people that is on the way to a more permanent home. As Ina Ferris states significantly: 'Wiebe's characters, exiled in the wilderness, search for the Promised Land that will transform existential chaos into meaningful form.'[51] This tension among Mennonites between longing for a physical homeland and the ideal beyond the material world is effectively expressed by the conversation between John Reimer and old Jakob Friesen who has just arrived from Russia. John Reimer says to Friesen:

> 'You know the trouble with Mennonites? They've always wanted to be Jews. To have land God had given them for their very own, to which they were called ... Wherever they got pushed ... they try to prove to themselves they are building that land.'
> [Friesen] 'They came close in Russia.'
> [Reimer] 'Closest there, I think. Unfortunately. But they are still trying to find it, and it isn't anywhere on earth.'[52]

I shall conclude this survey with cursory references to four young Canadian-Mennonite poets who are beginning to make a mark not only in the Mennonite literary world but also in the rest of Canadian society and beyond.

Menno Wiebe, a native of Manitoba, writes mostly religious poetry, but his poems bear little resemblance to the Mennonite poets of the past. Like John Reimer in *The Blue Mountains of China*, he 'challenges the old isolationist views'[53] of Mennonites and non-Mennonites alike. 'Some of his poems reveal a distinct impatience with those who are too slow to adapt their Christianity to the needs of a larger human family.'[54] For example in his 'ekklesia' he prays for unity and love among Mennonites: 'bind us again / renew our bonds / to avoid / the frazzlement / that dissects / and scatters / lifeless limbs / of the intended / organic / beautiful body / we call brotherhood.'[55]

In the poetry of Clint Toews there is expressed a definite sense of loss. He laments the loss of land, home, and values, and his criticism of loveless religiosity can be devastating as, for example, in the poem 'The Harlot and the Holy': The faces of the church leaders 'were quite old and / very, very angry.' The morally fallen girl finds no understanding among them. 'Their purist minds were very strong / and holiness condemned her on that day / They washed their hands and all agreed / to cleanse her heart from sin. / With one accord they drew their swords / and justly drove it in / In Jesus name amen.'[56]

David Waltner-Toews, a native of Winnipeg, who travelled in Indo-China and worked in India and Vancouver, is a practising veterinarian. His first collection of poems, *The Inescapable Animal*, was published in 1974, followed by *The Earth Is One Body* in 1979. This promising young poet is a fine craftsman, using images and symbols effectively and in a novel way. In the poem 'Homestead,' the building of 'this place' becomes a symbol of a developing poem,[57] and in 'The Birth of a Poem' the poet is handed after prolonged birth pangs 'a slippery / red-faced, incoherent quatrain.'[58] In many of his poems Waltner-Toews addresses himself both to the Mennonite conscience and to that of Western society. In describing a colonial setting and a life of ease in the poem 'In an Old Colonial Mansion (Guadeloupe),' he concludes with the lines: 'How easily appearances might hold a conscience captive, / and a sunset justify a thousand slaves.'[59] In 'A Calcutta Street, 1967' the poet's portrayal of poverty and squalor is most vivid:

> It is a red brick, cobbled street
> ...
> A sick rat, bloated, deformed
> drags itself half-way across the cobblestones
> and is run over by a black Mercedes;
> flies buzz around the entrails.
>
> Children in tattered rags crawl, run, scramble
> along the street.
> They are caked with dirt.
> One of them is missing an arm.
> One is missing an eye.
> They urinate on the rat.[60]

Patrick Friesen, born and raised in rural Manitoba, 'is the consummate artist in his use of the English language, both in his turns of phrases and in his skillful use of imagery.'[61] Friesen has published three volumes of poetry, *The Lands I Am*, *Bluebottle*, and *The Shunning*. This talented poet is most conscious of the Mennonite past with its rootedness in the soil and in traditional values, but the past is for him merely the base from which he moves into the modern world of city life, science and technology, and the fears and joys related to human existence. In the poem 'Patriarchal light' the poet stumbles between the rocket and the moon 'trying to balance, / to keep dignity and grace. / I will not be old or new, / I will not be stapled to the sky. / I did not know the patriarchs, / I am not sure which was their light. / I was not born in a simlin, / though my feet lovingly touch the ground.'[62]

The Shunning, a narrative poem dealing with two brothers, Peter and Johannes Neufeld – the one dying by his own hand after he is excommunicated and shunned and the other dying a natural death – is Friesen's greatest achievement to date. In this poem Friesen 'remembers' the past, the time when Mennonites (and humanity) still lived in another world, in Eden. Allusions to, and images dealing with, Adam and Eve, the tempting serpent in the garden, and toil on the land abound. The sense of loss is overwhelming in this poem: 'If I could live / find something from my people / something to hold / ... / from all those days going back / if I could find love / that grabs ... / ... / if I could know each day of our 400 years / take them in hand and say this is what it is / simply something / to hold to live for / to bring the kingdom here.'[63]

Friesen's criticism of modern Mennonites is as damning as his lament for their lost values: 'You know about some of our businessmen. The sharp ones who pay their workers dirt. Who live in their big houses and say God has blessed them. I always thought we were to share   give our only coat to the man without one. We were to build a heavenly mansion not an earthly one. ... You see how I don't understand things anymore.'[64]

Whether Friesen describes work in the field or garden, love-making, a Fundamentalist conversion, a Jew's attempt to sell some article to shrewd Mennonites, or the course of Mennonite history – the lines are always few, 'the images and symbols vivid and fresh, and the 'message' clear without moralizing. In a review of the *The Shunning*, Al Reimer's praise for Patrick Friesen's poetry is strong in its endorsement: 'What a revelation it is to have a genuine poetic vision of our very own humble, prosaic, taken-for-granted Mennonite World! ... He is revealing our own world to us in all its muted colors and dark illusions, a world that is as real and significant and worthy of being projected into the timeless forms of imaginative literature as any other.'[65]

The poetry of even the young writers who write in English is 'ethnic in origin, an outgrowth, as it were, of a conflict between the irreconcilable values of past and present,' as Peter Pauls has pointed out. 'Such conflicts and the resulting uncertainties will probably continue to inspire more poetry. It is inevitable, however, that these young poets, exposed as they are to the myriad literary influences of the English-speaking world, will opt for citizenship in and loyalty to a community much larger than their ethnic family. It is this new enlarged vision which distinguishes the new Mennonite poets from the old.'[66]

In summary, Canadian-Mennonite literature had its origin in the upheavals connected with the Communist Revlution of 1917 and the following civil war when the Russian-Mennonites saw their carefully constructed world collapse almost overnight. While there were some writers of note who had begun writing fiction around the turn of this century, it is doubtful whether Mennonites would have discovered and developed their creative genius without the destruction and loss of Russian Mennonitism. The literature which emerged from the chaotic times and continued to develop until Mennonites began to write in English deals predominantly with themes of suffering, loss, and senti- mental nostalgia. It is only in the more recent Mennonite literature, written by young Canadian-Mennonite poets and novelists, that themes of social responsibility and a search for identity have come to the fore. But even in the new literature the Mennonite past is 'remembered' and it is remembering those values, roots, and 'homeland' which enable Men- nonites in today's society to promote and maintain their identity as a faith-people and not merely as an ethnic group.

With regard to the literary value or quality of Canadian-Mennonite literature, the following observations may be in place. The value of any artistic work must not be measured according to standards that do not apply to it. Literary works of a period, tradition, or a particular people must be evaluated on their own terms and not be judged on the basis of how they measure up against established literary norms of other periods, traditions, or people.[67] Mennonite literature grew out of a certain socio-religious milieu and took on forms and contents characteristic of a particular ethnic people. The Canadian Mennonites have a story to tell, a story uniquely their own. Whether their narrative art compares favour- ably or unfavourably with Classical, Romantic, or modern German or English literature is beside the point. It is Mennonite literature and as such it must be taken seriously and on its own terms. As we have seen, the early Russian-Mennonite writers were still under the influence of older forms, but here and there they struck an original note, especially when they told their story of suffering and loss with sincere emotion and heartfelt piety. Such writers as Fritz Senn and Arnold Dyck were among those who had a story to tell and they told that story with style and originality. They rank among the best literary artists of the early period. Among the younger writers who write in English, the poet Patrick Friesen and certainly the novelist Rudy Wiebe rank among the very best creative writers in Western Canada. In drawing from their rich cultural and spiritual heritage they also have a story to tell and as accomplished artists they are able to pour that story into innovative artistic forms, something their forebears were unable to do. With them the Canadian-Mennonite literary tradition is coming of age and its further development is assured.

NOTES

This article was first presented as a paper on 8 February 1982, before the Mennonite Historical Society, Goshen College, Goshen, Indiana.

1 'Ein Homer hätte keinen Achill, ein Goethe keinen Faust gedichtet, wenn Homer ein Achill und wenn Goethe ein Faust gewesen wäre.' *Werke in drei Bänden*, ed. Karl Schlechta (München: Carl Hanser Verlag, 1966), II, 843.

2 See Victor G. Doerksen, 'From Jung-Stilling to Rudy Wiebe: "Christian Fiction" and the Mennonite Imagination,' *Mennonite Images: Historical, Cultural, and Literary Essays Dealing with Mennonite Issues*, ed. Harry Loewen (Winnipeg: Hyperion Press, 1980), pp. 197–208.

3 For a brief biography of Bernhard Harder and examples of his poems, see Peter M. Friesen, *The Mennonite Brotherhood in Russia (1789–1910)*, trans. from the German and ed. J.B. Toews et al. (Fresno, California: Board of Christian Literature General Conference of Mennonite Brethren Churches, 1978; 2nd rev. ed., 1980), pp. 945–58.

4 J.H. Janzen, 'The Literature of the Russo-Canadian Mennonites,' *Mennonite Life*, 1:1 (Jan. 1946), 23.

5 See Friesen, *The Mennonite Brotherhood in Russia*, pp. 703–4; 949–58.

6 John L. Ruth develops the idea that Mennonites were opposed to art because they saw it as idolatry, worldly sophistication, individualism, and artifice. Moreover their emphasis on asceticism, practicality, and edification caused Mennonites to identify art with 'the world.' *Mennonite Identity and Literary Art*, Focal Pamphlet 29 (Scottdale, Pennsylvania and Kitchener, Ontario: Herald Press, 1978), pp. 33–42.

7 See the significant article by Victor G. Doerksen, 'The Anabaptist Martyr Ballad,' *Mennonite Quarterly Review*, 51:1 (Jan. 1977), 5–21.

8 See Johannes Heinrich Janzen, *Das Märchen vom Weihnachtsmann*, ed. Waldemar Janzen (Winnipeg: CMBC Publications in Verbindung mit dem Verein der Freundinnen der Ersten Mennonitengemeinde, 1975).

9 Arnold Dyck, 'Jacob H. Janzen – Writer,' *Mennonite Life*, 6:3 (July 1951), 34.

10 Al Reimer, 'The Russian-Mennonite Experience in Fiction,' *Mennonite Images*, ed. Loewen, p. 225.

11 Janzen, 'The Literature of the Russo-Canadian Mennonites,' p. 23.

12 On Gerhard Loewen see Arnold Dyck, 'The Poet Gerhard Loewen,' *Mennonite Life*, 3:1 (Jan. 1948), 22–3.

13 Janzen, 'The Literature of the Russo-Canadian Mennonites,' p. 23.

14 Dyck, 'The Poet Gerhard Loewen,' p. 23.

15 Ibid.

16 Janzen, 'The Literature of the Russo-Canadian Mennonites,' p. 23.

17 Dietrich Neufeld, *A Russian Dance of Death: Revolution and Civil War in the Ukraine*, trans. and ed. Al Reimer (Winnipeg: Hyperion Press, 1977), p. 15.

18 Ibid., p. 4.

19 *Mennonite Mirror*, 4:7 (April 1975), 10.

20 Hans Harder, *No Strangers in Exile*, freely trans. from the German, ed. and expanded by Al Reimer (Winnipeg: Hyperion Press, 1979).

21 Ibid., p. 125.

22 Reimer, 'The Russian-Mennonite Experience in Fiction,' p. 227.

23 Janzen, 'The Literature of the Russo-Canadian Mennonites,' p. 24.

24 Gerhard Toews (Georg De Brecht), *Die Heimat in Trümmern: Deutsche Schicksale im Russland der Anarchie* (Steinbach, Manitoba: Warte Verlag, 1936), p. 238.

25 On *Verloren in der Steppe* as a *Bildungsroman*, see Michael Hadley, 'Education and Alienation in Dyck's "Verloren in der Steppe" : A Novel of Cultural Crisis,' *German-Canadian Yearbook*, 3, ed. Hartmut Fröschle (Toronto: Historical Society of Mecklenburg Upper Canada, 1976), 199–206. Concerning the lost world motif in Dyck's writings, Walter Schmiedehaus writes: 'die Heimat, die den Hintergrund all seines [Dycks] Dichtens bildet, die noch hier in der "neuen Welt" seinem Schaffen den eigentlichen erzeugenden Odem einhaucht und selbst seinen lustigeren Erzählungen einen Zug der Wehmut – oder soll man sagen der Schwere? – verleiht, diese Heimat ging zu seiner, zu unserer Zeit verloren ... für immer.' 'Der Schriftsteller Arnold Dyck,' *Mennonitische Welt*, 5:1 (Jan. 1952), 8.

26 Reimer, 'The Russian-Mennonite Experience in Fiction,' p. 232.

27 Arnold Dyck, *Two Letters, The Millionaire of Goatfield, Runde Koake*, trans. and ed. Elisabeth Peters (Steinbach, Manitoba: Derksen Printers, 1980).

28 George K. Epp, 'Dialekt und Hochdeutsch im Schrifttum der Mennoniten,' *Annalen II: Symposium Deutschkanadische Studien*, ed. Karin Gürttler and Friedhelm Lach (Montreal, 1978), p. 76.

29 J.H. Janzen, 'Die Belletristik der Canadischen Russlanddeutschen Mennoniten,' *Warte-Jahrbuch für die Mennonitische Gemeinschaft in Canada 1943*, 1 ed. Arnold Dyck (Steinbach, Manitoba: Prairie Press, North Kildonan, Manitoba, [1943], 87.

30 Fritz Senn, *Das Dorf im Agendgrauen: Gedichte*, ed. Elisabeth Peters (Winnipeg: Verein zur Pflege der deutschen Sprache, 1974).

31 *Mennonite Mirror*, 4:7 (April 1975), 10.

32 *Unter dem Nordlicht: Anthologie des deutschen Schrifttums der Mennoniten in Canada*, ed. Georg K. Epp (Winnipeg: Mennonite German Society of Canada, 1977), p. 8.

33 Ibid., p. 9. In *Unter dem Nordlicht* this poem has been erroneously attributed to Fritz Senn.
34 Janzen, 'Die Belletristik der Canadischen Russlanddeutschen Mennoniten,' p. 88.
35 Valentin Sawatzky has published the following collections of his poetry: *Friedensklänge: Gedichte* (Selbstverlag, 1971); *Heimatglocken: Lyrik und Balladen* (Selbstverlag, 1962); *Abendlicht: Gedichte und Märchen* (Selbstverlag, 1977).
36 *Unter dem Nordlicht*, ed. Epp, pp. 75–83.
37 Ibid., p. 66.
38 Ibid., p. 71.
39 Ibid., p. 70.
40 Janzen, 'The Literature of the Russo-Canadian Mennonites,' p. 28.
41 See *Unter dem Nordlicht*, ed. Epp, for poets who are still writing in German. Such Mennonite papers as *Der Bote* and *Mennonite Mirror* carry poetry and prose written in High German and Low German.
42 The following are the full-length novels Wiebe has written: *Peace Shall Destroy Many* (1962), *First and Vital Candle* (1966), *The Blue Mountains of China* (1970), *The Temptations of Big Bear* (1973), which was named winner of the Governor General's Award for Fiction, and *The Scorched-Wood People* (1977).
43 *Mennonite Mirror*, 4:7 (April 1975), 10. On the universality of Wiebe's novelistic themes, see the following: Elmer F. Suderman, 'Universal Values in Rudy Wiebe's *Peace Shall Destroy Many*,' *Mennonite Life*, 22:4 (Oct. 1965), 172–6; Elmer F. Suderman, 'The Mennonite Character in American Fiction,' *Mennonite Life*, 22:3 (July 1967), 123–30; Stephen Scobie 'For Goodness' Sake,' *Books in Canada*, 9:2 (Feb. 1980), 3–5; Sam Solecki, 'Giant Fictions and Large Meanings: The Novels of Rudy Wiebe,' *Canadian Forum*, 60:707 (March 1981), 5–8, 13.
44 Wiebe, *Peace Shall Destroy Many* (Toronto: McClelland and Stewart, 1962; paperback edition, 1972), p. 82.
45 Ibid., p. 83.
46 Ibid., pp. 236–7.
47 Wiebe, *The Blue Mountains of China* (Toronto and Montreal: McClelland and Stewart, 1970), p. 13.
48 Ibid.
49 Ibid., pp. 214–16.
50 Ibid., p. 214.
51 Ina Ferris, 'Religious Vision and Fictional Form: Rudy Wiebe's *The Blue Mountains of China*,' *A Voice in the Land: Essays by and about Rudy Wiebe*, ed. W.J. Keith (Edmonton: NeWest Press, 1981), p. 89.
52 Wiebe, *The Blue Mountains of China*, p. 227.

53 Peter Pauls, 'Mennonites Poets Possess Potential to Rank with Canada's Best,' *Mennonite Mirror* (Oct. 1975), p. 11.

54 Ibid.

55 *Harvest: Anthology of Mennonite Writing in Canada* ed. George K. Epp et al. (N.p.: Centennial Committee of the Mennonite Historical Society of Manitoba, 1974), p. 79.

56 Ibid., p. 87.

57 David Waltner-Toews, *The Earth Is One Body* (Winnipeg: Turnstone Press, 1979), p. 9.

58 Ibid., p. 50.

59 Ibid., p. 28.

60 Ibid., p. 26.

61 Pauls, 'Mennonite Poets,' p. 12.

62 *Harvest*, ed. Epp et al., p. 85.

63 Patrick Friesen, *The Shunning* (Winnipeg: Turnstone Press, 1980), p. 35.

64 Ibid., p. 87.

65 Al Reimer, 'Listening to the Gift of Poetry with Pat Friesen,' a review in *Mennonite Mirror*, 10:7 (March 1981), 15.

66 Pauls, 'Mennonite Poets,' p. 12.

67 See Hartmut Fröschle, 'Gibt es eine deutsch-kanadische Literatur?' and Heinz Kloss, 'Bemerkungen zur deutschkanadischen Literatur,' *German-Canadian Yearbook*, 3 (1976), 174–92. See also Epp, 'Dialekt und Hochdeutsch im Schrifttum der Mennoniten,' p. 72.

Henry Kreisel ⟩ഖ⟩ഖ⟩ഖ
A Canadian Exile Writer?

KARIN GÜRTTLER

Henry Kreisel, professor of English and Comparative Literature and author of two novels and short stories, all written in English, was born in Vienna in 1922. He fled to England in 1938, was arrested in 1940 as enemy alien, deported to Canada, and held in internment camps in the eastern part of the country for almost a year and a half. He is primarily known for two novels, *The Rich Man* and *The Betrayal*, published in 1948 and 1964 respectively. If Kreisel's life and *oeuvre* are examined within the context of the generally accepted time-frame of (German) exile literature, that is the period between 1933 and 1945, he can hardly be classified as an exile writer. Nevertheless, a case can be made for examining his novels within this context, since in both novels the writer's exile experience is of central importance. *The Rich Man* and *The Betrayal* reflect the transformation into literature of Kreisel's personal exile experience; significantly, this extends in Kreisel's case far beyond the actual period of exile and points to a more general connotation of the term 'exile.'

The case for examining the two novels within the context of exile literature could be made on the basis of a biographical approach. The novels in question contain numerous references to Kreisel's personal experiences in exile: he gives the names of the various internment camps; he refers to his mother's arrest on a train and her subsequent commitment to a concentration camp; he reminds the reader of his (Kreisel's) deportation from the Isle of Man to Canada; he refers to his work in a textile factory and mentions a number of other biographically verifiable details and events connected with his exile experience. In order to answer the question 'Is Henry Kreisel a Canadian exile writer?' a biographical approach might therefore be justifiable, especially in view of what Peter Laemmle aptly points out when he writes: 'What really connects the exile writers to each other is the mutuality of their biography: the experience of the exile situation.'[1] The exile experience common to all exile writers is undoubtedly an important aspect. However, the question arises to what degree the exile experience was really relevant to their creative process. There are some examples of writers in exile whose experience was not transformed into art. Within this context Jost Hermand's typological classification of exile literature according to the degree of political engagement against the Third Reich – he refers to 'resignedly escapist, consciously humanistic and actively antifascist currents'[2] – is of somewhat limited use; it seems a somewhat too convenient makeshift formula. It is, after all, possible to include under the term 'resignedly escapist' almost anything which does not fit into one category or the other. A typology of exile literature, in my estimation, is of questionable value, since the process of transforming the exile experience develops along different lines and manifests itself quite differently in individual authors. For this reason, I consider the suggestion of Egon Schwartz, who proposes a phenomenology of exile as reflected in the work of art itself,[3] to be more appropriate. Under this definition, I consider the exile experience as the generative principle in text production, whereas exile structures make up the operational model within the different levels of the text. Within this context of exile structures I should now like to focus on Henry Kreisel's novels *The Rich Man* and *The Betrayal*. The emphasis will be on the following particularly relevant aspects: 1/the narrative structure of *The Rich Man*; 2/the narrator in *The Betrayal*; 3/the symbolic use of paintings in both novels. Although models may be different, a comparative analysis of exile novels could discern a recurrence of narrative patterns; similarities in the function of the narrator may become evident and might lead to establishing distinct analogies between, for example, Joseph Conrad, Thomas Mann, and Henry Kreisel; likewise, similarities in the author's use of mythological patterns or in polyphony could beome evident.

THE NARRATIVE STRUCTURE OF 'THE RICH MAN'

The Rich Man, first edition 1948, is the story of Jacob Grossman, who when nineteen years of age leaves his home in Galicia and departs for the New

World. After several unsuccessful starts, he attains a modest livelihood through diligence, tenacity, and thriftiness, raises a family, and provides a reasonable education for his children. At the age of fifty-two, after thirty years of monotonous and hard work at the ironing machines of a Toronto clothing factory, he decides that he now, at last, can do what he had dreamed of all his life: return to the Old World and to Vienna, which rises in his fantasies of imperial Austro-Hungarian grandeur. He fantasizes a cheerful, carefree Vienna, singing and dancing to the waltz-strains of 'The Blue Danube.' It is the Vienna of glittering Hollywood sets and screen illusions. Jacob Grossman does not return to the Old World as a simple factory worker, who has put years of his savings into this trip, but rather as a man of success, as one who has made it, who has come to money and prestige, and who now enjoys abandoning himself to the pleasure of being gaped at and admired by his relatives during that short, immensely expensive period of a few weeks. He, Jacob Grossman, is the only one in the family who has achieved something, and the only one to have brought honour to the name Grossman.

This is the narrative model, which develops between the opposite poles of the Old World and the New World. It is the centuries-old myth of setting out for a new world and then returning to the old. It is the myth of the fairy-tale hero as well as of the Arthurian knight, and it is also the myth of the modern success-hero. In this case, it is the myth of the rich uncle from America, but the myth has undergone a significant modification in its traditional narrative structure. The New World does not fulfil the expectations of wealth and success, and, correspondingly, the expectations of refuge and salvation in the Old World also remain unfulfilled. The myth crumbles before the reality of down-to-earth everyday life, which is common to both worlds, and levels them down to a single world governed by the same laws. The myth becomes the anti-myth at the moment when the protagonist, moved by a false self-assessment, in his vanity and hubris attempts to appropriate to himself the behaviour and action patterns of the mythical hero, thereby violating the law of his own mediocrity, and thereby assuming a wishful identity and status which are not meant for him and cause him to fail.

The Old World–New World polarity appears continuously in a two-fold refraction, in the refraction of fiction and reality. On the manifestative level we are dealing with the categories of space, motion, and outwardly visible living conditions. Jacob Grossman's New World, Canada, is portrayed in his stories as a wide, open, and free space, as a country of unlimited opportunity, of success and of wealth. Indicators of this New World are given: comparisons of size (the Great Lakes area, Niagara Falls, population density in relation to the size of the country, and so on), geographic distances (a four-day trip from coast to coast), unrestricted freedom of movement (no compulsion to carry a passport, no controls), the outward appearance of the protagonist (a white suit made of sleek alpaca wool, white soft-leather shoes, the presents for his relatives, the Tassigny painting). All these indicators are façades and status symbols of an imaginary self; they are the wishful projections of his own mediocrity. Jacob Grossman's true living space in the New World is that of lower-middle-class restrictedness and modest living conditions. His outward appearance is in inverse proportion to his financial means, to his lifetime position as a simple factory worker, and to his condition of dependence on his employer, his wife, and his daughter.

Jacob Grossman's image of the Old World is limited to the city of his dreams, to nineteenth-century Vienna, to the imperial Austro-Hungarian monarchy, the waltzes of Johann Strauss, magnificent, ethereal, and full of *joie de vivre* – nothing but wishful projections of someone returning home. The living space of his relatives, however, the Vienna of 1935, manifests only restrictedness, seclusion, need, and poverty. It is not the city of the Hollywood movies, but a city of mass unemployment, of political assassination, and of the coming dictatorship along with its concomitant phenomena: secret police, arrests, newspaper bans, and underground activity. The Vienna of 1935 does not sing and dance; even the street musicians who roam the impoverished quarters, begging for a few pennies, are dispersed by the police. The 'Blue Danube' waltz only resounds like a dissonant funeral march. The indicators of the real Vienna in the novel are underground activity and concealment (the storeroom in Alfred Reich's bookstore, the cave in the Prater: 'It was almost like being in a small windowless room, pressed against a narrow corner,)[4] as well as restrictions on the freedom of movement, on the freedom of speech (the impossibility of travelling out of the country, the necessity of holding political discussions behind closed doors), and, finally the economic decline, and with it the loss of the basic necessities of existence.

The worlds of fictions disintegrate. Jacob Grossman's fiction of the Old World has been shattered, along with the imaginary role he intended to play in it, namely the realization of every immigrant's dream: to return home as 'a settled, prosperous-seeming man.'[5] His relatives reject the fiction of the New World, a world full of false promises and unfulfilled hopes. On the level of human values, it is not only Jacob Grossman who fails – Grossman who has been induced by his craving for recognition not to destroy the image his relatives have made of him, but instead to try to preserve it with complacent lies. Along with Jacob Grossman it is the New World that fails. Solidarity, the readiness to help, self-denial have become empty phrases. Confronted with the manifest indifference of the so-called Free World, and with the hopelessness of evading the catastrophe by emigration – 'for people who have no money, the doors of foreign countries are barred with steel'[6] – Jacob Grossman is left with nothing but the bitter feeling of being given up.

THE NARRATOR IN 'THE BETRAYAL'

The Betrayal, Kreisel's second novel, published in 1964, carries into the present the theme of guilt and complicity during the persecution of the Jews in Vienna, a theme which is preluded in the last part of The Rich Man. Once again the two poles of action are Canada and Austria, this time Vienna and Edmonton.

The young Canadian history professor Mark Lerner, whose name can be interpreted to mean 'teacher' as well as 'learner,' becomes inextricably involved in a whirlpool of moral conflicts, in which he is successively called upon to be a witness, a judge, and finally a counsel. He acts his part with reluctance and from the loftier view of the university professor, keeping his distance and avoiding rash conclusions. At the same time, Lerner represents the Canadian mentality vis-à-vis the stunning and irrational events in Europe's recent history. Canada is a young country, still in the state of innocence, as it were, a country that still believes in moral integrity. It is a country in which law and justice, though often misused, have never been shaken to their very foundations. Canada's standards of value are still intact, her historical consciousness is aimed at the future, unencumbered by a past filled with national catastrophes, which would have corrupted and perverted her at the very core. Canada is the outside spectator of world history – 'you Canadians have it so easy, so cozy, so rich, so beautifully settled in soft chairs to watch the world's drama.'[7] Canada, full of self-reliance and trust in the orderly course of things, is self-confident and possesses a kind of naïve self-righteousness. When Canada does intervene it is only in the role of a mediator avoiding implication, of a neutral referee looking for balance. In short, this is the Canada of the Lester B. Pearson era.

Lerner is also the narrator of the events. In his whole bearing he strives towards objectivity and respectful distance. He acts as the catalyst of passionate outbreaks and self-destructive moral conflicts. He is a narrator in the tradition of Thomas Mann's Serenus Zeitblom and Joseph Conrad's Marlow, but differs from these two in his personal detachment. At least one Canadian critic has noticed this: 'Professor Lerner ... is somehow too calm, too comfortably ensconced in his world to communicate powerfully the passions he has glimpsed. His aloofness is perhaps characteristic of the winter-bound Canadian consciousness – an irony of which Mr. Kreisel is undoubtedly aware.'[8] The impact of the plot of treachery and retaliation, of escape and persecution, is neutralized by means of the objective narrator. The dynamic force of the confrontation is reduced through reflection and self-analysis, and the plot is dissolved by argumentation. The novel thereby becomes a thesis novel. We may justly assume that this narrative attitude has as its underlying cause the author's own endeavours to distance himself from events which reflect his own bitter experiences, and to unravel the complex of inextricable involvement with guilt by means of an almost surgical analysis of the motives of human actions. By means of a reflective-analytical process the author attempts to shed a new light upon, and to make comprehensible, the phenomenon of the breakdown, under the pressure of violence and terror, of the moral principles governing human actions, and to set new standards of assessment. After all, the incomprehensible forces of a dehumanized time, when everything is out of joint, lie beyond the conventional norms of valuation. The monstrosities have assumed, in all their irrationality, such proportions that the categorizations of guilt and innocence, responsibility and irresponsibility have been invalidated, and in consequence, one can, at best, only inquire about degrees of guilt and responsibility. Only different shades of grey remain; there is no black or white.

The narrative scheme is quite simple: 'The hunter becomes the hunted and at last the victim.'[9] Joseph Held, who has helped escapees, becomes a traitor when he delivers a group of Jewish refugees to the Gestapo in order to save the life of his wife and daughter. Theodor Stappler, Held's pursuer and the only survivor of this group, has had the opportunity to warn his companions, one of them being his own mother, but he fails. All of them die in a concentration camp. At the end of the pursuit, the pursuer stands before himself: pursuer and traitor, Stappler and Held become one person. The vicious circle of entanglement with guilt is finally complete. The one seeking retaliation is now being accused, revenge makes no more sense, Held commits suicide, Stappler dies in an avalanche during a rescue mission in Canada's far north.

This narrative scheme is projected in the parallel of the Marat–Charlotte Corday episode in Mark Lerner's lecture on the French Revolution. Although personally dragged into the conflict of guilt and retaliation, Lerner does not undergo any significant change, and faithfully carries out his role as chronicler. He has become a bit more pensive, but he has not given up his Canadian attitude of non-involvement and non-commitment. He has, however, learned what it means when history lives up to its claim of being relevant to the present, by moving out of the secured zone of its historicity. He has learned that the answer of the succeeding generations turns out to be no different from that of the generation affected. 'I had often asked my students how we are to judge extreme situations and the reaction of fallible human beings to them. And now, asking myself the same question, my mind simply refused to come to grips with it. That was in a sense cowardly, an evasion of responsibility.'[10]

THE SYMBOLIC USE OF PAINTINGS IN THE TWO NOVELS

The significance of the paintings in these two novels is particularly great, firstly, because of their distinctive character within the novel's discourse, and secondly, because of the various levels of meaning that they connote. The ways in which these paintings and their meanings are transmitted to the reader are indeed complex. On the one hand, we are dealing with a fictional objective language, that is, the sign-language of the painting, which in itself has a connotative character. On the other hand, this objective language does not appear in its original form, that is as an image or a visible sign, but rather as a description in words, whereby this description itself is connotative, since it does not merely confine itself to a simple denotation of the elements of the pictures. Furthermore, the reader will also complicate the procedure by his or her reactions to the images connoted by the words. And finally, the painting in the text is a recurrent symbol that relates to all the other images and symbols and thereby attains a variety and multiplicity of meanings.

Now the fact that paintings or pictorial elements are mentioned or described in a literary text is not unusual. Their function, however, is normally limited to contributing to the frame of reference of a particular person, that is his social class, his education, his material situation, and so on. In short, the painting is used as a symbol of a socio-cultural framework. The Tassigny painting in *The Rich Man* also fulfils this function by helping to expose the incongruity between semblance and reality in Jacob Grossman's life, and in this respect it has the same symbolic function as the alpaca wool suit and the white soft-leather shoes. Significantly enough, this same discrepancy can be observed in Jacob Grossman's attempt to interpret the picture: his interpretation of Tassigny's *Entrepreneur* remains at the level of naïve analysis, that is it does not go beyond a simple enumeration of the individual elements of the painting. All his analysis achieves is a literal description of the picture; it comes nowhere near attaining the connotative level of the symbolic picture.

This symbolic connotation is achieved on two levels in the text: firstly, through the reactions of the journalist Koch and the statements of Tassigny himself, and secondly, through the recurrence of the painting as symbol throughout the text and through its association with other symbolic elements. Both levels of connotation are selective, they evoke more than they explain, and thus they are open-ended: the reader has to fill in meaning for himself.

The *Entrepreneur* shows, in the style of Expressionism, the figure of a man without a face, or, more precisely, with a black megaphone-like something instead of a face. His legs are oversized, taking up about three-quarters of the whole painting. A woman's face, thin and distorted, is partially obscured by the man's right leg. The predominant colour is a glaring green-yellow. These are the literal components of the painting.

On the second level of meaning the painting and its title connote a multiplicity of things. The title *Entrepreneur* refers to the man's function in society: the solicitation and exploitation of the masses by means of advertising. The painting further symbolizes his attitude and position, as exemplified by the relation of the man to the female figure: he is erect and dominating, whereas she is lying down and dominated. His nature is also symbolized by his anatomy: the oversized legs stand in sharp contrast to the absence of a head, which is represented merely by the neck. In other words, the intellectual and moral forces are subjugated by physical strength and brutality. The megaphone-like object in place of the head points to the excessive volume of the human voice caused by mechanical means of mass communication such as megaphone, loudspeaker, and radio, which reduce the human voice to nothing but screaming and thus annihilate the human and spiritual qualities of communication. In this context it is interesting to note that in modern art the existential crisis of our time, the loss of individuality and of human values such as character and integrity, is often represented by the symbol of the mechanical puppet. The distorted female face in the *Entrepreneur* painting denotes this lack of individuality, and it also symbolizes the crowd, a seduced and subjugated mass condemned to woe and misery. In keeping with all this is the colour combination green-yellow-black, which in its ecstatic disharmony works as a cry of despair. As Koch comments: 'All the agony and torture ... God damn it.'[11]

The terminology used by Tassigny belongs to the religious mythical world, and we thereby attain a further level of connotation, namely the artist Tassigny's apocalyptic vision of the modern seducer of the masses and of the mass exterminator. It is not reason that rules, but rather the diabolic voice of the modern propaganda machine, the incarnation of evil and dehumanization. This connotative level is complemented by the context into which the painting of the *Entrepreneur* fits: it is the political and historical context of the year 1935, with the German Nazis threatening to annex Austria, an annexation that finally took place in 1938 with terrible consequences. The Tassigny painting thus symbolizes the tyrannical rule of the Nazis: Tassigny, the artist, has transformed the threatening signs of the times into a vision of the coming inferno, and he thereby fulfils his role as prophet and as soothsayer in the original sense of the word: 'I think that a painter, an artist, must be a fighter and a prophet ... If people do not understand, I cannot help it.'[12] Every prophetic language is enigmatic, and the process of cognition implies at the same time a process of decision. In Jacob Grossman's case both take a negative course.

Just as in *The Rich Man*, a painting is also at the centre of *The Betrayal*. Very much as in the first novel the painting here brings into focus and symbolizes personal character traits, actions, and events in a compressed, symbolic language. The painting is an Emily Carr: a scene of the British Columbia forest, with its mighty tree trunks looming out of an impenetrable maze of intertwined roots and creeping vegetation. We are dealing here with two levels of connotation. With regard to the elements of the painting and its composition, the first level refers, speaking temporally, to the past, while the other indicates the potentiality of the future. One level refers to the gyratory principle of the vicious circle, the other to the dynamic principle of ever-present life. The polarity we encounter here is between two principles of life, between on the one hand the irrational and subconscious principle of the matrix, of chaos confined within the eternal circle of being and passing away, of birth and destruction, and on the other hand the rational and conscious principle of logos, of order, decision, and liberation. The jungle of intertwined roots and creeping underbrush symbolizes the impossibility of escaping the central conflict, as well as its disastrous effect, the moral entanglements and their inherent insolubility. The vertically rising tree trunks symbolize the young generation, in particular Catherine Held, who from the quagmire of past involvements with guilt and failure finds the straight path that leads to a bright future. Finally, this woodland scene of Emily Carr's is also a symbol for the Old World and the New.

Lawren Harris's painting, *Snow Mountains in the Arctic Ocean*, with its powerful yet simple form and colour scheme, appears at the end of the novel as a complement to Emily Carr's woodland scene of British Columbia. As a symbol it is associated, in this context, with Theodore Stappler's last phase of life, thereby symbolizing death, but also purification and catharsis.

In retrospect then, the question 'Is Henry Kreisel a Canadian exile writer?' – asked at the outset and dealt with above by analysing his two novels with respect to the structure of *The Rich Man*, the attitude and the function of the narrator in *The Betrayal*, and the symbolic use of the paintings in both – can be answered positively. Besides the numerous autobiographical references to his own personal exile experience the novels contain clearly discernible exile structures. Kreisel is personally aware of the fact that the transformation of his exile experience is central to his writing, as is evident in his own statement: 'I would agree that, although I consider myself a Canadian writer, I belong (in the sense in which you have defined the issue) to a certain category of "Exilliteratur." I can even say that I was conscious of this fact, and it was because I wanted to explore the conditions of the psychological and literary conditions of exile that I proposed (and wrote) my doctoral dissertation, which has the title "The Problem of Exile and Alienation in Modern Literature."'[13]

BIBLIOGRAPHY

NOVELS

The Rich Man. Toronto: McClelland and Stewart, 1948, pp. 263; London: Heinemann, 1952, pp. 271; Toronto: New Canadian Library, 1961, pp. viii and 207; reprint 1971; Toronto: Simon and Schuster, 1975, pp. 207 (paperback)
The Betrayal. Toronto: McClelland and Stewart, 1964, pp. vi and 218; Toronto: New Canadian Library, 1971, pp. x and 218

STORIES

'The Travelling Nude.' *Prism*, 1:1 (Fall 1959), 7–17
– *More Stories from Western Canada*, ed. Rudy Wiebe and Aritha van Herk,
 pp. 73–86. Toronto: Macmillan of Canada, 1980
'Homecoming.' *Klanak Islands: A Collection of Short Stories*, pp. 7–15. Vancouver:
 Klanak Press, 1959
'Two Sisters in Geneva.' *Queen's Quarterly*, 67 (Spring 1960), 67–75
– *A Book of Canadian Stories*, ed. Desmond Pacey, pp. 270–94. Toronto: Ryerson
 Press, 1962
– *Modern Canadian Stories*, ed. Giose Rimanelli and Roberto Ruberto, pp. 262–70.
 Toronto: Ryerson Press, 1966
– *Tradition-Integration-Rezeption: Annalen Zweites Symposium Deutschkanadische
 Studien*, ed. Karin R. Gürttler and Herfried Scheer, pp. 132–9. Montreal:
 Université de Montréal, 1979
In German translation, 'Zwei Schwestern in Genf.' *Neue Zürcher Zeitung*, 8 Jan.
 1961
– *Kanadische Erzähler der Gegenwart*, ed. Armin Arnold and Walter Riedel,
 pp. 377–93. Zürich: Manesse Verlag, 1967
'Annerl.' *Prism*, 2:4 (Summer 1961), 35–42
'The Broken Globe.' *Literary Review*, 8:4 (Summer 1965), 484–95
– *The Best American Stories 1966*, ed. Martha Foley and David Burnett, pp. 115–65.
 Boston: Houghton Mifflin Co., 1966
– *Stories from Western Canada*, ed. Rudy Wiebe, pp. 92–103. Toronto: Macmillan
 of Canada, 1972
– *Perceptions in Literature*, pp. 98–106. Boston: Houghton Mifflin Co., 1972
– *The Best Modern Canadian Short Stories*, ed. Ivon Owen and Morris Wolfe,
 pp. 50–9. Edmonton: Hurtig Publishers, 1978
In German translation, 'Der verbeulte Globus.' *Moderne Erzähler der Welt: Kanada*,
 ed. Walter Riedel, pp. 252–64. Tübingen and Basel: Erdmann Verlag, 1976.
 The story has also been translated into Italian and Swedish, and it has been
 adapted for the stage.
'An Anonymous Letter.' *Wild Rose Country: Stories from Alberta*, ed. David
 Carpenter, pp. 115–28. Ottawa: Oberon Press, 1977
'Chassidic Song.' *Tamarack Review*, 75 (Fall 1978), 78–88
The Almost Meeting and Other Stories. Edmonton: NeWest Press, 1981, pp. 148

PLAYS FOR RADIO AND TELEVISION

He Who Sells His Shadow: A Fable for Radio. CBC Wednesday Night, 1956; CBC
 Stage, 1960
The Betrayal. CBC-TV Production for Bob Hope Theatre, Dec. 1965

ARTICLES, REVIEWS, EDITIONS, MISCELLANEOUS

'The Letters of Thomas Wolfe and D.H. Lawrence.' *Tamarack Review*, 2 (Winter 1957), 84–8
'Bad Lands Sculptors, the Work of Wilfred Hodgson.' *Encyclopedia Year Book*, pp. 35–7. New York: Grolier Society, 1957
'The Arts – Useless – But Expensive.' *Bulletin of the Humanities Association of Canada*, April 1958, pp. 7–10
'Joseph Conrad and the Dilemma of the Uprooted Man.' *Tamarack Review*, 7 (Spring 1958), 78–85
'R.G. Everson's *A Lattice for Momos*.' *Dalhousie Review*, 39:2 (Summer 1959), 277–9
Aphrodite and Other Poems by John Heath, ed. with an introduction by Henry Kreisel. Toronto: Ryerson Press, 1959
'The African Stories of Margaret Laurence.' *Canadian Forum*, 41 (April 1961), 8–10
 – *Margaret Laurence: Critical Views on Canadian Writers*, ed. William New, pp. 105–10. Toronto: McGraw-Hill Ryerson, 1977
'Eleanor Farjeon's *Edward Thomas*.' *Queen's Quarterly*, 68 (Spring 1961), 193–4
'Recent Criticism of the Novel.' *University of Toronto Quarterly*, 31:2 (Jan. 1962), 246–50
'Literature as Language.' *English Teacher* (June 1962), 100–5
'A.J.M. Smith's *Masks of Fiction*.' *University of Toronto Quarterly*, 31:4 (July 1962), 478–9
'Are We Neglecting Modern Writers?' *English Teacher* (June 1964), 34–40
'Dreams and Reality: John Marlyn's *Under the Ribs of Death*.' *Canadian Literature*, 21 (Summer 1964), 64–6
'A Place of Liberty.' *CAUT Bulletin*, 13:1 (Oct. 1964), 27–32
'The Prairie: A State of Mind.' *Transactions of the Royal Society of Canada*, 6, series 4 (June 1968), 171–80
 – *Contexts of Canadian Criticism*, ed. Eli Mandel, pp. 254–66. Chicago and Toronto: University of Chicago Press and University of Toronto Press, 1971
 – *Canadian Anthology*, ed. Carl F. Klinck and Reginald E. Watters, pp. 620–7. Toronto: Gage, 1974
 – *Horizon: An Anthology of the Canadian Prairie*, ed. Ken Mitchell, pp. 247–57. Toronto: Oxford University Press, 1977
'The Prairie Observed.' *Canadian Literature*, 61 (Summer 1974), 88–90
'Diary of an Internment.' *White Pelican*, 4:3 (Summer 1974), 5–40
'Bertolt Brecht's Berlin.' *Modernist Studies*, 2:1 (1976), 54–6
'A Familiar Landscape' (observations on the short stories of Margaret Laurence). *Margaret Laurence: Critical Views on Canadian Writers*, ed. William New, pp. 143–6. Toronto: McGraw-Hill Ryerson, 1977
'Certain Wordly Experiences.' Interview, *Sphinx*, 2:3 (University of Regina; Winter 1977), 10–22

'Sheila Watson in Edmonton.' *Figures in a Ground*, ed. D. Bessai and D. Jackel,
pp. 4–6. Saskatoon: Western Producer Prairie Books, 1978
'The Games of Martin Myers.' *Essays on Canadian Writing*, 11 (Summer 1978),
147–50
'Language and Identity' (a personal essay). *Tradition-Integration-Rezeption:
Annalen Zweites Symposium Deutschkanadische Studien*, ed. Karin R. Gürttler and
Herfried Scheer, pp. 105–14. Montreal: Université de Montréal, 1979
'The Humanism of George Faludy.' *Canadian Forum*, 58 (March 1979), 27–9
'Roy Daniells 1902–1979.' *Canadian Literature*, 81 (Summer 1979), 140–2
'On the Crossing of Frontiers.' *Crossing Frontiers: Canadian and American Literature*,
ed. D. Harrison, pp. 138–43. Edmonton: University of Alberta Press, 1979
'The Poet as Radical: Dorothy Livesay in the Thirties.' *Contemporary Verse II*, 4
(Winter 1979), 19–21
'Festschrift.' *A Political Art: Essays and Images in Honour of George Woodcock*, ed.
W.H. New, pp. 82–4. *Canadian Literature*, 84 (Spring 1980)

NOTES

1 Peter Laemmle, 'Vorschläge für eine Revision der Exilforschung,' *Akzente*,
6 (1973), 512 (my translation).
2 Jost Hermand, 'Schreiben in der Fremde,' *Exil und innere Emigration*, Third
Wisconsin Workshop, ed. Reinhold Grimm and Jost Hermand (Frankfurt
a.M.: Athenäum Verlag, 1972), p. 16 (my translation).
3 Cf. Egon Schwarz, 'Was ist Exilliteratur?' *Exil und innere Emigration II*,
Internationale Tagung in St Louis, ed. Peter Uwe Hohendahl and Egon
Schwarz (Frankfurt a.M.: Athenäum Verlag, 1973), p. 158.
4 Henry Kreisel, *The Rich Man*, 2nd edition (Toronto: McClelland and
Stewart, 1961), p. 118.
5 Ibid., p. 31.
6 Ibid., p. 67.
7 Kreisel, *The Betrayal*, 2nd edition (Toronto: McClelland and Stewart, 1971),
p. 150.
8 Hugo McPherson, 'Betrayal, Desertion, Atonement,' *Tamarack Review* 34
(Winter 1965), 108.
9 Kreisel, *Betrayal*, p. 3.
10 Ibid., p. 182.
11 Kreisel, *The Rich Man*, p. 164.
12 Ibid., p. 37.
13 Letter from Henry Kreisel, 7 Nov. 1980.

An Austrian in Ottawa 🖎 Carl Weiselberger's Canadian Experience 🖎🖎🖎

WALTER E. RIEDEL

The 20th of December 1945 marks the beginning of Carl Weiselberger's new career as art and music critic in Canada. On that date, the then proofreader of the newspaper the *Ottawa Citizen* made his debut with a short article entitled 'Wagner – Enjoyable Again,' an article reflecting highly personal feelings and experiences. The occasion was a radio broadcast of Wagner's *Meistersinger* performed at the Metropolitan Opera House in New York; Weiselberger wrote: 'Yes, I enjoyed the *Meistersinger* again, now that the dragon of force and conquest has been defeated and lies chained in a prison-dungeon in the very Nuremberg of the *Meistersinger* – awaiting judgement! I am cured of my Wagnerphobia. Hitler is dead, and Wagner is more alive than ever' (oc., 20 Dec. 1945).[1] These words are a sincere expression of relief by an Austrian Jew, who, like many of his compatriots, was forced into exile at the time of Hitler's *Anschluss* of Austria and who, after the end of the war, at age forty-five, found himself attempting to begin anew in another country whose language and culture were foreign to him. Weiselberger's feelings about Wagner in 1945 reflect that sense of his origins in the European tradition which was to become an essential part of all of his *oeuvre* written in Canada. Indeed, his Canadian experience may be interpreted as a perception of Canada through the eyes of a cultured Austrian Jew. This perception reflects the different stages of his sojourn in Canada: exile and internment, freedom and the new beginning in a foreign country. Of central interest to Weiselberger's Canadian experience is his positive response to the country – a response exactly opposite to the supposedly specifically Canadian posture of the victim which, for example, has become associated with Margaret Atwood's interpretation of the Canadian experience.[2] In his life and his *oeuvre* Weiselberger represents a remarkable variation of the Canadian experience.

When Carl Weiselberger came to Canada, he had already made a mark for himself in pre-war Vienna as a writer of short stories and a novel. Born on 4 March 1900 of middle-class Jewish parents who had a more than average interest in literature and the arts, he spent nearly four decades in the city of his birth. He attended public school, then the *Realgymnasium*, and there discovered his special interests in art, music, and classical and modern languages. Swayed by his uncle, a director of the Bankverein, Carl completed the *Handelsschule* (trade school) and prepared for a career in banking. His literary debut dates back to his days as a bank clerk in Vienna and reflects the social and intellectual climate of his origins. The city of Vienna, which had the dubious reputation of 'Gay Vienna,' was the cultural, economic, and political centre of Austria. During Weiselberger's time in Vienna, Austria experienced far-reaching historical and political events and profound changes affecting all areas of cultural life. These four decades encompass the *fin-de-siècle*, the First World War, the end of the Austro-Hungarian Empire, post-war inflation and economic depression, and, finally, the events leading to the *Anschluss*. Weiselberger witnessed the cultural upheaval which occurred in Vienna and affected such areas as literature, the arts, music, and psychology. Part of Weiselberger's Austrian experience was the *fin-de-siècle*, the turn of the century, which – in retrospect – had the psychological significance of both the end of an old era and the beginning of a new one. Not only for Austria, but for all of Europe it was an era for reevaluation, for defining and enunciating new programmes. In the arts, various movements from Naturalism to Impressionism and Expressionism followed each other in quick succession. Beer-Hofmann, Schnitzler, Hofmannsthal were writing when Weiselberger's interest in literature awakened. In music, Arnold Schönberg discovered a whole new realm in expressiveness with his atonality, and in psychology Sigmund Freud and Alfred Adler formulated new ideas and theories. These are just a few of the forces that were shaping intellectual development at the time.

Weiselberger's Austrian experience was affected by his consciousness of this intellectual upheaval. The new literature of authors as different as Arthur Schnitzler, Hugo von Hofmannsthal, and the German Expressionists left distinctive marks upon young Weiselberger as he began to publish his short stories in newspapers and periodicals in Austria, Germany, Switzerland, and Czechoslovakia, as well as a novel entitled *Die Zeit ohne Gnade* ('Time without grace'), serialized in the Viennese newspaper *Der Tag* (1937). This autobiographical novel, set in the chaotic inflationary times of post-war Europe, reminds the reader of Georg Kaiser's *Von morgens bis mitternachts* (*From Morn to Midnight*) and of Vienna as portrayed in Arthur Schnitzler's plays *Anatol, Reigen* (*La Ronde, Dance of Love*), and *Liebelei* (*Light-o'-Love*). The protagonist of the novel recognizes the illusory value of money, and, in his search for values during the chaotic 'time without grace,' finds meaning in the beauty and simplicity of a human relationship.

Weiselberger's *oeuvre* written in Vienna – some of it has been republished in the two collections entitled *Der Rabbi mit der Axt* (1973)[3] and *Eine Auswahl seiner Schriften* (1981)[4] – bears upon his Canadian writings. These first stories have been described as 'usually short, original pieces, sensitively conceived, with a humorous touch of irony and frequently of astonishing stylistic quality ... they deal both realistically and with much imagination with themes taken from the life of ordinary people and artists ... and reflect a very keen psychological understanding of human nature.'[5] Although the stories are of great variety in subject matter, theme, setting, and time, a few predominant themes and motifs recur with remarkable frequency. The short prose selections provide evidence of Weiselberger's predilection for what he himself called 'human-interest stories.' He seems to have had a special eye for the ironies of fate, for human aspirations, disappointments, and idiosyncracies. He portrays his characters with sensitivity, empathy, understanding, and a sense of humour. Many of these stories have themes and protagonists taken from the arts: from painting, music, and sculpture. Protagonists bear great names, such as Mozart, Beethoven, Michelangelo, Leonardo da Vinci, but there are also unknown artists struggling for recognition and eking out a meagre living or dying in obscurity, such as his poor violinist Hampl.[6] Often they are outsiders, eccentrics, oddities. Many stories deal with problems concerning the nature of the arts. The protagonist is often an art critic, an obvious projection of the author; frequently he is presented in a humorous, ironic, or satiric tone. Of special interest to Weiselberger are the stories behind a painting, and questions concerning the relationship between reality and its portrayal on the canvas. Again and again he explores the relationship between figures on a canvas and the real world. Sometimes he proceeds in the opposite direction: people of the real world remind him of a well-known painting. Another favourite subject is the quick-change artist, the man who appears before his audience with many faces, but has no real one. The theme of reality and appearance preoccupied him frequently: 'Wolken im Frühling' ('Clouds in spring')[7] is reminiscent of Hofmannsthal's poems 'Vorfrühling' ('Early spring') and 'Terzinen über Vergänglichkeit' (*'Terza rima* on transitoriness').

A significant number of Weiselberger's Viennese stories deal with protagonists whose mechanical work turns them into automatons: bookkeepers, bank cashiers, museum guards, salesmen; even a teacher is perceived as a geometry machine in the story 'Die Geometrie Maschine.'[8] These protagonists long for freedom from their routines, for far-away countries, or for retirement. Significantly, however, when they have attained their long-awaited goals, they find this state unbearable. In some stories, Weiselberger portrays pessimistic visions of the future where a totally mechanized form of life leaves no place for beauty and happiness. Implicit is a longing for other times, specifically the good old times. Thematically related to these stories are others whose central themes are journeys, escapes into a world of dreams or fantasy. Sometimes this flight goes back to childhood where the world is perceived through the eyes of a child. The contrast between then and now is central to these early stories.

A recurring structural element in Weiselberger's Viennese stories is his satirical perspective. He has a predilection for portraying characters who suffer precisely those flaws and foibles which they criticize in others: Professor Tümmelmolch in 'Ein Feind der Zeit' ('An enemy of time')[9] has such a busy schedule of appointments, lecturing about the dangers of automation, the need to take time, and the ideal of *la dolce far niente*, that he becomes an automaton himself. Similarly Weiselberger's Goethe scholar ('Der Goethe-Forscher'),[10] who spends his time painstakingly investigating whether Goethe preferred his chicken baked or roasted and on which side of his place he placed his wineglass, cannot remember what he has just eaten for dinner and scolds his wife for being hopelessly pedantic. These and other stories reflect Weiselberger's joy in exploring a situation, an encounter, or an idea, and in pursuing that matter to its conclusion; they reflect his pleasure in playing a game of ideas in order to amuse or entertain. In structure, these stories are often reminiscent of those of Schnitzler.

The events leading to Weiselberger's exile in Canada go back to Hitler's

Anschluss of Austria in 1938. The advent of National Socialism put a sudden end to Weiselberger's promising beginning as a writer in Austria. In April 1939 he fled to England. However, after the fall of Holland, Belgium, and France, England feared an imminent invasion and declared all Germans, Austrians, and Italians to be 'enemy aliens.'[11] Weiselberger was among many interned on 12 May 1940, on the Isle of Man, in a seaside resort which had been hastily converted into a barbed-wire camp. Two months later, on 14 July 1940, he was deported to Canada along with about seventy-seven hundred internees;[12] Weiselberger remained interned in a camp near Sherbrooke, Quebec till 11 February 1943. The internment experience was an unexpected turn of events, a severe blow for Weiselberger, who, having fled from the National Socialist regime in order to find asylum in England, suddenly found himself deemed suspect. He left a record of his experience of exile and internment in the form of some twenty short stories, all written in German. They reflect his attempt to come to terms with the political events and the experiences connected with internment: his loss of his home and everyone and everything that gave him a reason for being: his family, his friends, his very means of existence. He perceived his internment as a frustration over which he had no control; he describes it in these words:

> A great cage of people on the seashore with the war as a backdrop,
> the threat of invasion, panic, 3000 men between 16 and 60 were interned
> in a melting pot, thrown behind a wire fence, almost all of them refu-
> gees from Hitler, full of anxiety at what tomorrow might bring, involun-
> tary guests at a seaside resort, two to a bed, but otherwise with every
> comfort, a wondrous mixture of elegance and incarceration.[13]

Since the beginning of Weiselberger's Canadian experience was internment, his first perception of Canada was from the perspective of the barbed-wire compound, from that absurd world of rumours, fears, and uncertainty about the future. The predominant themes of the stories written during this time are the sudden outbreak of the irrational forces of war and destruction ('Apokalypse'),[14] persecution and flight ('Die Gehetzten'),[15] the absurdity of living a caged and useless existence, the escape from the arena of war to a far-away country, and the inability to help in the defeat of the forces which were responsible for his absurd situation. Again and again he depicts the monotony of life in the compound, the games the internees play in order to kill time, the caged existence 'between barbed wire and camp latrine,'[16] a world of resignation and stupor producing a condition the internees referred to as 'internitis.'[17] Beyond the compound looms the vast, unknown country symbolizing freedom, life, a new beginning, but at the same time producing fear of the unknown. Understandably, in some stories his thoughts go back in time to his former homeland, to a 'golden' past whose values have been betrayed and perverted. In some stories he portrays his own experiences as those of the eternal Jew, hated, persecuted, suffering, and eternally wandering.[18] His most significant internment story, 'Kain und Abel in Kanada,'[19] contains his personal message and philosophy: the resolve to search for a meaningful activity despite the absurdity of the events. This positive response to the challenge of facing adversity was a decisive step on his way to a new beginning. In camp he learned the new language, and, after his release in 1943, he served as interpreter and translator in the Canadian government's mail censoring office till the end of the war. Then, after beginning as a galley-proof reader for the *Ottawa Citizen*, he forged a new career for himself as art and music critic; he held this position from 1946 till his retirement in 1965.

All of Weiselberger's writing in Canada reflects a high degree of subjectivity in perspective. He refers to it as 'the literary display of one's beloved ego' and reminds those who advise a writer to strike out the 'smiling "I"' from their writing and to 'step back behind a curtain of Shakespearean objectivity' of the 'symbolic importance' of Goethe's autobiography, written less to harvest personal memories than to illustrate, through the medium of his own life, the intellectual development of the period' (oc, 11 Oct. 1947). Weiselberger would like to see his writing considered in terms of the 'symbolic importance' of his personal experiences. Central to his Canadian experience is the fact that he came to this country as a political refugee who experienced internment, freedom, and the elation to be able to begin anew. It is not surprising that he portrays Canada with enthusiasm and often in superlatives. However, mixed in with his feeling of elation is a gnawing realization that his limited knowledge of English puts considerable constraints on him in his aspirations as a writer. Especially during his early years in Canada, he feels that 'the most tragic loss was ... that of [his] language' (oc, 11 Oct. 1947). Weiselberger chooses a telling symbol for this loss; he compares himself to Peter Schlemihl, the fairy-tale protagonist of Chamisso's eponymous novella, who has lost his shadow to the Devil and who is 'condemned to wander through the world without casting a shadow.'

Weiselberger points out that, significantly, this fairy tale was written by a German poet of French origin, Adelbert von Chamisso, who had fled from France to Germany with his parents and who grew up 'between the nations, between the languages.' Though he had learned to write excellent German he felt 'that he was floating through the world without his own idiom, without casting, like everybody else, a natural shadow in the sunlight.' Weiselberger's experience of beginning to write in the country whose language and idiom were foreign to him is described in these words:

> Naturally, you go and build a plank patched up of dictionaries, a narrow bridge of careful translations, through which to reach the others. At first you feel the new language like a stranger's coat on your body, uncomfortable, embarrassing, with sentences too long or too short like misfitting arm-sleeves while the buttons of verbs and conjunctions, which could clothe two thoughts, are missing. Years of struggle until you get used to wear [sic] the new idiom. Your genuine shadow lost, you grow an artificial one. And a bit proudly, you walk your small *ersatz* shadow through the columns of English newspapers.   (oc, 1 Oct. 1947)

A fellow Austrian writer, Stefan Zweig, who also experienced exile, said in his autobiography, *Die Welt von gestern* ('The world of yesterday') that with the loss of one's passport one loses not only one's homeland but also one's space to breathe.[20] Stefan Zweig took his life in desperation; so did others. Weiselberger's strength of character overcame the victim syndrome. For him, mastering the idiom of the new language was a necessity, a matter of survival, but he responded to the challenge as if he wanted to outdo Joseph Conrad. In numerous columns he deals with questions related to Canada's bilingualism from his personal perspective. To him, the confusion in the *Tower of Babel*, Breughel's picture hanging in a museum in Vienna, does not look like 'a blasphemy asking for punishment'; to him, it presents 'an exciting spectacle and game, a saturnine, if not satanic experience, expansion of the human mind' (oc, 27 July 1954). He reproaches the opponents of second-language study in a bilingual country for standing in 'the gateway to broadened expression and understanding' (oc, 27 July 1954).

Despite the problem of language, Weiselberger made a significant contribution to intellectual life in Canada's capital as art critic of the *Ottawa Citizen* from the mid-forties until 1965. Beginning with a modest column, he soon progressed to half a newspaper page of 'Art Notes,' renamed in 1959 'Carl Weiselberger about Art' and extended during the sixties to a full page entitled 'Carl Weiselberger Talks about Art.' In the early years, his task consisted mainly of informing his readers of the current art scene, and especially of writing reviews of exhibitions. Perhaps his most impressive contribution was the series of articles entitled 'The Isms of Art,' which began in September 1958 and ran fortnightly till July 1959. He wrote eighteen articles demonstrating the changing 'Isms' of art. The occasion was a joint programme by the National Gallery and the *Ottawa Citizen* focusing on special exhibits from the gallery's permanent collection. In informative, easily understandable commentaries he brings the European tradition in the arts to his Canadian readers: using Corot's 'Le pont de Narni' as a point of departure, he deals with the developments in the arts from Romantic Idealism to the rise of Impressionism. In the subsequent commentaries, he focuses on Courbet's Realism, on Degas's solidly drawn human figures (his 'slices of life'), on Monet's use of pure colour during the rise of Impressionism, on Picasso's experiments, on Renoir's expression of the 'joy of living,' on the impressionistic landscapes of Cézanne, on the 'Crossroads of Styles' of Cézanne, Pissarro, Corot, Lautrec, and Van Gogh, on Fauvism, on Signac's Pointillism, on German Expressionism, on the 'Joyous Play of Form and Color' in Matisse's work, on the Geometric Cubist interpretations of Braque and Pissarro. Three articles focus on Canadian art: Alfred Pellan's Surrealism, Borduas's *automatisme*, and Jean-Paul Riopelle's *tachisme* or action painting.

During his twenty years as art critic of the *Ottawa Citizen*, Weiselberger also dealt perceptively and always with didactic intent with many of the fundamental questions concerning the arts. Some of the questions he dealt with in his articles were: what is art? is art necessary? what is the purpose of art? what is the purpose of art criticism? how do I judge a work of art? what is art and what is trash? what is the nature of abstract art? what will art look like a century hence? These questions and variations of them became the titles of his articles. Other aspects he discussed were freedom of art, art and the man in the street, art as a social commentary, the art of teaching art, and the portrayal of the nude in the arts of the ages.

Weiselberger's background made him particularly receptive towards the European tradition in Canada's art wherever he encountered it. His 'Art Notes' abound in references to the arts in the Old World. Thus he points out that many of Canada's important artists are in fact Europeans:

the British artillery officer Thomas Davies, stationed in Canada over two hundred years ago, painted remarkable 'naive-romantic' watercolours of the Canadian scene having 'the charm of a poetic story-teller from a romantic never-never land' (OC, 29 June 1957). In a sensitive commentary on the German-Canadian painter William Raphael's *Immigrants at Montreal*, Weiselberger relates the style to influences coming from the Berlin Academy at the time of Adolph Menzel (OC, 23 Aug. 1958). On the occasion of a Krieghoff exhibition, Weiselberger draws attention to the European past of this Canadian artist, who, in his painting of Canadian themes (Indians, landscapes, and so on), brought with him 'the typical European style of the middle of the 19th century as practised by folk limners and fashioners of popular genre scenes' (OC, 26 Aug. 1961). In a sensitively written article on the life and works of the German painter Rudolf Bergmeer, with whom Weiselberger identifies to a certain extent since Bergmeer's paintings were burned by the Nazi storm troopers before his escape to Canada, Weiselberger recognizes a highly individualistic style of artistic expression, a 'magic realism,' which Bergmeer could pursue as a hermit near an Indian village on Canada's West Coast (OC, 18 Sept. 1965). Likewise, associations in themes and styles of Canadian art come to mind as Weiselberger examines paintings of European masters: on the occasion of a visit of a Biedermeier exhibition to the Austrian Baroque Monastery at Gutenstein, the paintings portraying an idealized, idyllic past and the flattering portraiture by such artists as the Austrian Ferdinand Waldmüller remind him of Georg. T. Berthon's *The Three Robinson Sisters* (1946). 'Ontario Biedermeier,' Weiselberger muses, pointing to Berthon's Austrian origin (OC, 25 Aug. 1962).

In a relatively short time, Weiselberger was able to establish himself as a respected critic. In 1948 he won the award presented annually by the Ottawa Press Club for the best feature story of the year; his contribution was described as 'a scholarly and stimulating appreciation of the Murillo painting "Abraham and the Three Angels."' On the occasion of the presentation of the award, Percy Philip, Ottawa representative of the *New York Times* and one of the judges of the competition, paid a high tribute to Weiselberger when he said: 'The writer of this story revealed himself not only an expert at the subject but also showed that he could write very well. The newspaper that employed him found the right man to do the job.'[21] Such recognition provided him with the freedom to give a very personal imprint to the art page. Giving free rein to his predilection for teaching and entertaining his readers by exploring ideas or situations, he now invents scenes, situations, and encounters and presents his ideas in the form of short stories, dialogues, or playlets. Even from some of the titles the influence of the Socratic dialogue becomes evident: 'Mr. Socrates Discusses Bytown' (oc, 11 May 1951); 'Socrates and the Art Dealer' (oc, 23 Feb. 1963); 'A Chat between Picasso and Turner' (about modern art) (oc, 18 July 1964); 'A Conversation between Leonardo da Vinci and Michelangelo' (oc, 29 Aug. 1964); 'Two Citizens of Florence discuss That Bothersome Modern Art' (oc, 31 Dec. 1965). One of the most original conceptions is an amusing example of Weiselberger's imaginative use of the European cultural tradition in a Canadian context. It is entitled 'Don Juan and Doctor Faustus Visit the National Gallery of Canada' (oc, 21 Oct. 1961). Weiselberger listens in on a conversation about art – including Canadian art – between Don Juan, eternal pursuer of lust, and Doctor Faustus, passionate seeker of truth. While Faust argues that the creator of a work of art 'must think, not merely feel,' Don Juan is solely interested in the sensuous side of art, claiming that art is 'nothing but pleasure and entertainment.' Moving from nude to nude, Don Juan gets so carried away by an adorable young Bacchante, a sculpture of a nude by Bourdelle, that he wants to embrace her and carry her off. Faust brings him back to reality by pointing to the security guard and by reminding Don Juan of the fact that she is only an image which would eventually vanish as did the spectre of Helena which he, Faust, had attempted to seize.

The art page lent itself to amusing short prose selections dealing with the arts. Following the method of his mentor Ovid, Weiselberger brings to life the sculptures of a museum or a cathedral, the figures of a painting, or the characters of books shelved in a library. Choosing the midnight hour, he gives them the gift of speech and provides opportunities for most imaginative encounters: in 'Midnight in the Museum' (oc, 22 Feb. 1964), the world's most famous lovers discuss that 'knotty marriage problem.' In 'Midnight in the Public Library' (oc, 22 Feb. 1952), ghosts of classical authors whose books were stamped 'not for open shelves' hold an indignation meeting until, at one o'clock, the bells of the Peace Tower end the tumultuous conference and 'the whole revered assembly of authors with coattails lifted in their hands, rush back into their more or less dusty book-covers, on their shelves – open or "not open."'

A significant part of Weiselberger's work as a journalist can be described as that of a cultural mediator between the Old and the New World. Weiselberger identified with Heinrich Heine who, while in exile in France, wrote reports about letters in that country for a German newspaper, as well as reports about Germany for a French audience. While Weiselberger's art columns written for the *Ottawa Citizen* and his talks on radio and television brought the arts, especially the European tradition, closer to his Canadian audience, his reports on Canada – the country, its people, and their culture – written in German for newspapers and periodicals of German-speaking countries brought Canada closer to his readers in the Old World.

His journalism contains numerous references to the Old World; he portrays Austria's rich cultural tradition and presents an image of the Austrians as an adaptable people formed by the melting together of different people and intent on building bridges between East and West. He looks behind the clichés of 'Gay Vienna' and presents an image of Austria as he remembers it from his experiences, but with an ironical attitude of detachment (for example, OC, 11 April 1953). He points out that 'the Great Waltz Vienna idea' is due to 'a friendly mistake nurtured by Hollywood movies with too much Danube-blue and too gaudily arranged waltzes by Strauss and Lehar,' and that the 'gay' Viennese are 'famous for their pessimism, their perpetual nagging, drudging, grumbling, their ironical attitude towards the world and … themselves.' He focuses on the dissonances of his fellow Viennese as he writes: 'Halfway between the exuberance of the Viennese three-quartertime and the pistol of the suicide stands nostalgic resignation, self-pity, sarcasm, a unique talent to belittle the world, and, in the first place, to belittle oneself, a literature full of morbid, bored, playfully weary heroes like Schnitzler's Anatol' (OC, 11 April 1953).

The image of Canada which Weiselberger presents to his European readers is similarly subjective. His Canada is seen through the eyes of the exiled writer who responds with gratitude and enthusiasm to the new home that enabled him to make a new start. Ten years after his arrival in Canada, the journalist muses in retrospect, still somewhat disbelievingly: 'I fell into a picturebook. Ten years ago … A thorny hedge has grown over my German. I marvel at the fact that I am sitting in an editor's office of an English newspaper in Ottawa, capital of Canada, on the North American continent. In dream-like reality, in a picturebook so to speak' (NÖ, 28 March 1948).[22] His Canada is a vast and beautiful country – thinly populated and having an immense potential for growth. He compares it to a young giant, strong and free, 'who is just rubbing the sleep from his eyes.' With enthusiasm and a sense of wonder, he portrays the Canadian landscape with its array of colours: the gigantic Rocky Mountains, the oceans, the fine nuances of the prairies – their 'grass-greens, earth-browns, yellow-earths, rust-reds and silver-greys in an eternal play of light and shade' (NÖ, 14 Sept. 1952). The titles of his articles are variations of the theme 'Canada: Fairy-tale and Reality' (NÖ, 14 Sept. 1942). The realistic aspect consists of 'practically thinking' people of different backgrounds and national origins, living together in peace, and engaged in building up their rich country. They are builders, architects, farmers, engineers, miners, fishermen, oil-speculators – people whose attention is focused on things of this earth: new deposits of uranium, aluminum, gold, silver, nickel, oil, and the transforming of huge forests into newsprint. He contrasts these practically oriented people with the 'morbidly sensitive artist-types' of his native Austria at the turn of the century, whose thoughts were focused on 'the sweet and naïve girl,' the *süsses Mädel*, and 'similar sublimated conceptions' (NÖ, 14 Sept. 1952). He welcomes progress and quotes impressive industrial and economic statistics as a measure of economic well-being. He regards cities, skyscrapers, and derricks as signs and symbols of progress. The steel-blue, rust-red, and aluminum-white elevators are, to him, 'the cathedrals of the prairie,' symbols of a 'practical earth-cult.' Significantly, in his enthusiastic portrayal of Canada, his new homeland, his thoughts go back to the country of his birth, to his cultural roots, and, striking a recurring chord, he writes: 'But sometimes one is nevertheless startled like Peter Schlemihl. Where is one's shadow? One does not throw a shadow in the bright sun! One has lost one's shadow, one's earth, one's origin, one's homeland. somewhere back there, in Europe. And one lives, quietly, ghost-like and unreal, between two languages, between the countries, their cultures, between memories' (NÖ, 28 March 1948).

Weiselberger's reports on the young country's search for its own expression in the arts reflect an enthusiasm similar to that in his reports on the country and its people. In an article in the Austrian periodical *Die Schau*,[23] he hails the achievements of the Group of Seven, for with them Canada outgrew its colonial tradition in the arts. The portrayal of Canada's landscape through European eyes gave way to those who 'began to see Canada with new, Canadian eyes and portrayed it with highly individualized simplification, yet capturing the essence of the Canadian landscape.' He characterizes the Group of Seven with these words: 'Every one of them, a Columbus or a Don Quixote of the palette, fought for the artistic discovery of the country, which extends from the

Atlantic to the Pacific Ocean, with picturesque harbours, fishing villages, great lakes and streams, endless prairie with steelblue jutting silos, glaciers of the Rocky Mountains and the mystic Arctic Northland.' In discussing Emily Carr's paintings, he lauds her perceptive portrayal of Indian villages with fantastic totempoles and of the deep silence of the forests of British Columbia – a portrayal of the very idea of growth. And in the modern interpretations of such artists as Alfred Pellan, B.C. Binding, and David Milne, Weiselberger recognizes the strong, interesting, striking elements that remind him of the recent European tradition – of Impressionism, of the Fauves, of Expressionism – proving to him that 'the world, including the lonely world of Canada, has become one' in the development of the arts.[24]

Weiselberger's cameo portraits of German and Austrian writers are of special significance within the context of his Canadian experience. The cameos, written in German, are short sketches, 'portraits,' written from memory, that is without the use of reference books. Weiselberger deliberately concentrated on essentials, 'recalling what [he] could remember, simply noting down what had not leaked out into oblivion from [his] deep well of memories,' as he explains in the Preface.[25] Using freely invented scenes and situations, he wrote word-portraits of such writers as Goethe, Schiller, Hölderlin, Kleist, Lenau, Heine, Raimund, Schnitzler, Nietzsche, and Kafka. There is, for example, Goethe, who, in the form of a spirit, inspects his birthplace, rebuilt after destruction in World War II. There is a portrait of Heinrich Heine sending Weiselberger a letter marked 'general delivery' from Purgatory, where he, with other mockers, awaits purification. There is a portrait of Nietzsche embracing a horse, saying 'O you, my Brother!' – an occasion which leads Weiselberger to speculate at length on the species of horse it might have been.

These cameo portraits can be considered as a significant document of Weiselberger's exile experience, but also of exile in general. In the Preface he states somewhat dramatically that the cameo portraits were written 'in the cold walls of a Canadian city, a distance of six thousand kilometres and thirty years separating him from their language.'[26] Their purpose, according to him, was 'to bring back the lost ones – those who had turned to thin shadows, blurred by the foreign atmosphere and the foreign language.' What he hoped to attain is expressed in his telling words 'And who knows, perhaps by calling their names, the portraitist himself will suddenly come to life again, to reality, and will regain the shadow, which he had lost to the Devil.'[27] The Devil is of course Adolf Hitler, the shadow a symbol for Weiselberger's losses – material, spiritual, and intellectual – which he experienced as a result of Hitler's rule. Within the context of the cameo portraits, the loss refers to the loss experienced as a writer, that is the loss of the German and the Austrian cultural tradition and reading public.

Exile inspired him to write the cameos. Central to any exile experience is the tension brought about in a writer as a result of being transplanted from the cultural tradition in which he grew up and which had become an integral part of him to a new and foreign one, so that he sees the new in terms of the old, or the now in terms of the then. Weiselberger's exile experience is shared by other exile writers, such as Heine, Mme de Staël, Heinrich and Thomas Mann, Bertolt Brecht, Stefan Zweig, and numerous others. Common to all is the attempt to clarify, redefine, win anew their own personal relationship to their cultural traditions. Werner Vordtriede, an exile writer himself, considers all great exile literature as 'Rettungsversuche für die abgebrochene Tradition' (attempts to find a way back to a broken tradition).[28] Weiselberger's cameo portraits, too, can be considered as such an attempt to clarify and redefine for himself and to win anew his cultural tradition which had been 'perverted and betrayed' (as Vordtriede says) during the time of the National Socialist regime. The Wagner quote at the beginning of this essay is a case in point.

Weiselberger's most remarkable creative achievements on his arduous road to using English as his medium of artistic expression are his short stories written in English. Returning to the short prose form which he had practised successfully during his time in Vienna, he once again wrote short stories with themes taken predominantly from music and art. Among them is a thematically unified series about an autobiographically conceived figure named Adrian Stonegate. Weiselberger's Stonegate is a well-to-do art collector and dealer. He owns an art gallery with a collection of modern art and a few old masters. Stonegate is a cultured man, well over sixty, curious, good-natured, a man with a great deal of imagination, intuition, wit, and humour, one who has travelled to the great cities of Europe – London, Paris, Munich, Madrid – a man always eager to hear and to tell a new story. He is a master impersonator of comical characters, a superb raconteur who likes to mix fact with fiction and produces sometimes exaggerated, sometimes imaginary, sometimes entirely spurious portraits or stories – as Weiselberger puts it: 'like a 17th Century heavily overpainted Baroque painting which may or may not be by Rubens or Van Dyck, or a brazen 19th Century forgery.'[29]

What makes Stonegate such an interesting character is his personal relationship to 'his' artists – great names as well as less known or sometimes entirely unknown ones. Stonegate's favourite pastime is talking about his life, his travels, his artists. Indeed, just as Weiselberger did in the Viennese stories, Stonegate seems to cultivate a predilection for odd, bizarre, sometimes absurd or frustrated artists, those who 'despite talent somehow missed the mark, the market' as Weiselberger puts it in the Preface to the Stonegate stories. To be sure, Stonegate is interested in their pictures, but more interested in the story behind the pictures, the life story of the painter. He has, after thirty years of being in business, come to think 'that the "human angle" ... was still more interesting than line, color, composition,' as shown in, for example, the following stories. In 'The Works of Mercy,' Stonegate leafs through a folder containing the most remarkable Italian drawings of a once promising artist from a small Manitoba prairie town. He had been so fascinated by the Renaissance frieze, by Italy, and finally by an Italian girl, that he stayed, even giving up painting altogether in favour of life itself. In 'The Quick-Change Artist,' Weiselberger explores the human story behind a much-talked-about surrealistic painting of the same title, showing the many faces of the man who seemed to have no face of his own. In 'The Equestrian Statue,' Stonegate is one of a jury that is to choose a statue commemorating the deeds of a local general from four dozen works ranging from traditional to a 'four-wire-on-a-base interpretation' of a cavalry man. Being unable to pick any of these, he is carried away by his imagination and visualizes the horses rebelling, laughing, neighing, and flying off. In another story, Stonegate tells how one of his finest graphic collections was the outcome of a joke: a poor, timid artist who always dreamed of a trip around the world collected tourist-information leaflets and postcards, shut himself in, and produced a series of most remarkable stylized etchings of the cities of the world and their famous attractions as proof of his travels.

Besides the artists, Stonegate is also interested in other collectors, especially the unusual ones, such as the one who bought spurious paintings but believed steadfastly in their authenticity. Other stories deal with gallery visitors: the widows of oil millionaires from Texas and Alberta, or the two middle-aged ladies who could always recognize objects in modern abstract paintings. One of the most outstanding creative achievements is the story 'Begone, Machine Devils!' – a marvellous portrait of the two elderly demoiselles Bergeron, living in a museum-like residence on a beautifully tranquil island in the Seine near

Notre Dame Cathedral, shunning radio, telephone, and all modern conveniences, surrounded by paintings the most modern of which are no later than Fouquet and Dürer, and considering Beethoven and Mozart standing 'with one foot in our disastrous modern times.'

With the Stonegate stories we have come full circle. The autobiographically conceived Stonegate reflects Weiselberger's own rich imagination, his gift as a raconteur, entertainer, and remarkable creative writer, whose Canadian experience has finally reached the stage that Stonegate describes with the words 'art is life.' Like Stonegate, Weiselberger as art critic has successfully created a world for himself, a world of the arts. This is indeed a remarkable achievement for a writer who for political and religious reasons had to leave his native country, who came to Canada as an exile, and who, like Joseph Conrad before him, wrote for a new audience in a language not native to him. His response to Canada was one of enthusiasm and gratitude. In his best writings, the short stories, Weiselberger has transformed personal experiences to imaginative literature to which can be applied the famous dictum 'le style est l'homme-même.' Behind Weiselberger's Canadian experience is his Austrian origin, which is manifest both in his stories written in Vienna and in his Canadian journalism and fiction. The late Carl Weiselberger deserves a place in Canada's literature as a writer of German and English short prose works, as an art critic and a cultural intermediary who experienced the New World in terms of the Old and whose Canadian experience was profoundly determined by his Austrian origins.

NOTES

1 In order to reduce the number of notes, all quotations from the *Ottawa Citizen*, the newspaper that was Weiselberger's main place of publication, are given in the text in abbreviated form as oc, with date of publication.

2 Cf. especially Margaret Atwood, *Survival: A Thematic Guide to Canadian Literature* (Toronto: Anansi, 1971); Robin Mathews, 'Margaret Atwood: Survivalism,' *Canadian Literature: Surrender or Revolution* (Toronto: Steel Rail Educational Publishing, 1978), 119–30. Cf. also Northrop Frye, Conclusion to *Literary History of Canada: Canadian Literature in English*, ed. Carl F. Klinck (Toronto: University of Toronto Press, 1965).

3 Carl Weiselberger, *Der Rabbi mit der Axt*, ed. Herta Hartmanshenn and Frederick Kriegel (Victoria: Morris Printing, 1973).

4 Weiselberger, *Eine Auswahl seiner Schriften*, ed. Peter Liddell and Walter Riedel (Toronto: German-Canadian Historical Association, 1981).

5 Liddell and Riedel, Introduction to Weiselberger, *Auswahl*, p. 3.
6 Weiselberger, 'Gottlieb Dominik Hampls Glück und Ende,' *Der getreue Eckart*, 13:2 (Nov. 1935), 131–2.
7 Weiselberger, 'Wolken im Frühling,' (typescript in Weiselberger Collection, University of Victoria, Victoria, BC.
8 Weiselberger, *Der Rabbi*, pp. 188–93.
9 Ibid., pp. 175–9.
10 Ibid., pp. 126–30.
11 Three recent studies dealing with the internment of 'enemy aliens' in Britain, Canada, and Australia are' Peter and Leni Gillmann, *Collar the Lot! How Britain Interned and Expelled Its Wartime Refugees* (London: Quartet Books, 1980); Ronald Stent, *A Bespattered Page: The Internment of 'His Majesty's Most Loyal Enemy Aliens'* (London: André Deutsch, 1980); Eric Koch, *Deemed Suspect: A Wartime Blunder*. (London, New York, Sydney: Methuen, 1980).
12 Figures based on Koch, pp. xiv, 262.
13 'Carl Weiselberger – Author, Critic and Writer in Exile,' in Weiselberger, *Auswahl*, p. 5.
14 Weiselberger, *Auswahl*, pp. 45–62.
15 Weiselberger, *Der Rabbi*, pp. 79–86.
16 Weiselberger, *Auswahl*, p. 81 (my translation).
17 Stent, p. 134.
18 Cf. Weiselberger, 'Das Gebet,' *Der Rabbi*, pp. 13–34.
19 Weiselberger, *Auswahl*, pp. 63–73.
20 Cf. Stefan Zweig, *Die Welt von gestern* (Berlin and Frankfurt a.M.: Fischer, 1944), p. 374.
21 Citation of Ottawa Press Club Award; cf. *Ottawa Citizen*, 7 and 8 Feb. 1949.
22 All quotations abbreviated by N.ö. are from the Austrian newspaper *Neues Österreich* (my translation).
23 Weiselberger, 'Ein junges Land sucht seine eigene Kunst,' *Die Schau: Sonderheft Kanada* (Wien, May 1954), pp. 244–9.
24 Ibid., p. 248 (my translation).
25 Weiselberger, 'Vorwort. Drei Dichterkameen,' in Weiselberger, *Auswahl*, p. 187f.
26 Ibid., p. 187.
27 Significantly, this sentence reflecting the purpose of Weiselberger's cameo portraits appears in an early version of the manuscript of the Preface.
28 Werner Vordtriede, 'Vorläufige Gedanken zu einer Typologie der Exilliteratur,' *Akzente*, 15:6 (1968), 557.
29 All quotations referring to the Stonegate stories are from typescripts contained in the Weiselberger Collection of the University of Victoria, Victoria, BC. Some of these appeared, in part or in their entirety, as newspaper publications in the *Ottawa Citizen*; e.g. OC, 25 March 1954.

Charles Wassermann ᛞᛞ Life and *Oeuvre* in the Service of Mutual Understanding ᛞ

HELFRIED SELIGER

Among German-Canadian writers Charles Wassermann is in a class by himself. As the author of more than ten books in German – many of them on Canadian themes – and of more than two hundred radio and television plays, mostly in English, he clearly was a child of two cultures. Even three cultures, for he tried not only to bring Canada closer to his German-speaking readers but also to bridge the gap between Canada's own 'two solitudes,' between the French and the English. In his function as a professional radio and television correspondent for both the CBC and several European networks he went far beyond the task of mere reporting. To act as an intermediary between cultures was to become his life's task. To be as effective as possible in this undertaking, to reach as wide an audience as possible, Wassermann worked in various media.

Charles Ulric Wassermann (1924–78) was born into a family of writers. His father, Jakob Wassermann (1873–1934), was one of the foremost German novelists of his time and was recognized far beyond the shores of Europe. His home in Altaussee in the Austrian Alps was a meeting place for many of his famous friends, among them the writers Arthur Schnitzler, Hugo von Hofmannsthal, and Thomas Mann. It was in this atmosphere of culture that young Charles grew up. His mother, Marta Karlweis (1888–1965), was a psychoanalyst and a writer in her own right. The Austrian *Anschluss* forced the fourteen-year-old to leave for the Isle of Wight where he attended Bembridge Public School until his deportation to Canada in 1941 and his eventual internment. His mother, who had come to Canada the year before to lecture in Montreal, intervened on her son's behalf with Prime Minister Mackenzie King and got Charles released. After that he attended Lower Canada College in Montreal and entered McGill University from which he graduated with a BA in literature and history in 1945. He obviously had a gift for languages and quickly adjusted to his new environment, for as early as 1941 he had already won a public speaking contest at the college and during his years at McGill he became the editor-in-chief of the student newspaper.

Through a job with the Wartime Information Board he got into radio and later joined the CBC, first as a reporter, then as a writer-producer. In 1952 he married the French-Canadian actress and singer Jacqueline Desjardins. The following year he became the CBC's correspondent on Eastern European affairs and from then on he maintained two residences, one in Montreal, the other in Altaussee, Austria, where he had spent his childhood. In 1956, when he covered the Poznan riots in Poland and the Hungarian Revolution as a cameraman-reporter, he branched out into television. His experiences in Hungary led to his being asked to write a book in German for the Bertelsmann publishers. A resounding success, it led to the publication of eleven others, including two detective novels, two works of light fiction, and three books on Canada.

As a result of a serious case of food poisoning, Wassermann began to lose his eyesight in 1961 and two years later had gone completely blind. But this did not slow his hectic pace. It is a testimony to his tremendous courage, strong will, and boundless energy that he not only continued his work as a correspondent for the CBC but that he started to branch out. In the same year he joined the German-language service of the Swiss Broadcasting Corporation as a correspondent. After 1967 his documentary films for television were produced by his own film unit, Charles Wassermann Telefilm. He produced more than fifty films on Central, Eastern, and Southern European topics with special reference to political developments. As if this were not enough, he wrote, or rather dictated, four more books before his untimely death in 1978.

The sheer mass and variety of Wassermann's creative work in three different media – print, radio, and television – is, to say the least, impressive. Yet it would be wrong to limit the discussion of his unique 'literary perspective' to those of his works that appeared in print only and to disregard his radio and television plays, which amount to about half of his literary production. For the purpose of this study the plays written for radio and television will be considered as part of his published works as long as they have actually been broadcast.

Even a cursory glance at this part of his production reveals close interrelationships among his works in the various media. Sometimes, material he had used in a radio play would crop up as a scene in one of his books; at other times, a narrative passage would be dramatized and result in a radio play which in turn could be reworked into a play for television. As an expert in the techniques required by each medium, he knew how to emphasize particular aspects of a story in order to meet the specific requirements of the genre in question. His professional experience as a correspondent and commentator stood him in good stead in writing his first plays. He knew how to shape facts into a strong story, how to arouse his audience's interest and hold their attention.

By 1948 he had already received official recognition for his work in radio and film by winning two international prizes. Throughout his career he was to receive many more awards for his distinguished contributions as an author, playwright, and producer of television films.

During his early years in Montreal he had begun to study the social and political history of his new country and discovered his love for Canadian folklore in general and French-Canadian legends in particular, perhaps because they reminded him of the folklore of his native Austrian Alps. Soon he knew Canada, the land and its people and their rich cultural traditions, better than most Canadians. Long before the feelings of nationalism began to stir and before it had become fashionable to search for one's roots, the young refugee from Europe was fascinated by the wealth of local traditions that were waiting to be unearthed.

His first radio plays bear eloquent testimony to his unique sensibility to the essential aspects of the land and its people. Even at this early stage of his career the dual purpose which informs most of his life's work is clearly discernible: to tell Canadians about their own great country and themselves, and to publicize Canada and her achievements to the rest of the world.

In the beginning he based his plays on significant moments in Canadian history, described local legends and geographical oddities. The titles of the series for which he wrote them speak for themselves: 'Discovering Canada,' 'The Canadian Chronicle,' 'Now It's History,' and 'The Canadian Primer' (1949–51). The latter was Wassermann's very own series of thirty half-hour programmes of basic information on Canada, presented in the form of a whimsical radio 'class-room' with 'students' in communities across Canada. These 'students' were really radio commentators who presented basic facts about Canada in primer form, addressing their 'homework' to a 'teacher.' There was a programme for each letter of the alphabet (for example, 'F for Fishing'), three review programmes, and a 'final examination.' Broadcast by the CBC's International Service, the series won an international competition sponsored by the Institute for Education by Radio. The official citation praised the series for its 'courage to approach international problems with sprightliness and humor, for bringing to bear the best of radio techniques in this area and refusing to allow its mood to be weighted down by the challenge of international relations.'[1]

For the CBC's series 'Canadian Yarns' and 'Canadian Legends' Wassermann wrote a total of twenty-seven scripts, but it has not been possible to confirm whether all of these dramatized folk legends were actually broadcast. In the course of his research for these plays[2] he became a good friend of Dr Marius Barbeau, the renowned expert on the folklore and traditions of Canada and especially of Quebec. Later, Wassermann's intimate knowledge of folktales and legends was to prove valuable in his German books on Canada. The more immediate result, however, was his own series of radio plays entitled 'Fiddle Joe's Yarns' (1951–4). Unique in their attempt to acquaint English-speaking Canadians with the lore and customs of their French-speaking fellow citizens, they quickly developed a tremendous following. Although planned as a summer fill-in, the highly entertaining and instructive series proved so popular that Wassermann was asked to continue it. The series ran for four seasons and finally contained a total of 164 shows.

The weekly half-hour plays dramatizing the folklore of backwoods Quebec were set in the imaginary village of St Christophe in the Laurentians around the year 1905. The central character and narrator was clearly inspired by the boisterous lumberjack Jos Violin of the legend 'La Chasse Galerie'[3] which was used to open the series. Fiddle Joe – his full name is Joseph Orphe Atanase Busque – a lumberjack and the unofficial historian of the village, plays the violin at village dances and spends much time gossiping with the locals. Being the hub of village life, he sees and hears all things and forgets nothing. As a cheerful, gregarious, and entertaining original, Fiddle Joe is liked by his peers and enjoys their respect. Wassermann skilfully uses him and his many encounters with the village folk to create the fictional world of St Christophe with a whole array of reappearing characters and a wealth of intimate detail.

There is Hormidas Grenier, the village mayor for thirty-three years, owner of the general store, keeper of the town tavern, and postmaster, all in one person. A pompous individual, a wheeler and dealer *par excellence*, he tries to be reelected at any cost. We also meet Casimir Cousineau, the clownish and lively fellow who likes his whisky blanc and who is dominated by his no-nonsense wife Thérèse and bullied by his sons Théophile and Thélésphore. Then there are the lumberjacks Baptiste Levesque and Auguste ('Tigusse') Beaudoin and their boss Jack Boyd, the owner of the local sawmill. There is the miserly butcher Philéas Lachapelle, an unhappy creature, there are Monsieur le Curé and the morally corrupt 'La Belle Annette,' whose popularity among the local men is undisputed because she runs an illegal pub just outside the village limits where liquor can be had at all times of the night.

Wassermann used to spend his summers in a small Laurentian village and it provided him with some of the characters, the flavour, and the idiom. He kept a card index of all his major and minor characters with important details concerning them. Everything was done to make them and their surroundings seem real. For example, the village 'is situated where the Ste. Lucie River bends sharply to the south' in the county of Minnigouche, half an hour from the next settlement, Ste Marie de Hungerford. Fiddle Joe lives on the Rue Principale, not far from Grenier's store and tavern. No effort was spared to create the imaginary world of St Christophe with such a wealth of detail that it seemed real to the listeners.

The series acquainted the English audience with such legends as 'Rose Latulippe,' 'Grand Monarque,' 'Loup-Garou,' 'L'Arbre des Rêves,' 'St. Catherine's Gap,' and 'The Black Horse,'[4] but eventually Wassermann ran out of legends and the series continued as a satire on life in rural Quebec. The topics ranged widely, from the newly formed Chamber of Commerce which attempted to put St Christophe 'on the map' by attracting new industries to the activities of the local Dramatic Society, the problems connected with the introduction of the first automobile, and the local and provincial elections with their sometimes shady campaign methods. Much research had gone into the programme on the provincial elections of 1906 and Wassermann got his audience to participate by inviting them to mail in their ballots.

As Fiddle Joe tells of the lives of these people, he describes their beliefs and fears, their superstitions and habits together with all the things which shape their lives and ultimately make up their folklore and culture. The programmes opened and closed with a lively theme song which was to become famous in its day. It immediately set the tone and atmosphere:

CHORUS

Hey you! Don't you go!
The whole thing if you want to know,
Come and listen to Fiddle Joe!
(Pass the spittoon and please bow low!)
Sac-a-tabi, Sac-a-tabac,
All those who're deaf will please draw back.

SOLO

He'll tell you all you ought to know,
Some stories true and some not so,
The Story Teller, Fiddle Joe!

With the techniques of flashbacks and fade-ins and the presentation of the folksongs of French Canada (usually two or three per programme), the plays were full of variety, lively, and interesting.

The songs, some adaptations of old French songs, others modelled after the songs of the Indians, were sung by the actors who played the dramatic roles since this was found to be the most effective way to make the programme sound realistic and genuine. The cast, themselves mostly French Canadians, became critically involved in the production of the show, anxious to ensure that it present the French-Canadian way of life accurately to other Canadians. Some of the actors were J.R. Tremblay, Clement Latour, Henri Poitras, Jean Pierre Masson, Georges Toupin, Norman Taviss, Richard Kronold, Barry Morse, Yvette Brind'Amour, and Jacqueline Desjardins.

Apart from the plots and situations, much of the entertainment value was based on linguistic humour. Wassermann had an excellent ear for the idiosyncracies of the English idiom spoken in rural Quebec with its strong syntactical and grammatical resemblance to French. Difficult words are either used wrongly or confused with similar sounding ones. Thus 'intimidation' could become 'imitation' and 'intimated' could stand for 'intimidated,' a question of 'political importance' could ominously become one of 'political impotence.' Figurative and idiomatic expressions are often taken literally and French expressions seep in every now and then. Wassermann was careful not to ridicule this way of speaking. Enthusiastic letters to the CBC from French Canada attest to the fact that he succeeded in a faithful recreation of the linguistic atmosphere of Quebec. [5] Jack Boyd, the Irish-Canadian boss of the camp, served to motivate the French accent of the other characters, because they had to speak English to him and he was also the character with whom the English-speaking audience could identify while learning about French Canada. In the later shows Wassermann concentrated on the social and psychological problems which these French Canadians encountered in their contact with the English element.

The series was in excellent hands with Ken Withers as producer and Arthur Morrow as musical director. The reactions from the public and the press were excellent[6] and there were even negotiations underway to translate the series back into French as 'Pit Violin' and broadcast it as 'a double-edged drive to perpetuate folklore and music second to none in Canada' and as 'a means of bringing greater understanding to English and French Canadians.'[7] This plan did not materialize, nor did 'Fiddle Joe' make a successful transition to television. Only one pilot programme was produced in an attempt to see if 'Fiddle Joe' would 'prove as popular as the Plouffe Family.'[8]

For years, the programme was broadcast on the Trans-Canada Network on Sundays at 5:00 p.m., back to back with W.O. Mitchell's 'Jake and the Kid.' The many feature articles, complete with illustrations, which appeared in the CBC Times during the years of its broadcast are a certain measure of the series' success in meeting its double purpose of entertaining and instructing.[9]

Another spin-off of 'Fiddle Joe' was the Arthur Morrow Choir, which had been developed specifically for the presentation of the songs of the series. It became the centre of a new programme entitled 'Songs of Canada' for which Wassermann wrote the dialogues.[10] He had now become an expert in this field as well, having selected and often translated the French songs of the 'Fiddle Joe' series.

Space constraints preclude anything more than a superficial discussion of his dramatic work for radio and television and the following offers by no means a complete inventory of his work in this area. Basically, his plays fall into three groups: those which are pure creations of his poetic imagination, those firmly based on true events or personal experiences, and finally dramatizations of his own works or the works of others.

To the first group belongs a gem of a pedagogic play, 'Livin' Doll or Jamie's Trip to Nonconformia' (1954), a criticism of conformity in modern society which at the same time ridicules the excesses of psychiatry that regard 'being out of step' as a kind of sickness. 'No Candy for Bertha' (1954) is a tribute to shopkeeping and gossip, implicitly condemning the impersonal atmosphere of the supermarket. 'In Search of Loyalties' (1949) focuses on an individual of Scottish ancestry whose family had long before become totally absorbed into French-Canadian society. After generations of total integration, the emerging nationalism forces the hero to examine where his loyalties are, with French Canada, English Canada, or just Canada. 'The Harbour Beat' (1953) is a series of detective plays set in Montreal with Benoit ('Benny') Savoy, a private investigator with a shipping company, as its central character. Basically a first-person-singular narrative and flashback story, it reveals Wassermann's talent for creating suspense and reflects his intimate knowledge of Montreal's harbourfront where he had first started out as a reporter. In 'The Wanderings of Pierre' (1954) he deals with the disastrous effects of antiquated laws of inheritance and the problems of the migration to the cities. Pierre, who has worked on the family farm for eighteen years, is disinherited on his father's death because the father did not want to see the land broken up between his sons. In desperation, Pierre leaves his home for the first time to pursue the almighty dollar in the city and becomes thoroughly disillusioned.

The theme of social criticism gives way to political comment in the second group of plays. Written for CBC's prestigious 'Vancouver Theatre,' the three-part series 'Assignment Europe' (1955) was about a Canadian newspaper reporter, Mark Daily, and reflected the problems of post-war Europe. One episode, entitled 'Frustration,' was set in the province of South Tyrol which had been cut off from Austria by the Treaty of Versailles. It examined the situation of the tough mountain people, their aspirations and frustrations. The fact that they had become a linguistic minority within another land had turned some of the men into heroes for a lost cause. The episode 'Persecution' described an English couple's particular problem caused by the war. The wife, whose first husband had died a war hero, would never let her second husband forget that fact.

Based on recollections from Wassermann's early childhood, 'The Inner Landscape' (1952) gives an account of the times of the rise of Nazism when a few men like his father defied the Nazis and had to pay for their defiance. The moving and intensely dramatic story shows what can happen to people in a country that is slowly drifting into dictatorship.

The border between this group of plays and the next is somewhat vague. But one should, by all rights, include here the dramatizations of eyewitness accounts originally related in Wassermann's own books of non-fiction. 'With Courage to Be Free' (1957, for TV) is a first-person account of the fate of a determined freedom fighter in the final days of the

Hungarian Revolution. He leaves the safety of his basement hideout and confronts the Russian tanks in order to divert them while his friends make their escape.[11] 'The Imposter' (1964) was a hilarious play based on a true story which happened not far from Altaussee. It dealt with the exploits of a modern 'Captain of Köpenick' who duped the Nazis into believing he was an important *protégé* of Hitler's and then continued the life of an imposter in a different but just as successful way after the war. He enjoyed a life of pleasure by making false promises of marriage to a series of women. This famous double fraud had also inspired the imagination of other writers.[12]

The television play 'Miroslav's Four Seasons' (1970) relates the story of the heroic suicide by a Czech student who chose to die rather than turn government informer after the end of the Prague Spring.[13] Wassermann also produced a German version of the play which was broadcast by both the CBC and the Zweites deutsches Fernsehen. All in all, he did about ten television plays in German, most of which were actually broadcast.[14] Unfortunately, it has been impossible to locate the scripts.

The last group of adaptations is sizeable and significant. Wassermann translated and adapted two of Ugo Betti's stage plays, *Delitto all'Isola delle capre* and *Irene innocente*, as 'Goat's Island' and 'Time of Vengeance.'[15] The latter was performed at the York Playhouse off Broadway and ran for two and a half months in the winter of 1959–60.[16] He also spent considerable time and energy adapting the works of his father for radio and television. The most important achievement in this regard was 'The World's Illusion,' a dramatization of his father's most widely read novel, *Christian Wahnschaffe* (1919). Directed by Rupert Caplan and with the young Lorne Greene in one of the leading roles, the two-hour radio play was broadcast by the CBC in September of 1951.[17] Among Wassermann's unpublished papers in the National Library in Ottawa, there are several adaptations in various stages of completion of works by his father, notably of the famous novel *Der Fall Maurizius*.

Speaking about Charles Wassermann's 'Nachlass,' one should definitely mention his excellent Schiller adaptation 'Mary Stuart' (1953). Done in the elevated style and archaic idiom of Elizabethan drama and in blank verse throughout, the form harmonizes with its content and milieu. The skilful use of a narrator helps in abridging the play and making smooth transitions between the episodes. Unfortunately, it was never broadcast, although it had been written for CBC's 'Wednesday Night' series. It can only be assumed that it was rejected because of the criticism generally levelled against Schiller's play, namely that it is a travesty of history.

Of his own works, Wassermann turned both his detective novels *Geheimstollen 'K'* and *Lawine halb fünf* as well as the novel *Der Journalist* into plays for German television.

A retrospective look at the works he adapted from other sources reveals a common theme, the impossibility of achieving true justice in human society. The fault lies neither with the individual alone nor exclusively with society at large but rather with both. Good and evil, love and hate are inextricably interwoven and the actions described do not easily follow a cause-and-effect relationship. There is a deeper, mysterious force at work which makes for the discrepancy between the way people live and the way they ought to live, between what they are and what they seem. Also typical of Wassermann's own works, this search for justice, though mostly futile, definitely has religious implications. From it spring his concern for the individual and his endeavour to make society more tolerant as well as his plea for compassion in the midst of a world of brutality.

This concern for freedom and justice and the fight against brutality were the motive forces behind his first two books, *Tagebuch der Freiheit*[18] and *Unter polnischer Verwaltung*.[19] Written in diary form and richly illustrated with his own photographs, they give a touching eyewitness account of two trips in 1956 and 1957 which confronted the author with two major tragedies of post-war Europe. The merit of the two books is determined by their value as documents of history which have preserved the drama of the moment and convey to the reader that important sense of immediacy. The first deals with the unrest in Poland and Hungary that finally led to the revolution in 1956. Wassermann, who travelled as a Canadian journalist, quickly established close contacts with some of the freedom fighters and gained excellent insights into the events of late 1956, barely escaping with his own life when Russian tanks closed off Budapest from the rest of the world. He concentrated on showing how the lives of simple people were affected. Sharing with them the moments of ecstasy at the achievement of freedom, the moments of determined resistance and finally of utter dejection, he was no prey to rabid anti-communism. The larger questions of politics were left looming in the background, for the desperate and heroic fight of poorly armed individuals against a well-equipped army demanded his undivided attention. He hoped to support their fight for freedom by documenting it.

The second book is the result of an extended trip the author took together with his wife in the summer of 1957. The travel diary is unique in its kind and a historic document, for the Wassermanns were the first

Westerners to get permission to travel freely by car through the former eastern provinces of Germany which were now occupied by Poland. It must be remembered that millions of Germans had been expelled from these territories after the war and that the Poles, who themselves had lost their eastern provinces to Russia, tried to resettle their own refugees in those areas. The ensuing chaos and destruction, the human misery on all sides, constituted a serious threat to peace in Europe.

Himself a former refugee from Nazism, Wassermann was aware of the horrors committed in its name, yet he tried to be as objective as possible in the face of what he witnessed there. He came well prepared, had studied the history of the region and brought old city maps and Baedekers along, trying to see what remained of the lands which were settled by Germans centuries ago and had become the frontier lands of Western civilization and culture. Where once there had been thriving cities, prosperous industries, and fertile fields, there were now – twelve years after the war – piles of rubble, fields of ruins, and neglected stretches of land that were slowly turning into steppe. At the sight of so much neglect, lack of ambition, and carelessness, Wassermann was clearly appalled. He expressed his bias in favour of German, and in a wider sense Western European, culture; yet he did not want to be unfair. He realized that frequently the people who were made to pay the price for Germany's actions had been least responsible for them. On the other hand, the new occupants had been expelled from their own homeland and could not be expected to develop an instant attachment to the new environment.

The book was a success in Germany because it presented the first detailed assessment of the contemporary condition of the territories. It found an avid readership among the many refugees from Silesia, East Pomerania, and East Prussia who now made their home in West Germany. In the spring of 1958 Wassermann accepted an invitation by various organizations of refugees from the east to go on a lecture tour. He literally criss-crossed West Germany giving slide talks to people who were eager for news about their former homelands. The following year he produced an English version of his account, entitled *Europe's Forgotten Territories.*[20]

Later he had mixed feelings about the fact that his honest and objective documentary had often been used as a political weapon by these refugee organizations and he admitted that his attitude towards the whole problem of the eastern territories had considerably changed. This was not to say that his reporting had been wrong or dishonest but that in retrospect he would have gone about it differently.[21] His intentions were good and it was his concern for his fellow men which had moved him to share his experiences. This was brought out by the hope expressed in the concluding paragraph of his book: 'Whatever may be the future of these territories, – it is at least to be hoped that continuing peace and growing human insight will help to end the sadness, the gloom and the hopelessness. May the people who live there, be they German or Poles, be granted an existence worthy of the civilized christian world.'[22]

At about the same time, Wassermann did his only translation of an English novel into German, namely Ross Lockridge's *Raintree County*.[23] Though he had found it a thankless task and vowed never to do anything like it again, the translation was successful and went through several printings.

After the impact of his depiction, he was asked to do something similar on Canada for the Bertelsmann Lesering, the German equivalent of the Book-of-the-Month Club. The result was a richly illustrated combination travelogue and history of Canada under the title *Das Land der Zukunft*, 'Land of the future.'[24] Crossing the country from coast to coast with the occasional side trip to the North, he covered all regions with the exception of the Northwest Territories and Prince Edward Island. After several years of working in Europe, he had developed an acute sense for what the European reader would expect from such a work.

As a masterful composer, he succeeded in telling the story of Canada in a compelling way, using descriptions of the contemporary scene as an opportunity to make excursions into Canada's past, interlacing much useful factual information on the country, its government, and its people in general with interviews with Canadians of all walks of life. The inclusion of several local legends that hail from the days of the Indians, the Eskimos, and the early settlers is an attractive addition.[25] They help to round out a work that contains a host of information on all aspects of Canadian life and culture, right down to statistical material on the standard of living. Published together with an Italian version[26] at the height of post-war immigration from Europe, it conveyed the author's pride in and love for his country to countless prospective immigrants for whom this work became the first truly meaningful encounter with their new homeland.

Spurred on by the success of his endeavour to tell Europeans more about Canada, Wassermann embarked on a new project and wrote a history of the Canadian Pacific Railway. *CPR: Das Weltreich des Bibers*[27] was written for the general public and avoids the pitfalls of a history written in the dry style of academics. As a versatile narrator who has mastered the art of arousing the reader's interest, Wassermann embeds the historical chapters in a brief frame by having a well-informed modern traveller aboard The Canadian muse about the era of bygone days. By employing a technique common in the radio play and thus writing a kind of flashback story, Wassermann brings the past alive by imitating the workings of human recollection. We do not remember tables of statistical data but we do recall significant individual moments and scenes which have impressed themselves upon our memory. We recall the conversations and discussions of the people involved, their personalities and special characteristics, perhaps even seemingly unnecessary details which, in retrospect, determine the general atmosphere. In other words, important historic events are dramatized and brought to life without changing the basic historical facts: Wassermann knows that dramatizing history can be an effective mnemonic device. In the end, the sketchy frame allows him also a smooth transition to the description of today's CPR as a globe-spanning, multifaceted enterprise.

It is unfortunate that there is no equivalent treatment of the subject available in English. Wassermann's is by far the most readable account and has the advantage that the related facts can be readily absorbed. In this regard it compares quite favourably with the popular history by Pierre Berton.[28] It is a sad reflection indeed that none of the authors who dealt with the subject subsequently[29] took cognizance of a competent study which contained much information not found anywhere else.[30]

The year before, in 1961, Wassermann had published two short detective novels under the pseudonym Charles Ulrik. Both are set in the Alps and centre upon the detective Joseph Emile Colbert from Montreal, a perfectly bilingual Canadian, whose formerly fluent German (war years!) had become somewhat rusty. Wassermann admitted that he was still somewhat insecure in German when he wrote these stories.[31] He made the best of it by providing his protagonist with a background which accounts for these linguistic deficiencies and at the same time imparts to the story what until the mid-seventies was a *sine qua non* for the detective story in Germany: the English or American atmosphere. His choice of pseudonym was definitely part of this consideration.

In *Lawine halb fünf*[32] Colbert proves his marvellously analytical mind by solving the murder of Sir Robert King, a wealthy fitness freak and expert mountaineer, who is apparently killed by an avalanche. The atmosphere of Alpine mountaineering is impressively recreated but the suspenseful novel is marred by its somewhat contrived end.

From the point of view of literary craftsmanship and the creation of suspense, *Geheimstollen 'K'*[33] is the better of the two novels. It embroils the East and the West in a dramatic search for an important formula left by an atomic physicist who had refused to reveal it to the Nazis. He died with his secret but not without leaving some clues as to its whereabouts. Before Colbert can solve the mystery, he gets involved in a frantic and murderous race for the formula hidden inside a painting that had been taken for storage into a secret tunnel of an abandoned salt mine.

His many years of experience as a foreign correspondent and commentator at some of the cold war's trouble spots made Wassermann thoroughly familiar with the ins and outs of his trade. And it is this hectic world of international journalism that provided the background and determined the action of his first full-fledged novel. Written towards the end of 1962, *The Journalist*[34] is set in the capital of the imaginary state of Morania, which is caught between the two power blocks and is in the throes of revolution. Civil war seems inevitable, leftists and fascists fight open battles, Soviet Russia is ready to intervene, while France attempts to avert the impending catastrophe. Against this chaotic atmosphere of hectic conferences, assassinations, conspiracies, and deceptions, the luckless Swiss journalist Ulrich Hilti is embarking on a frantic and unscrupulous hunt for the big news story that would make the world's headlines and restore his crumbling professional reputation. When he does happen upon this coveted news story in the house of his lover – her father is engaged in top-secret negotiations with France which might save the country from the abyss – he puts his personal journalistic interests above all other considerations. He triggers more than just sensational headlines, he causes a political catastrophe. For France is forced to deny that negotiations took place and the country quickly slides into a Communist dictatorship, ironically robbing Hilti of his great story about Morania's imminent salvation.

Although definitely a work of light fiction, the book addresses a serious problem: in the free world where there are no restrictive press laws each journalist has to be his own judge regarding the consequences of his actions. Carried to the extreme, the freedom of the press can often endanger human liberties. Man has a certain freedom of action but this in turn imposes duties and responsibilities, for laws cannot enforce what each individual has to do on his own.

For his next publications Wassermann returned to the technique he had so successfully used in his book on the CPR. After considerable research in archives, he produced two more fictionalized histories. *Kämpfer ohne*

Waffen (1965)[35] examines the role of the International Red Cross in twelve wars, from the Abyssinian Campaign in 1935, the Spanish Civil War, and World War II right down to the bloody conflicts in the Congo, Algeria, Laos, and Cuba. After a brief history of the organization itself there follows a series of short, gripping narratives recreating the authentic experiences of Red Cross delegates, their sacrifices, their heroic achievements, and their bitter frustrations. Though adhering to strict rules of neutrality often limited the effectiveness of its undertakings, the organization's record in the face of seemingly insurmountable odds is impressive. Touching and heart-rending as some of the stories are, they avoid pathos. It is not Wassermann's aim to elicit an emotional response from the reader but rather to show that in a world of injustice and brutality suffering can only be alleviated by individuals who believe in the ideal of human brotherhood and who are prepared to pursue this ideal to the point of self-sacrifice.

Himself a diabetic since the age of twenty-four, Wassermann was a grateful admirer of two important Canadians who had been inspired by this very ideal of serving mankind. *Insulin* (1966)[36] traces the fascinating history of one of modern medicine's greatest breakthroughs, the discovery of an effective specific for diabetes by Frederick Banting and Charles Best of the University of Toronto.

The result of solid research and several personal interviews with Dr Best in Toronto, this account makes for exciting reading by layman and expert alike. Wassermann draws a detailed picture of this drama of medical research, of the people it involved, their personalities, their individual sacrifices and contributions. Recreating history in a fictionalized account involved no idealization of past events. On the contrary, Wassermann does not gloss over the bitter academic infighting that almost saw the chairman of the department, J.J.R. Macleod, take credit for the achievements of the two young scientists. To a large measure he did succeed in robbing them of the recognition they deserved, for when the Nobel Prize was awarded for the discovery of insulin, it was not Best who shared the prize with Banting but Macleod, the person who had originally opposed the project and who at no time had ever been personally involved in the research. The discovery was only the beginning of a long story of further research that eventually led to the mass production of insulin, a story in which Canada played and continues to play a major role. Wassermann carried this history right up to the mid-sixties, informing his readers of the latest advances in the treatment of diabetes.

With the story of insulin he could finally combine two of the concerns which had always been close to his heart. It afforded him the opportunity to publicize a truly Canadian achievement and to return to the theme that evil, injustice, and suffering can only be fought by compassionate individuals.

Wassermann produced another work of light fiction with *Die Nacht der hellen Stunden* (1974),[37] setting it like his first in the world of journalism. Advertised on the jacket as a novel of 'love, eroticism, jealousy, and human insights,' it tells of Stanley Cattin, forty-two, who works in an East European capital as a correspondent for an American radio and television network. The novel is set against a background of political turmoil highly reminiscent of the events of the Prague Spring of 1968, and although it is nowhere specifically stated, it is highly autobiographical in nature. For Cattin has to overcome a terrible handicap: he has lost his eyesight. Since he is determined to hold on to his job, he has to develop new techniques of carrying on an interview, of taking notes with a tape recorder, of sometimes even working with two tape recorders at the same time, listening through an earphone to his notes from one machine while recording his reports onto a second. Making all these adjustments, he is careful to keep the secret of his handicap from his superiors in New York for fear of losing his job. As long as he can remain ahead of the competition he has nothing to fear.

Working under such pressures, he tries to live a normal life with his wife, Joan, forty-seven. On the one hand he depends on her increased protectiveness, on the other he resents it because it makes him aware of his handicap. The new assistant Christina, twenty-six, cheerful and attractive, but also a ruthless manipulator, quickly wins Cattin's love by granting him the pleasure of a sexual conquest and thus restoring his self-confidence as a man. However, Christina is not capable of a lasting relationship and gets involved with a student behind Cattin's back. Tormented by jealousy, he has to concentrate on his work since the hardliners within the government are gaining the upper hand. Already a clampdown has caused a return to political oppression. Perturbed and frightened, Christina flees the country on learning of the politically motivated suicide of her most recent lover. The Cattins witness the total collapse of the liberal regime, are expelled, and go to Vienna where they hope to rebuild their relationship.

Far superior to *Der Journalist* in literary craftsmanship, the novel leaves no doubt about Wassermann's talent as a writer. Rising above the standard of the category of light fiction, it is more than an interesting plot attractively packaged for easy consumption. It offers the political insights of someone who has lived in Eastern Europe for many years and it gives the reader a rare glimpse of the psychological problems a blind person must learn to cope with before he can hope to remain a useful and productive member of society. Quite fittingly, the novel starts with Wassermann's own translation of Milton's sonnet 'On His Blindness.'

By the mid-seventies the information contained in his first book on Canada, *Das Land der Zukunft* (1957), urgently needed updating. Rather than revise the combination travel diary and history, Wassermann decided to write an entirely new book. The result was *Kanada. Land der Zukunft* (1976),[38] which was to become a standard work on Canada in German.

He divides it into six parts and paints a comprehensive picture of the country and its various geographic regions, its history and its people, their culture, their institutions, and their system of government. Wassermann could draw on his intimate knowledge gained through years of studying the Canadian scene and countless trips to all parts of the land and he succeeded in creating a truly exemplary portrait of Canada. In his frank yet objective manner, he addresses himself also to some of the traditional and more recent problems that beset the country: the economic recession; the difficulty of holding a nation together whose various regions often have stronger economic and cultural ties with the neighbour to the south than with the rest of the country; the growth of separatism in Quebec and the West; the question of the settlement of native land claims; the sometimes exaggerated new nationalism that threatens to strain the traditionally friendly relations with the United States; and so on.

Though Wassermann generally refrains from expressing his personal opinions, he cannot hide the fact that the treatment of Canada's native peoples gives him cause for concern. Despite Canada's official policy of multiculturalism that supports the preservation of ethnic heritage, the traditional way of life of Indians and Eskimos is slowly being destroyed by the relentless push for the development of the North. Yet as the title of the book indicates, in spite of all these problems Wassermann had not lost his love for the country or his faith in its future.

In his last years Wassermann felt the need for a revised edition of his book on insulin. By its very nature it had contained much useful information for diabetics which now had to be brought up to date. In the hope that he himself might indirectly contribute to the fight against diabetes, he had all the while kept abreast of the latest advances in the treatment of the disease. What had started out as a purely Canadian story had turned into an international saga in which Canada continued to play a significant part. The thoroughly rewritten and greatly enlarged version[39] carried the story right up to the death of Dr Best in 1978. Just one month later, on 1 May 1978, Charles Wassermann's own life was to end.

It is ironic, perhaps even typical, that an author of such narrative and dramatic talent is virtually unknown in his own country. Granted, the scripts of radio and television plays do not make for easy reading, nor do they easily lend themselves to publication. Granted also, his published work was written almost exclusively in German and appeared outside Canada, and he was strongest in the writing of non-fiction and that borderline category of fictionalized history. But this is no excuse for totally ignoring an author who has written about Canada and Canadian themes in such a meaningful and effective way. It is to be hoped that Charles Wassermann will eventually be accorded the recognition in his own country that he truly deserves.

NOTES

1 Wassermann's unpublished papers are kept in the Ethnic Archives of the National Library, Ottawa. My special thanks go to Mrs J. Wassermann for much useful information, for granting me access to the papers, and for the generous permission to quote from them.
2 Mainly done at the Collection Gagnon of the Montreal Municipal Library.
3 Cf. Charles Marius Barbeau, *The Tree of Dreams* (Toronto: University of Toronto Press, 1955), pp. 35–42 and p. 111.
4 For most of these see Barbeau.
5 Part of the Wassermann papers, Ethnic Archives, National Library, Ottawa.
6 Cf. anon., 'Werewolves and Flying Canoes,' *Time*, 6 Aug. 1951, p. 28, and Margaret Ness, 'Meet Me at St. Christophe,' *Saturday Night*, 17 Jan. 1953, p. 32.
7 Letter of 16 July 1951 from Wassermann to M. Ouimet, director of the French network of the CBC. Ethnic Archives, Ottawa.
8 Dusty Vineburg, 'Amusing Fiddle Joe's Yarn Makes T.V. Debut Tonight,' *Montreal Star*, 6 July 1956.
9 See *CBC Times*, 27 May–2 June 1951, p. 7; 3–9 June 1951, p. 8; 10–16 June 1951, p. 10; 17–23 June 1951, p. 12; 24–30 June 1951, p. 4; 1–7 July 1951, p. 11; 15–21 July 1951, p. 1; 30 Sept.–6 Oct. 1951, p. 5; 7–13 Oct. 1951, p. 10;

11–17 Nov. 1951, p. 5; 18–24 Nov. 1951, p. 8; 9–15 Dec. 1951, p. 10; 17–23 Feb. 1952, p. 4; 24 Feb.–1 March 1952, p. 10; 28 Sept.–4 Oct. 1952, pp. 7 and 10; 2–8 Nov. 1952, p. 9; 21–7 Dec. 1952, p. 7; 17–23 May, 1953, p. 4; 27 Sept.–3 Oct. 1953, p. 3; 1–7 Nov. 1953, p. 9; 20–6 Dec. 1953, p. 5; 27 Dec. 1953–2 Jan. 1954, p. 3; 18–24 April 1954, p. 7; 25 April–1 May 1954, p. 9; 13–19 June 1954, p. 7.

10 Cf. *CBC Times*, 1–7 June 1952, p. 5.

11 Cf. the Janos episode in Wassermann, *Tagebuch der Freiheit: Als Reporter in Ungarn und Polen* (Düsseldorf: Bertelsmann, 1957 and Hamburg: Blüchert, 1957), pp. 275–313.

12 Cf. Alexander Klein, *Grand Deception* (Philadelphia: Lippincott, 1955) and Joseph Wechsberg, 'The Man Who Fooled Hitler,' *Atlantic Monthly*, April 1951, pp. 50–4.

13 Based on the events that led to the Vasil Risak plot in chapters 9–11 of Wassermann, *Die Nacht der hellen Stunden* (München, Berlin: Herbig, 1974; also as pocket book, Reinbek: Rowohlt, 1977), pp. 300–67.

14 Some of the titles: 'Kettenreaktion,' 'Der Kurier,' 'Die Bucht der sieben Inseln,' 'Wir waschen diesen Schandfleck ab,' and 'Der Baum der Träume' (Christmas programme of 'Fiddle Joe' series).

15 Wassermann used French translations as the basis for his version.

16 Brooks Atkinson, '"Time of Vengeance" Arrives at York,' *New York Times*, 11 Dec. 1959, p. 39, col. 1, and B. Atkinson, 'Time of Vengeance,' *New York Times*, 27 Dec. 1959, sec. II, p. 12, col. 1.

17 See Wassermann, 'The World's Illusion,' *CBC Times*, 16–22 Sept. 1951, p. 3.

18 See note 11.

19 Wassermann, *Unter polnischer Verwaltung: Tagebuch* (Gütersloh: Bertelsmann, 1957 and Hamburg: Blüchert, 1958).

20 Wassermann, *Europe's Forgotten Territories* (Copenhagen: R. Roussell, 1960). Amazingly, the text is marred by the odd Germanism.

21 Letter of 10 Dec. 1962 from Wassermann to Dr Hans Geert Falkenberg of the Kindler Verlag. Ethnic Archives, Ottawa.

22 Wassermann, *Europe's Forgotten Territories*, p. 272.

23 Ross Lockridge Jr., *Das Land des Regenbaums* (abbreviated edition taking into account the first translation by Harry Kahn from the English, rendered and reworked by Charles Wassermann; Gütersloh: Bertelsmann, 1958; also Zürich, Stuttgart: Fretz and Wasmuth, 1958, and Zürich, Schweizer Druck- u. Verlagshaus, 1964).

24 Wassermann, *Das Land der Zukunft: 20000 Kilometer kreuz und quer durch Kanada, mit 71 Schwarzweissfotos und 16 Farbfotos* (Gütersloh: Sigbert Mohn, 1960 and 1961; also Gütersloh: Bertelsmann, 1961). It is interesting to note

that a book with an almost similar title had been published twenty years earlier: Heinrich Hauser, *Kanada: Zukunftsland im Norden* (Berlin, 1941).

25 Four of the stories were among those on which he had based his early radio plays for the series 'Canadian Legends,' namely 'Big Chief Napeo' (pp. 39–43), 'The Legend of Frank Slide' (pp. 189–94), 'The Story of the Wishing Pool' (pp. 248–53), and 'Sable Island' (pp. 291–4).

26 Wassermann, *Il Canada*, trans. G. Gentilli (Milano: A. Garzanti, 1961).

27 Wassermann, *CPR: Das Weltreich des Bibers* (Gütersloh: Sigbert Mohn, 1962 and Gütersloh: Bertelsmann, 1966). A slightly revised version with the addition of more modern illustrations was published under the title *Canadian Pacific: Die grosse Eisenbahn* (München, Berlin: Herbig, 1979 and Gütersloh: Bertelsmann, 1979).

28 Pierre Berton, *The National Dream: The Great Railway 1871–1881* (Toronto and Montreal: McClelland and Stewart, 1970) and *The Last Spike: The Great Railway 1881–1885* (Toronto and Montreal: McClelland and Stewart, 1971).

29 Cf., among others: Harold A. Innis, *A History of the Canadian Pacific Railway* (Toronto and Buffalo: University of Toronto Press, 1971); Robert Chodos, *The CPR: A Century of Corporate Welfare* (Toronto: James Lewis and Samuel, 1973); and J. Lorne McDougall, *Canadian Pacific: A Brief History* (Montreal: McGill University Press, 1968).

30 For instance, the CPR's 'Austrian Adventure' as related by Wassermann in chapter 4. Only Innis, p. 170, mentions it in passing, without reference to Wassermann.

31 See note 21.

32 Charles Ulrik, *Lawine halb fünf* (Gütersloh: Bertelsmann, 1961).

33 Ulrik, *Geheimstollen 'K'* (Hamburg: Verlag der Freizeit-Bibliothek, 1961 and Gütersloh, Bertelsmann, 1962).

34 Wassermann, *Der Journalist* (Gütersloh, Bertelsmann, 1965 and Hamburg: Mosaik, 1965).

35 Wassermann, *Kämpfer ohne Waffen. Das Rote Kreuz in 12 Kriegen* (Hamburg: Mosaik, 1965). Also under the title *Helden ohne Waffen* (Gütersloh: Bertelsmann, 1967).

36 Wassermann, *Insulin* (Gütersloh: Sigbert Mohn, 1966 [with frontispiece] and Gütersloh: Bertelsmann, 1966 [with 20 photographs]).

37 Wassermann, *Die Nacht der hellen Stunden* (München, Berlin: Herbig, 1974; also as pocket book Reinbek: Rowohlt, 1977).

38 Wassermann, *Kanada: Land der Zukunft* (München: Herbig, 1976, and Gütersloh: Bertelsmann, 1976).

39 Wassermann, *Insulin, Der Kampf um eine Entdeckung* (München: Langen-Müller, 1978; also as pocket book, München: Heyne, 1989).

Ulrich Schaffer ❧ Seeking a New Landscape of the Spirit

PETER LIDDELL

> First follow Nature and your judgment frame
> By her just standard, which is still the same:
> Unerring Nature, still divinely bright,
> One clear, unchang'd and universal light,
> Life, force, and beauty, must to all impart,
> At one the source, and end, and test of Art.
>
> Alexander Pope, Essay on Criticism, lines 68–73

> I have tried not merely to theorize or intellectualize, because I am convinced that whenever we report genuinely and directly on ourselves we will create a bridge to others. In the last analysis our questions, joys, problems, and experiences are not that different from those of others. But we must not hide them from each other.
>
> Ulrich Schaffer, Im Aufwind, p. 78

Ulrich Schaffer is an anomaly among German-Canadian writers. He is a prolific, unusually successful author who has lived in Canada for thirty years, but who is scarcely known to Canadian readers. Although seven of his books are available in English, his main audience has been in German-speaking Western Europe, where fifteen of his seventeen books are still in print. To introduce him as a German-Canadian writer would therefore be a misnomer in one sense. Nor is it my intention in the following survey of his work to try to extract cultural affinities from among his themes, settings, or style, because his work is not easily localized, as will become clear in the course of discussion. Nevertheless, there is an underlying, fundamental purpose to Schaffer's writing which does compare ultimately with a central theme of many writers who try to reconcile two cultures or, indeed, of all writers who seek refuge from the loneliness of modern existence: namely, the urge to seek out an inner 'home.'[1]

Having fled the family farm in Pomerania in 1945, Schaffer's family settled briefly near Bremen before emigrating in 1953 in search of a more stable and promising future in Western Canada. After two years in Lethbridge, they moved to find work in the new town of Kitimat, BC, which had just been created to service a vast aluminum works. Although Schaffer had soon become fluent in English and first wrote in English as a tenth-grader, he decided at eighteen to write principally in German. His family's concern 'not to let their German slip' and his own reading of contemporary German poets had, according to Schaffer, created a sphere for German which was quite distinct from the 'English' world outside the home.[2] His first attempts at writing independently were influenced by favourite poets like Enzensberger and Fr. Mohn and published in *Gurluana* (1964) and *Im Gegenwind* (1965), both now out of print. Schaffer describes them as experiments with words and forms, or 'poetry,' in contrast to the 'meditations' of his later publications.[3] As 'poetry,' they are less concerned with meaning than with poetic or (again in Schaffer's terms) 'literary' expression.

During the 1960s, as an undergraduate and graduate student at the University of British Columbia, Schaffer's sense of cultural affinity with Germany increased markedly. He acknowledges several important influences then which affected his writing from 1968–9 onwards: his study of German literature; the encouragement of professors with whom he discussed his writing; his first visit and subsequent year of studying theology and philosophy at Hamburg University; and, throughout, a close contact with the German Baptist Church in Vancouver. More directly, he recognized at first hand, in public readings at UBC, the pitfalls of writing for effect. At the same time, through his youth work in the church, he found himself more and more dealing with what he calls 'the big questions: Who am I? Why am I here? Where am I going? Is there a God?' When this became the focus of his writing too, he found the core of meaning his work had lacked earlier.

The young people in the church group were by and large the children of

German immigrants of the early 1950s, like Schaffer himself. Their group discussions were conducted in a German which had become anglicized after fifteen years and increasingly remote from modern colloquial German. Schaffer remembers trying to express himself in good, modern German and treating the discussions as an opportunity for open, rather than formal, exchange. It is against this background that he began to write meditative verse on spiritual topics in 1968–9. In the Oncken Verlag he found a publisher with an interest in religious books; and with the acceptance and the initial success of his first collection, *trotz meiner schuld* ('in spite of my sins') (1971),[4] the future direction of his writing became clearer. He quite soon found a wider readership of younger, somewhat disaffected Christians who were interested in undogmatic discussion of questions of faith and human relationships.

Between 1971 and 1978 seven more books of meditative verse appeared. Two, *kreise schlagen* ('making rings in the water') (1973) and *umkehrungen* ('U-turns') (1975), form a loose trilogy with *trotz meiner schuld*. They deal with questions of faith and personal relationships. A second group of three has human love and faith as its principal theme.[5] Both groups emphasize faith as part of daily life. The two other books in the earlier meditations are based on the Bible – *gott, was willst du?* ('what do you want, god?') on selected Psalms, and *jesus, ich bin traurig froh* ('jesus, i am sadly joyful') on Old and New Testament passages. They complement the two trilogies in that they relate the Scriptures to everyday life.

As a sometime painter and avid photographer, Ulrich Schaffer has the visual artist's eye for the connection between his text and the way it is presented visually. In designing and laying out his own books, he maintains strict consistency between groups of books which are thematically related. Of the eight earlier books of meditations, all but two (which contain photographs) are the same length. More significant for his purpose, though, is the uniformity of the text: all eight books are printed throughout in the lower case, which reduces the visual, symbolic impact of individual words (particularly, in German, of nouns); similarly, there is virtually no punctuation. The effect is to reduce the language, the medium, to a monochrome, as devoid of visual (that is external, aesthetic) effect as possible. Without graphic indicators, emphasis and separation is created by varying the length of lines and stanzas. Rather than presenting complex statements or ideas interrelated to one another, this style tends to segregate the individual ideas or statements, by juxtaposing (or, more often, superimposing) them. Each one stands isolated to a greater degree than in conventional script:

...	...
and they say to him	und man sagt ihm:
look out	pass auf
don't fall foul of people	stoss dich nicht an menschen
and he doesn't either	und er tut es auch nicht
but in the long run	doch auf die dauer
it is easier said than done	ist es leichter gesagt als getan
for he is looking for his lord	denn in den mitchristen
in his fellow-christians	sucht er seinen herrn
and doesn't find him	und findet ihn nicht
only narrow minds and rules	nur engherzigkeit und gesetze
not liberation but chains	keine befreiung sondern fesseln
he's looking for real community	hier sucht er wirkliche gemeinschaft
and finds only superficial togetherness	und findet oberflächliches
	beisammensein

(*kreise*, p. 29)[6]

The emphasis placed on individual phrases or ideas through the script reflects Schaffer's concern to have meaning predominate over form in his earlier writing. He tried deliberately to avoid what he calls 'literary' language, so that the audience should not be 'lost in nice images or metaphors.' His early meditations are thus noticeably devoid of conventional poetic devices, but above all lack strong imagery. Evidence of how consciously he avoided poetic images can be seen in his treatment of the Psalms, where the original images are either omitted (for example, in Psalm 1) or replaced by modern idioms, as in the version of Psalm 14: 'theorien sollen die sünden zudecken' ('theories are to cover up sin') (*gott*, p. 20). Where images are used, they are usually colloquial metaphors which lack any literary qualities, because their pictorial, imaginative character is suppressed – sometimes with incongruous results: 'today i stood between people once again who are light years away from me' (*jesus*, p. 30). Occasionally the metaphors are so tightly compressed that they lose all individual plasticity in an amorphous mixture:

i want to walk in your light	in deinem licht will ich wandern
breach the walls and bonds	durchbrechen die mauern und fesseln
cloaked in your secure mantle	ummantelt mit deiner sicherheit
saved from the abyss	errettet vor dem abgrund
that opens up before me and in me	der sich vor mir und in mir auftut

(*kreise*, p. 24)

Such profusions of colour proclaim an intense but undifferentiated yearning and to that extent serve Schaffer's 'unliterary' purpose.

Few images are extended or sustained through a meditation in the earlier books. When they are, like the 'chains' of convention (*schuld*, p. 45) or the 'sand in the works' of dehumanizing systems (*kreise*, p. 28), they are stated with a declamatory force which appeals to the emotion rather than the imagination. The link between the worldly and the spiritual meaning of the metaphor is then made as a leap of faith, as at the end of 'ketten' ('chains'), where a litany of 'binding' social restrictions and reservations concludes:

what keeps us back from love	was uns von der liebe abhält
is a chain of fear	ist eine kette aus furcht
which only the one lord can smash	die nur einer sprengt
with his love	mit seiner liebe

(*schuld*, p. 45)

The most effective metaphors in the early meditations are those that contrast worldly and spiritual concerns, usually in the form of irony or paradox:

when i am still in charge of my life	wenn ich selber noch über mich verfüge
i am in chains	bin ich gekettet
and even the chains	und auch die ketten
that seem like wings	die wie flügel erscheinen
are chains	sind ketten

(ibid.)

Using paradox to express spiritual or religious truths is, of course, a well-established tradition (cf. the Sermon on the Mount, Matthew 5–7). Schaffer, however, uses everyday images in paradoxes that suggest metaphysical truths as freely as he uses conventional metaphors like the chain:

we make rings in the water	wir schlagen kreise
by our actions	wenn wir handeln
and rings when we do nothing	wir schlagen kreise wenn wir nichts tun

(*kreise*, p. 7)

If paradox can be a two-edged sword, irony can act like a dagger. In the earlier works in particular, Schaffer uses irony frequently, especially to prick the bubble of complacency: a meditation on the convenience of having rules and guidelines ('Grenzen' – borders or, loosely, fences) in life ends with the following twist:

good fences	gute grenzen
guarantee	garantieren
security	sicherheit
against	vor dem
life	leben
and often death	und oft tod
to the world around us	unserer umwelt

(kreise, p. 56)

Where Christian ethics are concerned, the irony may be humorous, as in this epitaph:

'The christian's first duty is to keep the peace'	'ruhe ist die erste christenpflicht'
was the motto of his life	stand über seinem leben
...	...
between his life	zwischen seinem leben
and the grave	und dem grab
there was little to choose	war wenig unterschied zu merken

(kreise, p. 11)

or more puckish: 'noah was an "egoist" / when he had to save himself' (*kreise*, p. 27). The particular targets of the irony are façades, labels, or generalizations of any kind that impede personal commitment or conceal the essential individual.

Schaffer's insistence on probing deeper and independently into questions of faith led, in 1971–2, to difficulties with his church which eventually brought about his expulsion. This still causes him much regret, although, in retrospect, he appreciates the freedom to speak as an individual not as a spokesman for a particular denomination. At the time his writing reflects sadness and some bitterness at being excluded. The irony is particularly pointed where he castigates the 'patent solutions' preached from the pulpit ('nach der predigt'; 'after the sermon') (*schuld*, p. 30) or the congregation that excludes the unconventional young from worship, in 'reihe um reihe' ('row upon row,') (*schuld*, p. 32): 'first you have to convert to the pious pose / then perhaps you may convert to jesus christ.' Later, the tone gradually softens to a more general malaise about institutionalized religion: 'we have been looking after you pretty well now for 2000 years' (*kreise*, p. 50). There is even irony at the expense of his own attempts to lead religious youth groups: 'anyone who leads a group knows that / you have to put in time and love / now we've finally made it through / but god says: "you fools"' (*kreise*, p. 32).

In the broader sense, institutions or shibboleths of all kinds – religious, intellectual, or social – are suspect: the 'kingdom of God' is not to be found in worldly institutions, buildings, schedules, titles, or human talents ('reich gottes') (*schuld*, p. 61); the worldly optimism of humanistic thinkers like Goethe, who hold that man was created to strive to be 'noble and good,' is, for Schaffer, utterly confounded by the magnitude of man's atrocities in the twentieth century, 'as if mankind could pull itself out of the muck by its own hair' ('edel und gut – notiz zu goethe,' *kreise*, p. 41). Ultimately, Schaffer believes, anyone who looks for worldly answers to spiritual questions is deceiving himself – both the seller and the buyer of the 'patent solutions': not only the manipulators, such as the communications media (*kreise*, p. 36) and the 'advertising experts and fork-tongued politicians' (*gott*, p. 55), but also the manipulated, the timorous, self-denying, ingratiating ones who debase themselves and those around them by excessive concern to react to others (*schuld*, pp. 26, 62; *lieben*, p. 45). According to Schaffer's belief, the first prerequisite for a truly purposeful life is independence from the blandishments of the world, but never at the cost of denying the responsibilities of the world. Those who forsake their family and social duties for a life of church service merit equally ironic treatment (*kreise*, p. 53; *umkehrungen*, p. 29). True unity and purpose depend on looking beyond the often antithetical signs of worldly appearances, in Schaffer's view.

Stripping off the veils to look for the unity beneath the multiplicity involves courage – the risk of being ground to dust even as one acts like 'sand in the works' of the system (*kreise*, p. 28). There is loneliness involved in overcoming man's social leanings in order to pull down the façades of convention (*umkehrungen*, pp. 38, 49), and ruthlessness in constantly evaluating oneself, not taking credit alone for one's activities ('why should i give thanks to [god]?' *schuld*, p. 16). Above all, Schaffer stresses the need to recognize the duality of life, the conflicting properties of man's worldly existence. In his own case, for example, he has a writer's respect for the power of words to deceive both himself and the reader by their intrinsic allure (*kreise*, p. 4; *Journal*, passim). Paradoxically, silence can sometimes say more than words – even, or perhaps especially, the involuntary and humbling silence when inspiration fails (*Im Aufwind*, p. 68).

Contrast and antithesis are as essential to Ulrich Schaffer's philosophical position as paradox and irony are to his style of writing. In the first trilogy, on faith and relationships between man and God and man and man, the duality is expressed from a single perspective ('ich'). The mode is highly subjective, but avoids idiosyncrasy and egocentric bias through the constant spirit of self-evaluation that pervades all. These early meditations are addressed as monologues to God or an invisible, indefinite third party, but express the duality of life in the wide spectrum of their contrasting moods: pensive, active, inert, energetic, angry, joyful, despairing, hopeful, suspicious, receptive, and so on.

In the second trilogy, on human and divine love, the perspective changes perceptibly. *ich will dich lieben* is typical of all three: the irony ('and the slogan of the day is make love / and they produce love / in one sector of their lives,' p. 33) and the paradox ('to possess is to lose,' p. 33) are still in evidence; but the meditations are no longer addressed to the cosmos at large – God, or a faceless third party. Now they speak to the partner in love and thence to God as the God of love.

Similarly, as their titles imply, the two books based on biblical passages both seek to engage God/Christ in a meditative dialogue. The sometimes defiantly subjective tone of the earlier trilogy ('today i am going to clear the decks with you / jesus / the dirty clumps on my feet / are slowing me down / and i have one or two things to say to you,' *schuld*, p. 38) gives way in the later meditative texts to a more conciliatory approach, closer to dialogue than simple acclamation or confrontation ('jesus / i stand before you / once again unable to really love,' *lieben*, p. 44). Indeed, the foreword to *jesus, ich bin traurig froh* expressly encourages the readers to read the numbered sections aloud with separate speakers, to emphasize the sense of a discussion taking place between an individual, or several participants, and God (p. 5). In this respect, the duality in life and the contrast between worldly and spiritual concerns, which had been expressed earlier through figures of speech, here begin to evolve into a dialectical discussion aimed at eliciting the truth progressively.[7] It represents Schaffer's increasing belief that God can be experienced 'more and more in the other person, [so] that faith becomes real in human interaction ... , putting human relationships on a par with the man-God relationship.' The changing perspective was to have a profound effect on Schaffer's writing.

Having consciously reduced the 'literary' effects of his writing in the early 1970s, Schaffer began to feel, through his unusually close contact with his readers,[8] that, 'after years of shared experiences,' they could accept a 'more ambitious' literary style. This, coupled with the new shift towards dialogue (that is, the need to acknowledge other perspectives), leads to a more allusive style, appealing to the imagination rather than proclaiming. In order to suggest, not theorize about, the metaphysical world, Schaffer relies increasingly on imagery in place of direct assertion.

The new emphasis on metaphor coincides with the gradual introduction of photography in *wachsende liebe* and *mit kindern wachsen*, two of the 'love' trilogy. The majority of the pictures in both books show adults or children in poses reflecting the different moods and topics of the meditations. A small number of photographs of non-human subjects, however, introduce a new element by pointing to a metaphor in the accompanying text. The metaphor may be implicit, as it is in 'loslassen' ('setting free') (*wachsende liebe*, p. 55), but the theme – that links must not become bonds – derives obviously from the ambiguous connotations of the chains (cf. English 'bonds') in the accompanying photograph. Elsewhere, a striking and central image may be taken from the text and presented in a picture which is itself symbolic. This has the effect of intensifying the metaphor: in the meditation 'auswege' (loosely: 'rationalizings'), which reflects on the hiatuses that occur between a married couple, the otherwise sombre tone is relieved by one outstanding image: 'these are the dry reaches, the deserts around and within us' (*wachsende liebe*, p. 44). The photograph opposite picks up the metaphor and at the same time indicates the optimism of the conclusion of the meditation: a single, thin sea-grass plant is shown silhouetted against the grainy, barren-looking sand that nevertheless sustains it.

Schaffer explores this highly metaphorical combination of text and picture in his third trilogy, the larger-format, hardback volumes *Im Aufwind* (available in English as *Searching for You*), *Überrascht vom Licht* (*Surprised by Light*), and *Wurzeln schlagen* ('striking root' – not available in English).[9] As a unit – all are eighty pages long and very similar in layout – the three represent one of two significant innovations in Schaffer's more recent work, as he tends increasingly to view life as a metaphor for the spirit. In this case, the metaphor is nature and the medium is meditative poetry (in Schaffer's sense of the word) combined with symbolic photography. The other innovation, prose, will be discussed later.

Since Schaffer introduces the metaphorical view of life in the 'photographic' trilogy and the pictures themselves play such a prominent part in enriching the metaphor, or simply making it more explicit, a brief general comment on the photographs themselves should be added here. The keynote is simplicity, a straightforward, uncluttered image and a finish which emphasizes line, pattern, silhouette, and contrast. Schaffer prepares the black-and-white photographs in his own dark-room with these characteristics in mind, as the technical notes to each volume explain. The effect is not artificial, but symbolical. Above all, though, it is the subject matter which creates the symbolical effect. Few photographs include people, and those that do convey no sense of their individuality. They are simply figures in a landscape – distant silhouettes either integrated into, or almost overwhelmed by, the surrounding shapes and masses. Equally, few pictures show man's works either, except where they are clearly, and almost timelessly symbolic, like a field of stooked wheat, fishing nets, chains, windows, doors, and boats. Since these objects, like the human figures, are shown for what they represent or evoke, there is little sense of locality or time – there is little information in the photographs themselves to indicate exactly where or in what year they were taken. Their importance lies in the associations they arouse, not their individual identity. Thus the same scene may, with different lighting or perspective, evoke quite different echoes (cf. the lone rock in the ocean, the last image in both the black-and-white volumes, *Im Aufwind* and *Wurzeln schlagen*, p. 77).

In the same spirit of not localizing the scene, not showing it only to illustrate the beauty of a certain place at a certain time, none of the pictures stress motion or action. Their effect is certainly visible, in the contorted limbs of a tree or weather-worn rock or wood; but it is the lasting state that the picture reveals, not a momentary effect. Trees and grasses lean without moving and beaches lie corrugated by unseen waves, expressing the stability of the rhythms and lines of nature, the patterns of adaptation and recurrence that are the only real portents of permanence and survival.

The fragility of existence emerges in the many images of lone, exposed figures in a calm but obviously potentially hostile setting – a distorted pine on the High Sierra, a cottonwood copse on a Cariboo prairie, grasses and trees protruding starkly from sand or water, a small sapling struggling for light on the forest floor, or a rocky outcrop in the ocean topped by trees in imminent danger of collapse. Woven throughout are pictures of translucent or luminescent leaves or transparent drops on a spider's web, embodying one of Schaffer's most important images and suggestive of the 'transparency' of Creation and of man's striving to reveal and illuminate the spiritual purpose of existence. The moods of the photographs may vary considerably, alternating from the peace of a Greek sunset to the ominous gloom of a North German forest of twisted oaks, or from the delicate balance of hawthorn berries iced by the first frost to the inscrutable solidity of a windowless villa; but the sense of seeing a moment of calmness in a lasting struggle is reminiscent of Winckelmann's Classical ideal of life as a progressive conflict between order and confusion and beauty as the moment when they are in perfect balance.

The dominant image in the text of all three photographic books is Light: it is the source of illumination but also of blindness. It gives life, inspiration, and insight but in excess causes death, despair, and deceptiveness (cf. *Überrascht*, p. 49). Man's eternal struggle to reach beyond his earthly limitations in search of ultimate truths is conveyed by the metaphor (which takes many forms) of the individual seeking the source of the light beyond the contrasting effects that it produces. However, those conflicting signs exist within his own dual, worldly and spiritual, nature, as well as around him in the worldly demands of everyday life. In seeking the source of light he is the observer and the observed. If he is to see clearly, he must learn to distinguish between his two natures – roughly equivalent to the persona (which adapts to worldly stimuli) and the anima (which reflects the unique individual within – his essential or divine spark). And he must learn to distinguish at all times and in all changing circumstances, because the conflict between the claims of the spirit and the demands of the world is constant.

According to Schaffer's imagery, the process of differentiation, or isolating and nullifying the persona, means the 'death' of the worldly self (*lieben*, p. 52); but it must go on constantly, so that life becomes 'a series of days for dying' (*umkehrungen*, p. 7). More often than not these 'deaths' are involuntary, caused by unexpected turns in the ways of the world man perceives with the senses:

the world rushes in on us	Die Welt stürzt auf uns ein
and overwhelms us.	und überwältigt uns.
But then our senses feel too confining,	Aber dann werden uns die Sinne zu eng,
the framework bursts open,	der Rahmen zerspringt,
and we come upon that yearning	und wir begegnen der sehnsucht,
that far transcends our senses.	die weit über die Sinne hinausgeht.
We enter into the presence	wir treten in die Gegenwart
of the spirit of God.	des Geistes Gottes.

(*Überrascht*, p. 31)

These personal 'crucifixions' (ibid., p. 14) reduce the individual, now bereft of persona, to a state of existential loneliness, isolated from the world, but therefore closer to the 'transparent' state that reveals the spririt within himself and enables him to recognize it in others:

...	...
And around me I discover others in their loneliness.	Und um mich entdecke ich andere in ihrer Einsamkeit.
Overwhelmed by the same force of light	Überwältigt von der gleichen Lichtgewalt
they too are transformed into new men.	werden auch sie in neue Menschen verwandelt.
Oh God	O Gott
your light is so beautiful!	wie schön ist dein Licht!

(*Wurzeln*, p. 53)

'Transparency,' the momentary state of insight, can make one impervious to the 'rifle-shots' of the world's fortunes (*Überrascht*, p. 64), but there is no permanent guarantee of sanctuary. 'Death,' or that state of helpless self-lessness, comes unexpectedly and cannot be forecast or planned. It may occur at the moment of greatest despair, when the world seems desolate, which is why Schaffer endows images like 'death' itself, 'stillness,' 'emptiness,' 'gravity/heaviness' ('Schwere'), 'darkness,' 'abyss,' 'anxiety,' 'blindness' (to take only the examples of *Im Aufwind*) with such ambivalence. Because these moments offer the hope of insight, they should not be feared and avoided, regardless of whether they consist of nothing more than a dull, uninspired day for one individual or a cataclysm in the affairs of man. Spiritually there is no distinction between man's errors as an individual and his collective sins: 'Vietnam is as horrifyingly close / as the fellow human being whom I do not really love' (*schuld*, p. 50). It is thus possible, if regrettable, that God finds it necessary to visit mass murder on man as a reminder of his inscrutable purpose (*Journal*, pp. 246–7).

Schaffer is sensitive to the criticism that his writing is too introverted, too little concerned with the problems of the world.[10] His response is that his relationship to the world depends on his relationship to God (*Im Aufwind*, p. 78), which, as has been shown, is a constant effort to look beyond the affairs of the world. The 'truth that lies hidden behind reality' (ibid., p. 33) lies not in the 'broken pieces' of reality itself (*schuld*, p. 53), nor in acquiring more and more knowledge about the world. Such solipsism can lead to dogma and 'send others through fire and water' (*umkehrungen*, p. 53). By this token, the world and all its institutions – even the various churches (*umkehrungen*, pp. 54–7) – are suspect in so far as they serve their own, worldly ends. Then, too, they are fragments of a greater whole.

Beginning with the three photographic books and continuing in the prose writing, Schaffer treats the world itself as the source of faith. That is, instead of emphasizing that the conflicting signals of a higher purpose can only be reconciled by faith in God, he looks at the contradictions and antitheses of worldly life themselves as the sign of a higher purpose. The earlier sense of faith despite the world ('du liebst mich trotz meiner schuld'; 'you love me in spite of my sins,' *schuld*, p. 6) is gradually, in the photographic trilogy, replaced by the holistic view that the signs of a higher unity can be found in the complexities of the parts.

The apparent unity among the three books of the photographic trilogy – their format, imagery, themes, and subject matter – conceals a subtle progression from a faith which broadly depends on a perceived revelation from above to a faith which seeks substantiation though this world. Significantly, mention of God decreases through the trilogy in direct proportion to the increasing emphasis on his works. Meditations which were addressed to God in the first black-and-white volume are addressed to friends in the other, the last volume of the three. In between, the volume of coloured photographs, *Überrascht vom Licht*, still addresses the man-God relationship, but it celebrates God in Creation and man as the 'creation and partner of God' (p. 78).

The first volume, *Im Aufwind*, consists of meditations written during the period 1973–7. They closely resemble others written at the same time, with one minor visual exception – conventional punctuation and a lapidary, rune-like, upper case script, both of which lend strength to the words themselves, emphasized by the accompanying photographs. The picture often reflects the metaphor in the text, but occasionally suggests one, such as a starkly outlined jetty aligned with a meditation on waiting for God's grace (pp. 28–9). Where there is no obvious linking metaphor, Schaffer intends 'to draw the reader deeper into questions of faith' by meditation (p. 78).

The dominant attitude of *Im Aufwind* is humility and supplication, which is reflected in the rather sombre tones of the photographs. By deliberate contrast, *Überrascht vom Licht* is a celebration of nature which, because it is in colour, is 'willy-nilly more positive and life-embracing' (p. 78). Not only is it conceived as an aesthetic contrast to *Im Aufwind*, it also deliberately educates the reader into viewing the world it now embraces as a metaphor for the spiritual relationship described in *Im Aufwind*. The use of conventional script and normal punctuation together, which begins with *Überrascht vom Licht*, signifies a new phase, when meaning no longer completely dominates form. Now the reader is explicitly encouraged to appreciate the imaginative quality of the imagery, whereas in *Im Aufwind* the metaphorical link between the spiritual and the physical worlds was implicit, by association between the text and its accompanying picture. In *Überrascht vom Licht* a majority (approximately two-thirds) of the meditations relate directly to 'their' photographs: some do so by referring to them elliptically, in the opening lines ('*These* leaves' or 'We wonder what is behind *them*'); or the reader may be led to the image by a simile – otherwise a very unusual figure of speech in Schaffer's writing ('like nets,' 'like a branch'); or the text may trace a spiritual picture of the photograph ('deeper than any abyss' ... 'at every bend' facing a scene with a meandering stream disappearing into dense, dark forest). The gentle didacticism shows through most plainly in a poem that refers outright to pictures/images ('Bilder') like those in the book itself and to their role in reflecting the 'landscapes that inhabit my inner being' and helping the writer 'become transparent like the landscape and translucent for a different light' (p. 52). In the other one-third of the text where there is no specific mention of, or any apparent direct connection with, the picture, and in the case of the three carefully spaced, double-page photographs, Schaffer encourages the reader to meditate independently on the associations they evoke (author's comment, p. 78).

The transition to seeing the world as a metaphor of the spirit is completed in *Wurzeln schlagen: eine Feier des Miteinanders*. Rather than being inspired by a spiritual idea, these meditations are inspired often by Schaffer's relationship with a specific friend, which is then reflected in the visual metaphor of the accompanying photograph.[11] In this dialogue, God is a third party, referred to obliquely as 'the Law,' 'the heart of the light,' 'he who waits,' 'he who is life,' and so on – images drawn from the human world. There is one cardinal exception – a meditation superimposed on the only double-page photograph in the book. Here God is acclaimed ecstatically as the source of the blinding, illuminating light of the spirit. The familiar metaphors of loneliness, vulnerability, and transparency are reflected in the photograph of a solitary, half-dead tree, lit by a single beam from a theatening sky. The human characteristics predominate here and in other poems in this volume that allude variously to the coldness, confusion, or enchantment of a metaphorical scene. These characteristics and the human images of God are then linked in the person of the friend who inspired the poem, as in the example of the poem on limitations, or reaching the edge ('Rand') of one's abilities: 'All my experiences show me limitations in myself / through which I can really recognize you and him for the first time' (p. 49). God, or a higher spiritual purpose, is no longer 'like' the images of this world, but is *in* the relationship between the individual and his world, if he can only see it in the proper light. But like the photographs, which are now provided with a contrasting black or white surround 'to increase the light in the picture' (p. 78), the world requires the appropriate 'frame' before it can reveal its essential spiritual meaning.

Viewing the world metaphorically led to a second innovation in Ulrich Schaffer's writing – a growing interest in extending the human metaphor into fictitious characters and events, in prose. So far, he has published two volumes of fiction, both in the shorter prose genres: *Der Turm* ('The tower') is a collection of twenty parables, and *Das Schweigen dieser unendlichen Räume* ('The silence of these endless spaces' – taken from a favourite quotation from Pascal) is a novella-like study of a suicide. Both works are elliptical and highly symbolic. God, as an entity, is replaced entirely by abstract human concepts such as authority, justice, love, or extraordinary perception (hearing or sight). Rather than in search of God, or meaning, in an inscrutable world, characters tend to be shown at a personal borderline, facing the unexpected prospect of controlling their own fate. That is, they tend to walk along the same fine teleological line between self-reliance and dependence that marked Schaffer's meditative poetry; but only in *Das Schweigen* is the imagery drawn from nature, in keeping with its setting – the 'inner landscape' of its main character. The parables on the other hand draw on biblical, Germanic, or fairy-tale archetypes for their allegorical settings and characters: the seer, the prophet, and moments of great revelation; the ominous figure from the North (conscience?), pure, morally persistent female figures, contrasting with battling males; a giant, a tower, castles,and medieval villages.

Schaffer's preference for shorter prose forms, archetypal situations, and aphoristic, limpid prose makes comparison with Kafka perhaps inevitable. Kafka's influence had been visible even in the meditations, for example in two passages from *Im Aufwind* which strongly recall the cryptic parable *Vor dem Gesetz*:

> He creates such a longing in you that you almost expire
> He lets you envision Paradise even if you can not yet enter.

(p. 18)

and in this image:

> We wonder what might be behind them
> and over and over we find there are no answers
> but still we are drawn to them again
> those many doors in life

(p. 22)

The major, and decisive, difference is that Schaffer does not share Kafka's existentialistic, nihilistic view of the countryman waiting futilely and awestruck at his entrance gate to the inner light, until he dies:

> [God] shares out the waiting
> as a gift and a burden
> because he wants to be
> the only one who calms our hunger pangs

(p. 18)

Schaffer, like Kafka, concentrates on the precise moment of the critical confrontation between the individual and his destiny, For that reason he, too, often creates a timeless suspension of reality. The graphically detailed, agonizing suicide by stabbing described in 'Der langsame Tod' ('Slow death') (*Der Turm*, pp. 59–63) is comparable to the twelve-hour execution in Kafka's *Penal Colony*. At the most critical moments of self-examination time virtually stops, as in Schaffer's 'Gelähmt' ('Lamed'), the episode of a prisoner so consumed by anxiety about being left alone that past and future disappear as he concentrates his whole mental and spiritual energy on his fears; eventually, unable to make the simplest decision to act and find out if he is actually alone in the dark, he dies of his palpitations (ibid., pp. 28–30). As in *Vor dem Gesetz*, total self-absorption cripples the ability to act, a moral which Schaffer draws clearly, unlike Kafka, thereby avoiding the potentially absurd, parodistic possibilities of his prisoner's timeless self-preoccupation.

The fragmented style of Schaffer's story *Das Schweigen* corresponds to the fragmented perception of its main character, Steffen. For him, life has no connecting strands to relate past, present, and future in a coherent purpose. His inner landscape is 'like an American prairie ... , vast distances, no vegetation of note, grey grass, a gigantic sky, and nothing else. No hint of human presence in this expanse' (p. 11). Perversely, instead of trying to people the landscape through a fulfilling relation-ship, he tries to sharpen his understanding of the empty spaces by introducing an arbitrary time-limit to his life (p. 17). This solipsism changes nothing – life continues to be timeless, without cohesion, until he reaches the point of incoherence himself. Like his life, his thoughts and words are a meaningless jumble. After the allotted two months he is, in the image of the book's cover picture, 'a dying tree on the foreshore ... among driftwood that looks like people' (p. 62). At the moment when his death seems inevitable he is saved by the one force which can people his barren inner landscape – warmth for another human being. Like Kafka's man from the country 'before the law,' he gains a glimpse of the light that gives meaning; but unlike him, he lives on to make use of the glimpse. His life, as the continued fragmentation of the prose shows, remains fragmented, but there is hope for a new, purposeful future in the final lines: 'The landscape does not stay empty. Even the endless spaces are filling with warmth. Look! A tree is blossoming, as bright as a man in love. The outstretched hand is reaching out to catch the falling man' (p. 91). Like the inner landscapes earlier in his life, this 'transparent' mixture of natural and human metaphors will be familiar to those who know the meditative poems.

Schaffer's most recent and perhaps most ambitious work continues his vision of the human experience, rather than faith alone, as the key to spiritual insight. In *Journal: Aufzeichnungen september 1980–dezember 1981* he himself becomes the metaphor, 'invited by God to discover His realm in me and also to stand up and be seen as His son' (p. 8). Consisting of up to ten notes of varying length on each day of the fifteen-month period, *Journal* is a spiritual diary. It is a highly conscious, extensive record of a more or less arbitrarily selected period. Because it is not the events but the comments that they provoke that are recorded, even trivial events take on a symbolic quality: '8th July. At the dentist: every tooth even seems to have its own way of hurting' (p. 214). As a montage of reflections compiled through strict daily routine and altered little before publication, the diary has a sense of authenticity which Schaffer emphasizes by dating each entry and by recording the trivial event and the sombre (such as a visit to Bergen-Belsen) with equal consideration. It is not the events themselves but their capacity to provoke reactions, to reveal the individual experiencing them, that causes them to be included. To that extent Schaffer succeeds in letting the world 'shine directly through' his eyes and words (p. 10). However, 'transparency' also involves revealing the unifying purpose underlying the events. Without that, they remain disconnected fragments of existence and the diary remains 'opaque.' Equally, to inherit the 'legacy of the Enlightenment' and follow the 'urge to reason and prove,' by imposing religious or philosophical patterns on the events, would, in Schaffer's view, distort the essential significance of the individual event (p. 11). It is the fundamental dilemma of all his writing stated in terms of the author's dilemma: the conflict between formless authenticity and contrived artifice.

In viewing the world – social interaction, nature, personal experience – Ulrich Schaffer is not looking for empirical evidence of God. The evidence of a higher purpose is not, he believes, found in any single object, event, or image, but in the contrasts between worldly phenomena, those intellectual connections of opposites which only man can make. The contrastive style of his earlier writing, the dualistic imagery of the photographic trilogy and the decisive borderline moments of his fiction are all concerned with linking opposites, not similarities. The spiritual perspective he seeks is not to be gained by comparative overview, scanning time for a better understanding of the present, or predicating today's activity on future plans. In one recent poem in *Wurzeln schlagen* he describes the sense of finding and experiencing each moment for itself, 'which is all that we really have,' as 'being.' To 'be' means 'throwing off the past and future like ballast' (p. 35). In the *Journal*, this emphasis on the timelessness of each moment is to be seen in a strict insistence on immediately recording his thoughts and in the avoidance of direct comparison of events or people. On arriving for a prolonged stay in Germany, for example, Schaffer comments: 'People are different here. But to go into that more closely would be too dangerous' (p. 234). National differences, like other generalizations, lead nowhere spiritually. The purpose of being anywhere at any given time is not to be divined by comparison with other places, people, or times but in truly being in that place at that time, as opposed to the alternatives. In this respect, in the urge to 'be,' one senses the common urge of all those who seek a spiritual 'home,' a reconciliation between the two natures of man, and perhaps between the deep ties of the old and familiar and the challenges of the new. In this essential, existential and spiritual urge, Schaffer shares the experience of all migrants:

14 June. En route somewhere in B.C.: I try to look into the photograph I am taking as if I belong in this landscape, even if I am only here on holiday. The need to be at home everywhere that I enjoy being, to hide the fact that in the end I am always on the move.   (p. 202)

That particular irony is never lost on a poet who seeks the contemplative peace and the landscapes that describe man's spirit in his North American homeland, but must travel abroad to Germany and Europe to find his natural audience, the resonance he needs.

BIBLIOGRAPHY

References are included in the text of the article, using the abbreviated titles indicated below. Titles are grouped to correspond to the groupings discussed in the article. Unless otherwise stated, all books are published in Wuppertal, by Oncken (o) or Brockhaus (B).

POEMS

Gurluana and *Im Gegenwind*. Karlsruhe: K. Rüdiger, 1964 and 1965. Out of print

MEDITATIONS

1 *trotz meiner schuld: gedanken und gebete*. 1971. (o)   (*schuld*)
  Kreise schlagen: gedanken, gebete, gedichte. 1973. (o)   (*kreise*)
  umkehrungen: gedanken, gebete, gedichte. 1975. (o)   (*umkehrungen*)
2 *ich will dich lieben: meditationen über die liebe*. 1974. (B)   (*lieben*)
  mit kindern wachsen: meditationen, zwiegespräche und fotos zum verhältnis eltern zu kindern. 1975. (o)
3 *gott, was willst du? nachdenken über psalmen*. 1976. (o)   (*gott*)
  jesus, ich bin traurig froh. fragantworten und selbstgespräche. 1976. (B)   (*jesus*)

MEDITATIONS AND PHOTOGRAPHS

Im Aufwind, mit Gedanken und Gedichten. 1977. (o)   (*Im Aufwind*)
Überrascht vom Licht: Gedanken und Meditationen. 1980. (o)   (*Überrascht*)
Wurzeln schlagen: eine Feier des Miteinanders. 1981. (o)   (*Wurzeln schlagen*)

PROSE FICTION

Der Turm. Gleichnisse. (Zeichnungen: Fr. Peter). 1979. (o)   (*Der Turm*)
Das Schweigen dieser unendlichen Räume. Eine Erzählung. 1981. (B) (*Das Schweigen*)
Siljas geheimer Plan. (Zeichnungen: T. Shoji). 1978 (o). A children's story on
respecting Creation

PROSE NON-FICTION

Journal. Aufzeichnungen – september 1980–dezember 1981. 1982. (o)   (*Journal*)

NOTES

1 Books written by Schaffer have appeared in seven languages so far, and
  sales exceed four hundred thousand. His writing and other related publications and activities have earned him a sufficient level of financial independence that he has recently resigned his post as instructor in European
  Literature at a community college in the Vancouver region, where he has
  taught for twelve years. Biographical notes and quotations not otherwise
  attributed derive from an (unpublished) interview conducted at Schaffer's
  home in July 1981. I am indebted to him for his patience in answering so
  many questions.
2 Schaffer pursued his interest in German poetry and literature through mail
  orders and subscriptions to periodicals like *Akzente.* Apart from speaking
  German at home and reading contemporary German writers, he also acknowledges a debt, as a writer, to the discipline of writing 'good' German to
  pen-friends in West Germany.
3 Of the fifteen books still available, eleven consist of meditations or, more
  recently, meditative poetry. Schaffer continues to write what he calls
  'poetry,' but has yet to publish it.
4 Italicized English titles have been published in English; otherwise the
  translation is mine. Schaffer writes or rewrites, or translates, his own work
  into English. Translations into other languages are made by others.
5 The 'love' trilogy consists of *ich will dich lieben, wachsende liebe,* and *mit
  kindern wachsen* (i want to love you,' 'growing love,' 'growing with children').
6 For the sake of consistency, because not all English texts were available at
  the time of this writing, all translations are mine. The original German
  accompanies the longer quotations for linguistic or stylistic comparison.

7 The idea of searching for truth through dialectical discussion had first arisen in 'im gespräch' ('in conversation') (*umkehrungen*, p. 32). As Schaffer points out in several forewords, conversation with a goal formed an important part of his spiritual life at this time.

8 Through over one hundred readings, correspondence, discussion groups, retreats, and creative workshops, principally in German-speaking Western Europe, and also in North America, Schaffer is in regular and close contact with a large proportion of his readership.

9 *Searching for You* and *Surprised by Light* were both published in San Francisco and London, England, by, respectively, Harper and Row and Lion, in 1978 and 1981. A recording of parts of *Im Aufwind* set to music and posters of excerpts from it have also been published.

10 Such criticisms are openly acknowledged in *Im Aufwind* (p. 78).

11 While writing, Schaffer set up a list of close friends to whom he addressed poems individually, as a dialogue (author's comment, p. 78).

Hermann Böschenstein ✍✍
A Swiss among Canadians

ARMIN ARNOLD

SHORT BIOGRAPHY

Hermann Böschenstein was born on 1 May 1900 in the town of Stein am Rhein, twenty kilometres from Schaffhausen, twenty-seven from Konstanz.[1] His grandfather had been a mailman; when he became an invalid, Hermann's father, then fifteen years old, put on the mailman's uniform and did the work in his father's place. Hermann's mother owned a grocery store; it provided much work and enough income that her husband eventually abandoned the mail service and began helping in the store. He inherited and bought several parcels of land, grew vegetables, and ran a poultry farm. He was a highly respected man and was elected town councillor. He was in charge of the 'städtische Asyl' (municipal home), where the town placed its old and poor and – temporarily – those families who had lost their providers, and also children who had lost their parents. Many of these children became members of the Böschenstein household, so that Hermann was rarely without 'brothers' or 'sisters.' In fact, he had had a real brother and a real sister, but both had died in an epidemic shortly before Hermann was born.

For nine years, Hermann was a pupil of the 'Volksschule' (elementary school) in Stein. Even at the ages of twelve to fifteen, he was an avid reader and poet; he wrote stories by the dozen. The main influence on him at the time was the popular Swiss author Ernst Zahn. In 1916, Hermann entered the Gymnasium in Schaffhausen, where, in 1919, he obtained his

'Matura' (university entrance). He was a difficult youngster and rather unruly; disciplinary measures did not improve matters, and it was clear that he would break out of his milieu as soon as he could.

World War I began in August 1914. Hermann and a friend made up their minds to join the German army and march on Paris. Their plan was discovered and the two would-be heroes were severely punished. The plan, however, was not abandoned. Like many other Swiss at the time, Hermann had the feeling that he was prevented from participating in the great events of history; he felt that the Swiss were a cowardly people who hid themselves behind their official neutrality. Six days of the week, Hermann travelled by train down to Schaffhausen and back; the railway line ran along the Rhine, the border with Germany. During his last year at the Gymnasium, he rented a room in Schaffhausen. At first, he was a good student at the Gymnasium; then he felt ashamed of seeming to be more ambitious than his fellow students and did everything in his power to lower his marks. He succeeded, and this raised the ire of his teachers. Now he stayed away from school for days and weeks, worked in his room, and wrote novels. The authorities decided that he should not be permitted to write the final examinations, but his teacher of German, to whom Hermann had shown some of his writings, intervened, and Hermann was allowed to graduate.

In the summer of 1919, Böschenstein went to Zürich – he wanted to become an actor. In autumn he travelled to Munich and registered in the 'Schauspielschule Otto König.' In Munich he completed the novel Die Mutter und der neutrale Sohn which was published in 1921 by Xenien-Verlag in Leipzig. The proofs of the novel were corrected in Posen. How did Böschenstein get there?

While in Munich, Böschenstein had heard that Poland was calling up troops in order to break through the Curzon line and occupy the region around Wilna. This was Böschenstein's chance. Many of his actor colleagues had fought in France and told stories about Verdun and the Somme and made it clear that they had nothing but contempt for someone like Hermann Böschenstein who had chosen to wait out the conflict beside his well-lit stove. Böschenstein went to the Polish consulate and asked to serve as a medical orderly in the Polish army. He was told that he was a fool, but he was accepted. He was put in a training camp and then participated in the march on Wilna. When peace was concluded, Böschenstein went back to Munich. He had now seen at first hand what war was like.

Böschenstein abandoned the idea of becoming an actor. He studied German literature, philosophy, archaeology, and history at the universities of Kiel, Königsberg, Berlin, and Rostock. In Rostock, he felt so much attracted by the personality of Emil Utitz 'that he completed his doctorate with Utitz with a thesis on the philosophy of J.P. Crousaz in 1924.'[2] Having obtained his D.Phil., Böschenstein returned to Switzerland, served his term in the Swiss infantry, then accepted a job as a tutor in Admont, Austria. He had continued to write and, in fact, had already gained the second prize in a short story competition in 1919, and again high praise in 1923 – in a novel competition.

In 1925, we find Böschenstein in Naples; he is a correspondent for the Swiss daily *Der Bund*, attends lectures at the University of Naples, and writes. From Naples, he travels to Paris, and from there, in 1926, to Canada. Humphrey Milnes, Böschenstein's late friend and colleague, tells the story of the next decades:

> Falling in with a group of students, he crossed the country by harvest train as far as Regina, where he helped with the crops long enough to earn passage to the west coast. There, mainly in Prince George, Vancouver and Victoria he worked as a lumberman, farm-hand, railway sectionman and janitor. You could not say that he was preparing for an ivory tower existence.
>
> In May 1928, he returned to Switzerland to stay and to marry Elisabeth Schoch. He did marry Elisabeth, but it was only two weeks before he decided not to stay. In August, 1928, they set out for Toronto, where Hermann gravitated towards the university. He worked at the Banting Institute and the University Library, and enrolled for philosophical studies with George Sidney Brett, the man in Toronto who came closest to being a kindred spirit of Emil Utitz. The shift in centre of gravity towards literary studies came with a sort of inevitability. Professor G.H. Needler of the University College German Department met him casually and recognised his potential. He appointed Hermann to the Department in 1930, and would have done it a year earlier, but for a slip of memory. It was about this time that Needler introduced the young couple to the Muskoka landscape and it was love at first sight. Needler had a fine parcel of land in a choice section of the Lake of Bays, opposite Bigwin Island, to which he regularly invited the Böschensteins and their young son Frank, and later Gertrude, Tom and Bill, as the family grew. The two families often shared the simple chores and pleasures of the northland. One had only to see Hermann stripped to the waist, cutting the long grass on the back forty with a scythe

to realise that underneath the urban exterior there lurked a pioneer spirit, clearing the wilderness. In the economy of the life of the scholar and teacher there was from the first a place for family recreation in the elemental and spirit-healing setting of the Canadian Pre-Cambrian shield.

His work in the department came to include responsibility for graduate work more and more as time passed and numbers increased. He proved without peer as guide and counsellor over a range of literary fields, the breadth of which is indicated in the appended bibliography. Range and versatility are the keys to appreciating a number of his other activities. An interest in things Canadian led to the monthly report he broadcast for Radio Basel and Bern, part of a program devoted to the cultural life and politics of the English-speaking countries of the world. Long before there was a Bi-Bi Commission, Hermann Böschenstein was reporting critically to his own multi-lingual country on both English and French developments in the Canadian novel. He also surveyed Canadian national achievements and failures in a regular way for the *Zürcher Tagesanzeiger*.

From 1942 to 1946 Hermann Böschenstein was on leave of absence from the University of Toronto to serve as the Director for Canada of the War Prisoners' Aid of the Y.M.C.A., a job for which his background and humanitarian impulses perfectly suited him.[3]

During his wartime activity, Böschenstein had an experience which he was never able to forget and which continued to torment him from time to time: 'Was mich für den Rest meines Lebens erschüttert, hängt mit einem Zusammenbruch von Ordnung, Gerechtigkeit und Menschlichkeit zusammen, den ich aus nächster Nähe mitempfinden musste, die Verurteilung und Exekution von vier deutschen Soldaten in Lethbridge während des letzten Krieges' ('Something that moved me deeply for the rest of my life was connected with a breakdown of order, justice, and humanity, and I experienced it at closest proximity: the sentencing and execution of four German soldiers in Lethbridge during the last war).[4]

In 1956, Böschenstein, who during the previous two and a half decades had gained an excellent reputation as teacher and scholar, became Chairman of the Department of German at University College in Toronto. He was a Visiting Professor in Zürich (1950), London (University College, 1956), Chicago (1963 and 1965), and Buffalo (1969). He published several important books on German literature (see bibliography), became a member of the Royal Society of Canada in 1957, and received an Honorary Doctorate from Queen's University, Kingston, in 1968. He retired from his administrative position in 1972. Böschenstein held post-retirement appointments at the University of Waterloo and at McGill University (Montreal) until 1976 when his wife died and he decided to devote the remaining years of his life to the writing of fiction and drama. In 1974 he published a volume of short stories, *Unter Schweizern in Kanada*; in 1977, a novel, *Im Roten Ochsen*, followed. While working on a third novel, he died in his home in Toronto on 21 September 1982.

'DIE MUTTER UND DER NEUTRALE SOHN'

It must be a rare phenomenon in literary history – an author who publishes two novels, one at the age of twenty-one and the next fifty-six years later, at the age of seventy-seven.[5] Another curious fact is that in both works one of the female protagonists is based on the same person: Böschenstein's wife Elisabeth Schoch. In the first novel she appears as Elisabeth in the speculations of Böschenstein's *alter ego* Kaspar, in the 1977 novel as Martha Schneblin-Zollinger.

Die Mutter und der neutrale Sohn is, on the one hand, a typical example of Expressionist prose; on the other, it is one of the earliest parodies of the Expressionist novel. It is a clever book – with several layers of meaning. It consists of three parts and an appendix. The central figure in the first part is Erika, the mother. Her biography is given in one short page, in the rapid notation invented by Kasimir Edschmid in 1915 (*Die sechs Mündungen*). The following sentence is typical: 'Sie ging nach Hause, schloss die Fenster ihres Zimmers und spielte ein wenig Violine, aber wie gesagt, zur Künstlerin war sie nicht schamlos genug' ('She went home, shut the windows of her room and played the violin a little, but as has already been said, she wasn't shameless enough to be an artist').[6] Characteristic of Böschenstein's kind of writing is the use of concrete expressions for abstract phenomena; for instance: 'Sie musste einen Glauben haben, um dessen Nacken sie die Arme schlingen, in dessen Gesicht sie ihre Augen drücken, dem sie sich ganz hingeben konnte' ('She had to have a faith, about whose neck she could wrap her arms, into whose face she could press her eyes, and to whom she could give herself completely') (p. 5).

The author's sense of irony and parody becomes apparent from the second page. A leitmotif of Expressionism is 'der Schrei,' the scream. Erika, meditating on a bench, hears a scream. She jumps up and finds a child on the bank of a river. A note left with the child explains that the child's mother has jumped into the water. In her surprise, Erika swears in

Swiss German: 'Gottfried Stutz!' (p. 6). There is an abundance of Expressionist pathos in the novel, but it is never sustained: in each case Böschenstein destroys the pathetic mood by throwing in Swiss dialect expressions, irony, and parody.

Erika is a 'superwoman' and a 'neuer Mensch.' Having found this child, she immediately changes her life and abandons her studies: 'jauchzend dringt es jetzt heraus: ich werde Kinderschwester' ('exultantly it forces its way out of her: I'm going to become a children's nurse') (p. 8). While working as a nurse, Erika brings up the boy she had found and joins – by pure accident – a left-wing organization. In Expressionism, things usually happen without apparent motives: 'Auf einmal wurde sie zur Präsidentin gewählt, stand nun vorne, wurde Brennpunkt aller Augen, fühlte sich schwindelnd emporgeschleudert wie ein tanzender Ball auf Wasserstrahlen, aus ihrem Zentrum drang heiliger Wille in schmeichelnde Düfte von Phrasen, sie sauste auf Flügeln rauschender Reden umher und wiederholte immer den einen Schrei, aus Glaube und Eitelkeit: Revolution!' ('Suddenly she was elected President and stood now out front, the focal-point of all eyes; she felt herself being hurled forward in a daze, like a ball dancing on a jet of water; from her centre a sacred will forced its way into flattering mists of words, she flew around on the wings of intoxicating speeches and constantly repeated one cry, out of both conviction and vanity: revolution!') (p. 13).

Internal evidence suggests that the second part of the novel begins on p. 13. (Parts I and III are indicated properly, but the figure II is nowhere to be found. I suspect the author did this intentionally, since, later in the book, he reproduces some passages from Kaspar's diary, numbering them 1, 3, and 4!) Erika has adopted the boy she found and, ironically, called him Kaspar. He is now about twenty years old, and she sends him out into the world: 'Sie schickte ihn in die Welt hinaus, er sollte Heerscharen sammeln und am Tage des Kampfes zu ihr stossen. Aber seine Erlebnisse waren andere, nach den ersten Schritten schwankte er, Farben, Mädchen und Musik verwirrten ihn' ('She sent him out into the world, he was to gather legions and on the day of battle join up with her. But his experiences were different, after his first steps he faltered, colours, girls and music confused him') (p. 13).

There follows a long series of letters which Kaspar writes to his mother – they explain the title of the book. While Erika (like Germany) is a revolutionary, Kaspar – and he is partly an autobiographical projection of Böschenstein — remains 'neutral,' just like Switzerland during the war.

Sometimes he feels like a coward, and in one instance he tries to impress a girl by telling her lies about his heroism in battle. The passage is a hilarious parody of Edschmid's style.

Again and again, Kaspar thinks of Elisabeth. Sometimes he soberly tells himself that it would be best to go home, marry her, and become a respectable and useful citizen. On other occasions he puts his longing for her into the form of a parody of Expressionist prose: 'Aufsprang er und fühlte Sehnsucht, gegen die man toben, schreien, springen, wandern, weinen, wund sich schlagen könnte, dass es eine Freude war. Rasch stürzte er ins Freie, warf sich in die Wälder, stemmte sich von Baum zu Baum, zog Schritt um Schritt aus weichen Feldern, erstieg die Müdigkeit ... ' ('Up he sprang and felt a yearning against which one was able to rage, scream, jump, wander, weep, and wound oneself, so that it became a joy. Quickly he plunged into the open air, threw himself into the woods, pushed himself from tree to tree, step by step crossed soft fields, overcame fatigue ... ') (p. 20).

Böschenstein's novel contains a number of amusing stylistic experiments. One of Kaspar's letters, written when he is drunk, is mainly composed of sentences from German 'Trinklieder.' Later on Böschenstein inserts dadaist prose and poetry. Several of Kaspar's letters contain hilarious anecdotes and humorous pseudo-philosophical reflections. Evidently, Böschenstein had read *Schloss Nornepygge* and/or other books by Max Brod and was familiar with Brod's 'Indifferentismus.' The high point of part II is, no doubt, the only letter Erika ever sends to her son – in answer to more than a dozen of his letters. The text is as follows:

Ich glaubte, Du wolltest die Erde zerstampfen, nun kriechst Du wie ein Wurm darüber hin. Würmer kann man nicht peitschen, nur zertreten. Ich habe grosse Lust dazu, Du rückenloses Wesen. Mir ekelt vor Dir, der Du unfähig bist der Strammheit aufragenden Leibes. Weiber und Lieder sind Dir in die Knie gefahren. Nun suchst Du Deinen Schlotter zu heilen mit Pfarrer und Bibelsprüchen. ... Raffe Dich zusammen! Lass Deine Wahnsinnswuchten kreisen und fräse hinein in die Paläste der Schlemmer, durch die Hälse der Prasser, und wandle lachend über die Zacken ihrer Trümmer. Führe mich zum Tanze unter den Bögen ihrer Blutstrahlen! Revolution! (p. 26)

(I thought you wanted to trample the earth, but now you are creeping over it like a worm. Worms cannot be whipped, only squashed. I have a strong inclination to do it, you spineless being. I am disgusted by you, who are incapable of the erect bearing of a body striving upwards. Women and songs have made you weak-kneed. Now you are trying to cure your trembling with priests and biblical sayings. ... Pull yourself together! Let the energies of your madness whirl around and bore into the palaces of the gluttons, through the necks of the debauchers, and wander laughingly over the jagged edges of their ruins. Lead me to the dance under the arches of their streams of blood! Revolution!)

Towards the end of the second part we find parodies of Edschmid ('Wie herrlich, sich selbst zu erahnen, sich erschauernd abzutasten, indem ich mit den Händen esse, in den Wagen eines reichen Mannes steige, hemdärmelig zur Kirche gehe, Frauen prügle, singe, fluche, miau mache und sonst alles, was der Leib nur kann!'; 'How splendid to gain a sense of oneself, to explore oneself with a shudder, as I eat with my hands, climb into a rich man's car, go to church in my shirt-sleeves, beat women, sing, curse, meow, and do everything else that only the body can do!' [p. 31], of 'Indifferentismus' ('Er fühlte, dass die Darstellung dieser vollkommenen Gleichgültigkeit einen Ausdruck verlangte ... ; 'He felt that the depiction of this indifference demanded expression ... ' [p. 35]), and of dadaism of the Kurt Schwitters variety:

Apfelmus auf deinen Händen
Hosiannah die Zigarre.
Den Papier geschnitten wenden,
Maienkäfer an den Wänden,
Alles feine frische Ware
Doch der Strohhut an den Füssen
Und der ganze Kegelklub,
Springen Hühner Hähne müssen
Dada – wada – lada wup.   (pp. 38–9)

(Apple puree on your hands
Hosanna the cigar.
Turn the paper cut,
Cockchafers on the walls,
Everything fine fresh wares
Yet the straw hat on your feet

And the whole bowling club,
Jump must hens cocks
Dada – vada – lada vup.)

Part II ends with Kaspar trying to become a new man; he pities and helps the poor, refuses to accompany his friend into the army, has visions and dreams and wants to be like a tree: 'Wie der Baum will ich sein! rief Kaspar, von allen Seiten nimmt er, nach allen Seiten gibt er' ('I want to be like a tree! shouted Kaspar, taking from all directions and giving to all directions') (p. 44). His friend dies in battle' in a way, Kaspar now feels ashamed, a coward, a 'Neutraler.' Kaspar drowns his sorrows: '[Er] stürzte mit Sicherheit entgegen seinem letzten, besten Freund, dem Wein' ('He plunged in certainty towards his last, best friend: wine') (p. 49).

Part III consists of two pages and is devoted, like part I, to Erika. Her search for justice has taken on gigantic proportions. In the end she is hit by a bullet. The appendix has three pages and is entitled 'Satyrspiel.' Kaspar travels to Germany. He has tremendous visions of a war and then dreams of a hunt and hangs himself with his suspenders. The last sentence: 'Er fiel, und die Hosenträger waren stark genug' ('He fell, and his suspenders were strong enough') (p. 55).

Böschenstein has called his work a 'Jugendsünde' (sin of youth). This little novel, however, is one of the most interesting pieces of Expressionist prose. Here is a highly intelligent man, familiar with the authors of the day – Edschmid, Frank, Sternheim, Schwitters – who intends to write a novel which will be largely autobiographical. Since he is acquainted with all Expressionist techniques of writing, he uses them – but while using them he feels that he is not being original, that he is artificially making up a style which does not really suit him. Hence the irony and the parodies. In a way, Böschenstein was in the same position as Cäsar von Arx, the Swiss dramatist, who tried to produce an Expressionist play and turned out a parody, *Moritat*. Von Arx, too, left Switzerland for Germany after the war and spent the years from 1920 to 1923 in Leipzig. Böschenstein's early novel is an inverted Expressionist tale: it is usually the father who is conservative and the son who is a revolutionary, while the mother, standing between father and son, suffers. In this novel, there is no father at all, the mother is the revolutionary, and the son the conservative. I know of no other Expressionist novel with this parodistic sort of constellation.

'UNTER SCHWEIZERN IN KANADA'

The eighteen short stories and anecdotes collected in *Unter Schweizern in Kanada,*[7] all told in the first person singular, cover the years 1926 to about 1947. They seem to be strictly autobiographical; they are written in an unassuming, polished German, reminding one of Meinrad Inglin's prose. Böschenstein is less interested in the Canadian landscape than in the characters he describes: mainly people he knew during his vagabond days in 1926–8 and during World War II. In 1927, Böschenstein worked as a hotel doorman in Victoria where he met a number of highly unpleasant immigrants: a conceited German who always knew better; immigrants who were too proud to adjust to a different way of life; ruthless crooks who had no scruples even about robbing those who had formerly helped them. Böschenstein's best stories are the bitter ones, and the unsavoury characters are most memorable. One of his outstanding figures is Wirz who, with thirty thousand dollars in his pocket, manages to cajole his poor compatriots into working for him and feeding him.

During World War II, Böschenstein travelled all over Canada, bringing relief to hundreds of Germans in prison camps. He describes a number of pleasant, unpleasant, and hilarious situations; the best story in this section of the book is devoted to McCurdy, conductor of the weekly train from Sioux Lookout to Port Arthur. Chronologically the last tale seems to be 'Richmond' – which describes the homecoming of a crippled soldier after World War II. To conclude from the tenor of the eighteen stories, Böschenstein is still a pacifist and more interested in lower-class people than in others. He has a good heart and, in regard to the idea of solidarity among men, an attitude halfway between Hemingway and the early Steinbeck.

In many ways, these sketches represent, from an artistic point of view, Böschenstein's most convincing book. The ambition, the literary cleverness, and the sense of parody which stood behind his Expressionist novel have disappeared. The sketches are the work of an older man who has gone through many hardships and who has few illusions left. But he has not become a cynic; he has preserved his good sense of humour and his irony.

'IM ROTEN OCHSEN'

There are at least three books to which *Im Roten Ochsen* can be compared:

Gottfried Keller's *Martin Salander*, and Wilhelm Raabe's *Stopfkuchen* and *Abu Telfan*. (Böschenstein published two books on Keller and wrote extensively on Raabe in the second volume of *Deutsche Gefühlskultur*; he also translated Barker Fairley's book on Raabe.) The style of *Im Roten Ochsen* is quite unique and personal, but in some ways reminiscent of Arnold Kübler's style.

The novel is told in the third person singular. Karl Schneblin (Böschenstein) returns with his wife Martha (Elisabeth) to Gandurum (Stein am Rhein) where they own an apartment. While Karl and his former school friends spend much time over drinks in the Gasthaus 'Zum Roten Ochsen' (it exists under this name in Stein am Rhein, and even Elsi, the waitress, is genuine), Martha often travels to Scafusien (Schaffhausen) where she has relatives. Karl and his wife do not come from Canada, but, like Leonhard Hagebucher in *Abu Telfan* and Eduard in *Stopfkuchen*, from Africa, where Karl (who has studied agriculture) runs a plantation. Hagebucher's purpose in returning was – says Böschenstein in *Deutsche Gefühlskultur*– 'seinen deutschen Zeitgenossen die Leviten zu lesen, ihnen den kritischen Spiegel vorzuhalten und bessere öffentliche Zustände zu erzwingen' ('to lecture his German contemporaries, to hold a mirror of criticism up to them and to bring about better social conditions).[8] *Martin Salander* was written with a similar purpose in mind, by a disillusioned and bitter man. Schneblin has little in common with Hagebucher or Salander, but resembles Eduard, who has not come in order to criticize, but to meet old friends and to hear the story of Heinrich Schaumann and Tinchen Quakatz. Raabe tells us little about Eduard, and we learn even less about Karl Schneblin's life after he left Switzerland. As in the case of *Stopfkuchen*, we are informed about the fate of those who continued to live at home. Böschenstein tells us how his compatriots had fared during the depression, during World War II, and during the 'Wirtschaftswunder.' Clearly, Karl has often been homesick; living in Africa, he has envied those who have been able to make their career in Gandurum. Many welcome him with enthusiasm; he has some sincere friends – people with golden hearts who could have stepped out of a novel by Leonhard Frank. There is some social criticism, mainly connected with the character Alfred, who has had a miserable life with his foster father; also, some of the local people had sympathized with the Nazis.

Karl devotes his time in Gandurum to two main tasks: he renews contacts with his friends of fifty years ago, and he writes down his memories in connection with the first 'Flugtag' (day of flight) in

Gandurum. This took place a few years before World War I. The story of
Pastor Gysi, who built Gandurum's first airplane ('Schwerer-als-die Luft'
– 'heavier-than-air'), and its pilot Gustav (a student at the Gymnasium
and, partly, a projection of young Böschenstein) has all the humour and
irony of Gottfried Keller's 'Novellen' about Seldwyla. It takes up more
than a third of the novel and is a masterpiece of historical realism, irony,
and humour. Gustav dies in the end, but one can just as well laugh as cry
about the fate of this revolutionary teenager.

As in his first novel, Böschenstein is quite self-conscious; why is Karl
writing a novel? He has made up his mind 'Gandurum auf die literarische
Landkarte zu setzen' ('to place Gandurum on the literary map').[9] But is he
capable of writing a good novel? He puts his own scepticism into the
mouth of the publisher to whom Martha has shown parts of the
manuscript. First, why write about Gandurum rather than about Africa? A
novel about Africa would find more readers. Second, is the author, after
spending so many years away from home, capable of dealing with this
very Swiss topic? ('Verfasser dürfte zu lange im Ausland gelebt haben,
um sich in der Seelenverfassung unseres Menschenschlages noch aus-
zukennen. Die Psychologie des Homo helveticus hat schon tieferen
Denkern, als Herr Schneblin einer ist, grosse Rätsel gestellt'; 'The author
seems to have lived too long abroad to be able to fathom still the spiritual
condition of people of our type. The psychology of homo helveticus has in
the past posed difficult riddles to profounder thinkers than Herr
Schneblin' [p. 139]). There are two more points which carry less weight.

Böschenstein's novel did, indeed, put Stein am Rhein on the literary
map. I passed through Stein in October 1977; the novel was prominently
displayed in the one little bookstore there. The press had received the
book with enthusiasm. Visiting the 'Rote Ochsen,' I met the lady called
Elsi in the book, and she confirmed that the novel was being read by
everybody in the region; the 'Rote Ochsen' was certainly profiting from
the book.[10]

ON SOME MANUSCRIPTS LEFT BY HERMANN BÖSCHENSTEIN

Böschenstein completed his second and last published novel, *Im Roten
Ochsen*, in 1976. In that year he gave up his last teaching appointment (at
the University of Waterloo) and began to devote most of his time to
writing. I knew from conversations with Mrs Böschenstein in 1972–5 that

her husband had hidden away a considerable number of manuscripts which he intended to revise for publication after retirement. She spoke mostly about short stories, but there are at least two novels and some plays among the many manuscripts. I asked Hermann Böschenstein to let me read those manuscripts which he intended to publish, and he kindly gave me his permission.

In 1976, Böschenstein decided to revise three plays and publish them, preferably in three small volumes which could also be used as 'Bühnenmanuskripte,' then do a novel. The revision of the plays was completed in 1980, and they are now being prepared for publication. Having disposed of the plays, Böschenstein began revising a novel which he had originally written in the thirties. While working on this novel, he died.

As mentioned earlier, Böschenstein had originally wanted to become an actor and had studied the art of acting in Zürich and Munich. By 1976, he was less interested in the theatre for the intelligentsia than in the 'Volkstheater' (popular theatre) – in the plays performed by local 'Theatervereine' (drama clubs) on 'Volksbühnen' (popular stages) for a clientele which is rarely seen at a 'Stadttheater' or 'Schauspielhaus' (municipal theatre). All the five plays I have read are written for this kind of public. Cäsar von Arx, the first Swiss dramatist of international reputation, wrote several such plays which are still performed (for instance *Vogel friss oder stirb!*), and it was Böschenstein's ambition to provide some of the texts for a possible revival and enrichment of the Swiss 'Volkstheater.' He felt that two of the five texts should not be published at the moment; one of these is a dramatized version of a novel (in manuscript, not for publication either), entitled 'Bachab' and concerned with the one-time opposition to women's suffrage in Switzerland. It is, of course, a comedy. The second play is entitled 'Der Schweizerische Wandersmann. Laienspiel in 15 Bildern.' The theme: three young Swiss friends travel to America; two stay there (against their will), one returns. The play is written in rhymed blank verse; there are sad and comical scenes; the public will learn what the one returning young Swiss has learned. Böschenstein was a teacher and a humanist, and his plays do teach (and moralize). Böschenstein points out what is important in life and what is not, what is honest and ethical and what is not; he advocates humanism, solidarity among human beings – but all this with a strong dose of humour. As in a Chaplin film, the public will laugh and cry simultaneously.

Let us glance at the three plays which are ready for publication.

'Dreimal Stiftungsfest oder Der Zürihegel. Eine Posse'
The play has three acts and is concerned with the development of a small
segment of a Swiss community: some members of a 'Quartierverein'
(district association). The time of the first act is 1912, of the second 1937, of
the third 1952. In each of these years, a 'Fest' is planned, and the highlight
of each of these celebrations is supposed to be a 'Festrede.' One family
emigrates to America in 1912, one son of this family returns in 1952.
Böschenstein succeeds admirably in creating the atmosphere of 1912, 1937
(the 'Ruckzuck' people are Swiss Nazi sympathizers), and 1952 (the
beginning of the 'Wirtschaftswunder'). The play is a comedy, and there
are so many jokes that the moral is quite unobtrusive; looking back after
the final curtain, the Swiss spectator will become conscious of the fact that
he has just lived through forty years of history, and that his parents' and
his own life are based on (and a consequence of) the events he has just
witnessed on the stage.

'Seefahrt tut not. Eine Parabel'
Two ships travel through the ocean of time and arrive on the shores of a
beautiful continent, populated by figures of ancient Greek myths (Ulys-
ses, Electra, Hercules, and so on). There is the admiral who stands for
political power and would rather blow up the world than limit his power;
there is Emil, the religious fanatic, who is no less evil. Then there are those
who accept the world as it is, who appreciate its beauty, who are happy in
their simple lives. There are symbolic meanings on several levels, but the
main message is clear: no bombs or missiles; let's not be fanatics of any
kind; live and let live; be tolerant and peaceful; don't be greedy, but share
with all; don't be an egoist, but think that others have a right to live as
well.

'Eulenspiegel in Babylon – Ein Traumspiel. Komödie in 14 Szenen'
Scenes 1 and 14 take place in an apartment among friends at Carnival time.
Scenes 2 to 13 are dream scenes. Three friends have taken a sleeping
potion and meet in their dreams – in the Orient. There is a great deal of
hilarious fun, but in the middle of it, the catastrophe takes place: war – the
complete destruction of Babylon. The few survivors slowly get together
and decide to travel to Achmed's farm which has been spared – a
paradise. But it turns out that nobody has learned anything: the general
wants troops and revenge, the bankers want guarantees and profits;

there is no hope in philosophy, in religion, in socialism. Everybody begins to quarrel and to kill again.

But this is no tragedy – at least not on the surface; the reader is laughing most of the time – at the parodies of scenes from classical plays, at the puns and misused proverbs, at the absurd situations and the many references to recent events. Many spectators would not be conscious of the fact that they have just witnessed the destruction of our world – until after the end. The audience has been led (to quote Friedrich Dürrenmatt) into a tragedy-trap (as for instance in Dürrenmatt's *Die Physiker*). Since 'Eulenspiegel in Babylon' is a dream play, some of the figures are 'strange,' 'unreal,' and the spectator cannot easily identify with them. This gives him, in spite of the laughter, a chance to watch from the outside, to reflect, to be critical of what is happening, to come to conclusions, to learn to behave differently.

The Novel (no definite title)
The central figure: a young man who leaves Switzerland as an emigrant. While *Im Roten Ochsen* is a 'Heimkehrerroman' (novel of return), this was to be an 'Auswandererroman' (novel of emigration). Böschenstein had begun writing the book in the thirties; when war broke out, he locked the eight hundred pages of manuscript away and did not look at them again for forty years. He found that he had to cut out most of the material, revise the rest and add a new part. On 11 January 1982, Böschenstein wrote to me: 'Jetzt fesselt mich der Gehalt, der aus einem Erlebnis- oder schon fast Abenteuerroman herausgepresst werden kann, und dazu bedarf es eines kleineren Gefässes. Es geht mir jetzt nicht so sehr um all das, was ein Einwanderer erlebt und erlitten hat, sondern um das Wenige, was er dabei an Nützlichem, Tüchtigem gelernt haben mag. Aus dem Auswandererroman ist – einmal mehr – ein Erziehungsromänchen geworden' ('Now I am fascinated by the content that can be squeezed out of a novel of experience or adventure, and for that I need a smaller container. I am now not so much concerned with all the things that an immigrant experiences and suffers, but rather with the small number of useful and valuable things he may have learnt. The novel of emigration has – once again – turned into a novellette of education').

Böschenstein had the reputation of being one of the most beloved and respected teachers in his field; certainly, the pedagogical element is always present, certainly in all the plays, and in most of his writings since

180   Armin Arnold

1928. But there is nothing to be said against this; Böschenstein is in excellent company there – in the company of his compatriots Pestalozzi and Gotthelf, Keller and Dürrenmatt.

BIBLIOGRAPHY

The following bibliography is adapted from *Analecta Helvetica et Germanica. Eine Festschrift zu Ehren von Hermann Böschenstein*, edited by A. Arnold, H. Eichner, E. Heier, and S. Hoefert (Bonn: Bouvier Verlag Herbert Grundmann, 1979), pp. 388–92. The compiler was Humphrey Milnes. It has been brought up to date, and a section of publications about Hermann Böschenstein has been added.

BOOKS

Das literarische Goethebild der Gegenwart in England. Breslau: Priebatsch, 1933, pp. 100
Hermann Stehr: Einführung in die Stimmung seines Werkes. Breslau: Priebatsch, 1935, pp. 92
'Irving Babbitt, amerikanischer Humanist und Kulturkritiker,' in *Kulturkritik und Literaturbetrachtung in Amerika*, by V. Lange and H. Böschenstein, pp. 42–76. Breslau: Priebatsch, 1938
Gottfried Keller: Grundzüge seines Lebens und Werkes. Bern: Haupt, 1948, pp. 178
The German Novel, 1939–1944. Toronto: University of Toronto Press, 1949, pp. viii, 189
Deutsche Gefühlskultur: Studien zu ihrer dichterischen Gestaltung. Band I, Die Grundlagen, 1770–1830. Bern: Haupt, 1954, pp. 379
Der neue Mensch: die Biographie im deutschen Nachkriegsroman. Heidelberg: Rothe, 1958, pp. 130
Gotthelf: Hans Joggeli der Erbvetter. London: Edward Arnold, 1961, pp. 63
Deutsche Gefühlskultur II, 1830–1930. Bern: Haupt, 1966, pp. 388
German Literature of the Nineteenth Century. London: Edward Arnold, 1969, pp. 170
Gottfried Keller. Stuttgart: Metzler, 1969, pp. 138; second revised and enlarged edition, 1977, pp. 176. Sammlung Metzler M84
Heiteres und Satirisches aus der deutschkanadischen Literatur. John Adam Rittinger, Walter Roome, Ernst Loeb, Rolf Max Kully, ed. with introductions in German and English by Hermann Böschenstein. Toronto: German-Canadian Historical Association, 1980, pp. 116

ARTICLES

'George Santayana.' *Schweizerische Rundschau* (Zürich), 28:8 (Nov. 1928), 732–43
'Die Psychologie in Amerika.' *Psychologische Rundschau* (Göttingen), 1:6 (1929), 189–96; 1:8, pp. 260–65
'Katholische Pionierarbeit in Kanada.' *Schweizer Rundschau* (Solothurn), 29:1 (April 1929), 58–68
'Behaviorism.' *Neue Schweizer Rundschau* (Zürich), 22:7 (July 1929), 497–507
'John Dewey und die amerikanische Erziehung.' *Neue Schweizer Rundschau* (Zürich), 24:1 (Jan. 1931), 5–22
'James Leuba und das religiöse Leben Nordamerikas.' *Raschers Monatshefte* (Zürich), 4:3 (Jan. 1931), 142–53
'Zur amerikanischen Religionspsychologie.' *Psychologische Rundschau* (Göttingen), 2:12 (1931), 373–8
'Zur Charakteristik der deutschschweizerischen Literatur.' *Germanic Review* (New York), 8:1 (Jan. 1933), 52–62
'Sprachstilistische Merkmale Hermann Stehrs.' *Germanic Review* (New York), 9:2 (April 1934), 130–9
'Zum Studium der deutschen Zeitungen in Amerika.' *Monatshefte für den deutschen Unterricht* (Madison), 26:4 (April 1934), 103–8
'Zu Ludwig Thomas "Andreas Vöst."' *Germanic Review* (New York), 11:3 (July 1936), 207–13
'Gotthelf oder Keller?' *Germanic Review* (New York), 14:2 (April 1939), 118–25
'Hermann Stehr, der Erzähler-Mystiker.' *Monatshefte für den deutschen Unterricht* (Madison), 33:3 (March 1941), 99–109
'Zum Aufbau von Otto Ludwigs "Zwischen Himmel und Erde."' *Monatshefte für den deutschen Unterricht* (Madison), 34:7 (Nov. 1942), 343–56
Articles on H. Federer, E. Gött, H. von Heiseler, F. Huch, R. Huch, G. Keller, F. von Saar, J. Schaffner, C. Spitteler, A. Steffen, H. Stehr, L. Thoma, and psychoanalysis in modern European literature in *Columbia Dictionary of Modern Literature*. New York: Columbia University Press, 1944
Articles on B. Constant, R. Dehmel, G. Hauptmann, G. Keller, C.F. Meyer, J.H. Pestalozzi, R.M. Rilke, A. Schnitzler, C. Spitteler, Mme. de Staël, Stefan George, F. Wedekind, F. Werfel, and Swiss literature in *Encyclopedic History of Literature*. New York: Philosophical Library, 1946
'Betrachtungen zur amerikanischen Goetheforschung der Gegenwart.' *Etudes Germaniques* (Paris), 2:3 (April–Sept. 1949), 291–311
All articles on Swiss literature in *New Century Cyclopedia of Names*. New York: Appleton-Century-Crofts, 1954
'On Rereading Jean Paul.' *Germanic Review* (New York), 29:2 (Feb. 1954), 119–30
'Jean Pauls Jugendroman 'Abelard und Helouise,"' *Hesperus* (Bayreuth), 12 (1956), 38–45

'Goethe's "Die natürliche Tochter."' *Publications of the English Goethe Society* (Leeds), n.s.25 (1956), 21–40

'Trends and Symbols in Contemporary German Fiction.' *University of Toronto Quarterly* (Toronto), 26:1 (Oct. 1956), 32–46

'Else Seel: Eine deutsch-kanadische Dichterin.' *German-Canadian Review* (Kitchener), 10:1 (Spring 1957), 17–19

'Tag- und Jahreshefte: A New Type of Autobiography.' *German Life and Letters* (Oxford), 10:3 (April 1957), 169–76

'Contemporary German-Swiss Fiction.' *German Life and Letters* (Oxford), 12:1 (Oct. 1958), 24–33

'The Germans Look at the Atomic Age.' *University of Toronto Quarterly* (Toronto), 28:3 (April 1959), 250–66

'Frederick Philip Grove.' *Festgabe für Eduard Berend*, pp. 257–71. Weimar: Böhlau, 1959

'Hugh MacLennan, ein kanadischer Romancier.' *Zeitschrift für Anglistik und Amerikanistik* (Berlin), 8:2 (May 1960), 117–35

'Von den Grenzen der Ironie.' *Festschrift für H.H. Borcherdt*, ed. A. Fuchs and H. Motekat, pp. 43–58. Munich: Huber, 1962

'Zur deutschschweizerischen Literatur der Gegenwart.' *Deutsche Beiträge zur geistigen Überlieferung*, vol. v, ed. Matthijs Jolles, pp. 146–64. Bern: Francke, 1964

'Is There a Canadian Image in German Literature?' *Seminar: A Journal of Germanic Studies* (Toronto), 3:1 (Spring 1967), 1–20

'Lorenz Oken.' *The Encyclopedia of Philosophy*. New York: Macmillan, 1967

'Observations on Otto Flake.' *Essays on German Literature in Honour of G. Joyce Hallamore*, ed. Michael S. Batts and Marketa Goetz-Stankiewicz, pp. 236–55. Toronto: University of Toronto Press, 1968

'Emil Utitz, der Philosoph aus dem Prager Kreis (1883–1960).' *Studies in German in Memory of Robert L. Kahn*, Rice University Studies (Houston), 54:4 (Fall 1971), 19–32

Articles on German-Swiss literature and a number of individual German-Swiss writers in *Cassell's Encyclopedia of World Literature*. London: Cassell, 1973

'Zur Erzähl-Thematik in der Literatur der DDR.' *Erfahrung und Überlieferung* (Festschrift for C.P. Magill), pp. 166–84. Cardiff: University of Wales Press, 1974

'Betrachtungen zur deutschkanadischen Literatur.' *Annalen I*, pp. 2–17. Montreal: Université de Montréal, 1976

'Das Konzentrationslager in der deutschen Literatur. Einige Bemerkungen.' *Formen realistischer Erzählkunst. Festschrift für Charlotte Jolles*, ed. Jörg Thunecke and Eda Sagarra, pp. 66–78. Nottingham: Sherwood Press Agencies, 1979

'The First World War in German Prose after 1945: Some Examples – Some Observations.' *The First World War in German Narrative Prose: Essays in Honour of G.W. Field*, ed. Charles N. Genno and Heinz Wetzel, pp. 138–58. Toronto: University of Toronto Press, 1980

FICTION

Die Mutter und der neutrale Sohn. Leipzig: Xenien, 1921; pp. 55
Unter Schweizern in Kanada: Kurzgeschichten. Basel : Gute Schriften, 1974; pp. 79
Im Roten Ochsen. Geschichte einer Heimkehr. Schaffhausen: Verlag Meier, 1977; pp. 231

TRANSLATIONS

Kanadische Lyrik. Übertragungen. Bern: Feuz, 1938; pp. 69
Fairley, Barker. *Wilhelm Raabe: eine Deutung seiner Romane.* Munich: Beck, 1961; pp. 261. Original title: *Wilhelm Raabe: An Introduction to His Novels.* 1960
Fairley, Barker. *Goethe dargestellt in seiner Dichtung.* Frankfurt a.M: Insel, 1968; pp. 175. Original title: *Goethe as Revealed in His Poetry.* 1932

ABOUT HERMANN BÖSCHENSTEIN

Milnes, Humphrey. 'Hermann Böschenstein.' Hermann Böschenstein Anniversary Number of *German Life and Letters*, n.s. 23:1 (Oct. 1969), 1–6
Arnold, Armin. 'The Fiction of Hermann Böschenstein.' *International Fiction Review*, 5:1 (1978), 52–8
Arnold, Armin. 'Hermann Böschenstein als Erzähler.' *Tradition – Integration – Rezeption. Annalen 2*, ed. Karin R. Gürttler and Herfried Scheer, pp. 82–90. Montreal: Université de Montréal, 1978
Milnes, Humphrey. 'Hermann Böschenstein.' *Analecta Helvetica et Germanica. Eine Festschrift zu Ehren von Hermann Böschenstein*, ed. A. Arnold, H. Eichner, E. Heier, and S. Hoefert, pp. 387–92. Bonn: Bouvier Verlag Herbert Grundmann, 1979

NOTES

1 I am grateful to Hermann Böschenstein for providing me with much of the information for the years up to 1926.
2 Humphrey Milnes, 'Hermann Böschenstein,' in Hermann Böschenstein Anniversary Number of *German Life and Letters*, 23:1 (Oct. 1969), 1.
3 Ibid., pp. 2–3.
4 Böschenstein, letter to the author, 11 Jan. 1982.
5 Chapters 2 to 4 are based on my paper 'The Fiction of Hermann Böschenstein,' *International Fiction Review*, 5:1 (1978), 52–8. I am grateful to the editor, Professor Saad Elkhadem, for permitting me to reprint parts of that paper.

6 Böschenstein, *Die Mutter und der neutrale Sohn* (Leipzig: Xenien Verlag, 1921), p. 5. From now on the page numbers of quotations will be given in the text.

7 Böschenstein, *Unter Schweizern in Kanada: Kurzgeschichten* (Basel: Gute Schriften, 1974).

8 Böschenstein, *Deutsche Gefühlskultur*, vol. II, 1830–1930 (Bern: Paul Haupt, 1966), p. 231.

9 Böschenstein, *Im Roten Ochsen: Geschichte einer Heimkehr* (Schaffhausen: Meier, 1977), p. 28. From now on the page numbers of quotations will be given in the text.

10 The text of chapters 3 and 4 is, in part, taken from my review of *Unter Schweizern in Kanada* and *Im Roten Ochsen*, published in *German-Canadian Yearbook*, 5 (1979), 247–50.

Contributors

ARMIN ARNOLD is Professor of German, McGill University. He has written on German and Comparative literature and is widely known for his studies on Expressionism, D.H. Lawrence, James Joyce, G.B. Shaw, and Friedrich Dürrenmatt. He has also translated Canadian short stories into German and edited numerous studies of German and Comparative literature.

KARIN GÜRTTLER is Associate Professor of German, Université de Montréal. She has published on medieval literature, exile literature, and Canadiana Germanica. She is organizer of German-Canadian Symposia and editor of Annalen.

GÜNTER HESS is Associate Professor of German, University of Western Ontario. His special research interests are Goethe and Walter Bauer. He is preparing a biography on Walter Bauer.

PETER LIDDELL is Assistant Professor of German, University of Victoria. He has published on the literature of the GDR, Canadiana Germanica, and the methodology of teaching, and has coedited a volume of Carl Weiselberger's writings.

HARRY LOEWEN is Professor of German and Mennonite Studies, University of Winnipeg. He is the author of studies on Goethe and Luther and on the literature of the Mennonites.

WALTER E. RIEDEL is Associate Professor of German, University of Victoria. He has published on Expressionism and reception of Canadian literature in German-speaking countries, and has coedited a volume of Carl Weiselberger's writings and translated Canadian literature into German.

ANTHONY W. RILEY is Professor of German, Queen's University. He has published widely, especially on Thomas Mann, Elisabeth Langgässer, Alfred Döblin, Anglo-German literary relations, and Frederick Philip Grove. He is responsible for the new critical edition of Alfred Döblin.

HELFRIED SELIGER is Associate Professor of German, University of Toronto. He is known for his study *Das Amerikabild Bertolt Brechts* and his work on German-Spanish literary relations.

RODNEY SYMINGTON is Associate Professor and Chairman of the Department of Germanic Studies, University of Victoria. He has published on Brecht and Shakespeare, has translated German literature into English, and has edited Else Seel's writings, along with the correspondence between Else Seel and Ezra Pound.

Index